POSTMODERNISM IN HISTORY

Postmodernism has significantly affected the theory and practice of history. It has induced fears about the future of historical study, but has also offered liberation from certain modernist constraints. This original and thought-provoking study looks at the context of postmodernist thought in general cultural terms as well as in relation to history.

Postmodernism in History traces philosophical precursors of postmodernism and identifies some roots of current concerns. It describes the core constituents of postmodernism and provides a lucid and profound analysis of the current state of the debate. Southgate's main concern is to counter 'pomophobia' (fear of postmodernism) and to assert a positive future for historical study in a postmodern world. *Postmodernism in History* is a valuable and accessible guide for students, teachers, and general readers alike.

Beverley Southgate is Reader Emeritus in the History of Ideas at the University of Hertfordshire. His numerous publications include *History: What & Why?* (1996) and *Why Bother With History?* (2000).

POSTMODERNISM IN HISTORY

Fear or Freedom?

Beverley Southgate

Routledge
Taylor & Francis Group

LONDON AND NEW YORK

First published 2003
by Routledge
11 New Fetter Lane, London EC4P 4EE

Simultaneously published in the USA and Canada
by Routledge
29 West 35th Street, New York, NY 10001

Routledge is an imprint of the Taylor & Francis Group

Typeset in Goudy by
Keystroke, Jacaranda Lodge, Wolverhampton
Printed and bound in Great Britain by
TJ International Ltd, Padstow, Cornwall

British Library Cataloguing in Publication Data
A catalogue record for this book is available from the British Library

Library of Congress Cataloging in Publication Data
Southgate, Beverley C.
Postmodernism in history : fear or freedom? /
Beverley Southgate.
p. cm.
Includes bibliographical references and index.
1. Postmodernism. 2. History—Philosophy. 3. Postmodernism—
Psychological aspects. 4. Postmodernism—Sociological aspects.
I. Title.

D16.9 .S67 2003
901—dc21

ISBN 0-415-30538-1 (hbk)
ISBN 0-415-30539-X (pbk)

For Sheila, again,
without
whom I'd be history;
and for Ellen, who shows
that history goes on . . .

CONTENTS

ILLUSTRATIONS

PREFACE

My title is ambiguous. It implies concern, first, with postmodernism in history as the past; and, second, with the possible implications of postmodernism in history as a present academic discipline. That ambiguity is deliberate: my concern is with both. I try here both to contextualise postmodernism as a part of intellectual history, and to assess its past and potential effects on the study of history.

In both cases the focus can be deduced from my subtitle. Indeed, my interest in the subject stems from observing manifestations of the *fear* that postmodernism seems to engender, and not least among historians: highly emotional responses to postmodernism seem to sit ill with the modernist ideals on which historians still insist – such virtues as 'rationality', 'fairness', 'balance' and 'detachment'. So what is going on? Is fear an appropriate response – or should we rather be celebrating greater *freedom*?

Many, of course, now protest that postmodernism *is* history – a thing of the past, an irritating intellectual fad that had its day in the late twentieth century and can now safely (and thankfully) be forgotten. On the whole, it's claimed, it told historians nothing that they didn't already know, though it may be conceded that a few of its minor insights have now been incorporated into existing historical practice. But that is a position that I can't accept: rather, I take postmodernism to be the continuing attempt to formulate a theoretical explanation for the situation that in practice (and by definition) we're all in – the situation itself of postmodernity. As such, it's not only an academic or theoretical matter that we are concerned with: on the contrary, postmodernism has very much to do with the practicalities, not only of history but of life – with the ways we choose to live as individuals, with the ways we interact with others in society, and with our choice of political agenda. And it has to do not least with our aspirations for the future.

No doubt overly ambitious, then, this book aims to be another 'Guide for the Perplexed'. It's for those who remain perplexed about what postmodernism is, and about how it relates in particular to history; and it's for those who are perplexed also about what has been diagnosed as 'pomophobia' – about why so many people seem to be in such an emotional and even fearful state about these apparently esoteric matters.

I have structured the work in three two-chapter parts: 'Fear' (of post-modernism in the present), 'Contextualisation' (tracing, or proposing, some precursors and parallels from the past), and 'Freedom' (pondering our prospects for the future). The first chapter, then, is concerned with diagnosing postmodernism and pomophobia generally, and the second with an analysis more particularly of the relation of postmodernism to history – with how traditional, modernist history has been undermined and is attempting now to reconstruct itself. The 'contextualisation' of Part Two involves, in Chapter 3, an examination of some claimed antecedents, tracing roots back as far as classical antiquity; and I then, in Chapter 4, propose some parallels to our current discomfiture in the early-modern upheaval that similarly provoked anxiety and fear by threatening long-established certainties. The proposal for future 'freedom' in Part Three involves, first, a consideration of some modernist constraints from which postmodernism might free us, and a final chapter indicating some possible options for a liberated history in postmodernity.

While inevitably interdisciplinary in approach, this book is essentially a work of intellectual history with a focus on the future. I hope, therefore, that it may be of some particular interest to historians, but that it will also appeal to others – whether from the standpoint of humanities, social sciences or general interest – for whom reflection on postmodernism, and on postmodernity itself, seems important.

ACKNOWLEDGEMENTS

I'd like publicly to express my thanks to my editor Victoria Peters for her interest, encouragement and advice; to (no longer anonymous) Routledge readers – Patrick Joyce, Alun Munslow, Jeremy Popkin and Barbara Tischler – for their sometimes conflicting but invariably constructive criticisms and comments (which is, of course, by no means to say that they agree with anything I say); to Keith Jenkins for his continuing intellectual stimulation, advice and encouragement; to Robert Burns and the other members of his Philosophy of History seminars at the Institute of Historical Research, London, for maintaining intellectual life even in the retired; and to John Ibbett for his intellectual and very practical friendship. My thanks, too, once again, to Lin (now Davidson) and to Jane Bloye at the University of Hertfordshire, who have contrived to make hard copy from obsolescent electronic images; and to Sheila (now Southgate) for everything.

The author and publisher thank the copyright holders for permission to reproduce illustrations: on page 23, Glenys Barton, photo Karen Norquay, and Angela Flowers Gallery, London; on page 43, photo Ben Southgate; on page 100, drawings Anne Duke; on pages 100, 148–9, illustrations National Portrait Gallery, London; and on front cover of paperback edition and page 165, photo Stan Douglas and David Zwirner Gallery, New York.

Part 1

FEAR (THE PRESENT)

1

POSTMODERNISM AND POMOPHOBIA

1 Introduction

'Britain is now dominated by "post modern" attitudes.' So the British Prime Minister was advised by a Cabinet Office report early in the year 2000.[1] Significantly, that news was reported to the public under the resounding headline: 'Warning for Blair over state of the nation'. In other words, postmodernity – or postmodernism, as denoting the intellectual attitudes associated with that condition – had well and truly arrived, but it carried a health warning: it was something to be concerned about. Or even feared. Pomophobia, too, had come of age.

Pomophobia, when defined as a fearful reaction to the sort of post-modern situation envisaged, could easily be understood. For, as the official report went on to explain, old-fashioned 'modern' attitudes, such as 'respect for authority, support for the family and allegiance to large institutions', were 'in terminal decline'. They had been replaced by 'a belief in self-expression, creativity and individual value systems'. And while there were clearly some advantages in those novelties, the corresponding dangers were all too obvious. People were likely to 'become less deferential to institutions such as Parliament and the courts', and indeed to lack any sense of national identity. And, perhaps most significantly of all, people would lack any moral framework, or any 'clear template'; and without that, they were in danger of making 'inappropriate choices', or of being so 'overwhelmed by choice' as to 'feel unable to cope'.

There were a number of things, then, that Prime Minister Blair's advisers believed that the already all-pervasive 'postmodernism' implied for society and for individuals. But the essence was that an essentially anarchic individualism was likely to endanger social and political cohesion, while individuals themselves would be unable to cope with their new-found freedom. That was clearly cause for some concern.

But that socio-political diagnosis served only to confirm anxieties that had been expressed about postmodernism in academia for several decades.

'The intellectual equivalent of crack', offered to innocent young people 'by devilish tempters', was how the traditionalist historian Geoffrey Elton put it some ten years earlier; in the United States Allan Bloom has referred to 'an intellectual crisis of the greatest magnitude, which constitutes [nothing less than] the crisis of our civilisation'; and Felipe Fernández-Armesto has more recently noted the 'mood of *uncertainty*' induced by postmodernism, and has urged his readers (supposedly and maybe quite properly 'perplexed' about the truth) not to abandon their children to be 'victims of delusions or doubt'. It's time, he insists, 'to prise ourselves free' from a pernicious intellectual movement which threatens to drag us all back to the Dark Ages. Civilisation itself is endangered: the barbarians, in the form of contemporary postmodern 'truth vandals', are already at the gates. In similar vein, the American historian Gertrude Himmelfarb has clarified her attitude by entitling her book on culture and society portentously as *On Looking into the Abyss*; and her study of America's 'demoralisation . . . from Victorian virtues to modern values' has been described by one critic as 'stridently apocalyptic in tone, celebrating the past, worrying over the present, *fearful* of the future'. The intellectual historian John Clarke, while conceding the recent development of more constructive forms, has written of postmodernism tending 'to exude a kind of scepticism that leads to cynicism and even despair, rather than to wisdom or spiritual growth'; and Susan Pederson has described how postmodernism has rendered academia a 'disquieting place in which to live'.[2]

Postmodernism, then, is well and truly impinging on us at levels both practical and theoretical; and pomophobia is what we get – is what we suffer from – when we just can't stand the disruption that it seems to threaten. Pomophobia indicates that our emotional balance has finally been lost, and that we can't cope any longer. It's what is manifested when we're no longer able to tolerate the uncertainties, ambiguities and doubts that postmodernism reveals and provokes (or that postmodernity entails).

However, the general proposition for which I argue in this book is that, while fear may well be an understandable reaction to our postmodern situation, it's none the less an inappropriate response. While it's natural enough, initially, to cower and seek refuge as the familiar edifices of modernity begin to crumble, it makes equally good sense thereafter to investigate the possibilities for new creations in the future. The end of one life need not imply just death, but the possibility of another and better life to come. The destruction of mediaeval certainties was the price to be paid for intellectual rebirth and subsequent enlightenment; and similarly, as modernism subsides, its new postmodern replacement can be (and should be, and perhaps must be) not so much feared as welcomed.

4

In this introductory chapter I shall try to indicate a little of what I understand by the central terms 'postmodernism' and 'pomophobia'.

2 Postmodernism: an attempt at diagnosis

So what is postmodernism? What is the postmodern challenge? What's all the fuss about? And the fear?

First, 'postmodernism' is a notoriously elusive concept: trying to define it resembles bare-handed fishing. In this slippery predicament one potential hook (admittedly a little blunted now by over-use, but serviceable still) is offered by Jean-François Lyotard, who famously wrote: 'Simplifying to the extreme, I define *postmodern* as incredulity toward metanarratives'.[3] By that he meant, in short, that all those 'grand narratives' of modernism (narratives characterised by such words as 'progress', 'secularisation' or anything that presupposes movement in a certain direction, and so bestows some meaning and purpose) can no longer be believed in or accepted. So at least we can conclude that inbuilt meaningfulness and purpose play no part in the postmodern condition; and it's not without some significance that Lyotard's definition appears in a work entitled *The Postmodern Condition*. As theorising a *condition* (the condition of postmodernity), postmodernism may well be fearfully resisted, but it can't forever be avoided.

A similar point emerges from another definition more recently proposed by Keith Jenkins, who writes of 'the era of the raising to consciousness of the "aporia"'.[4] 'Aporia' is a Greek word that can refer to both places and people. For the former, it indicates a difficulty in passing: it's hard to get through. In relation to people it refers to a difficulty in dealing with something that results in doubt and hesitation. So it's here perhaps best translated as 'impasse' – another imported word, but one that has been adopted into English to describe a road having no outlet; in the face of which we're at a loss as to how to proceed.

Jenkins himself, of course, is referring not to any physical road, but to every intellectual one where some sort of decision is required – whenever, for instance, we need to describe or to judge, as we constantly do in life and in historical study. And, following Derrida, he makes clear that every such decision is unique: circumstances are never exactly repeated, so that there can never be a blueprint, a set of rules or again a template that can simply be applied: always the particularity of a situation demands a starting again from scratch (though that's not possible either); there's no existing path that we can follow through or build upon, no absolutes against which we can measure or assess ourselves and our decisions, judgements and representations. So we're always groping in the dark – doing the best we can, but never well enough. Always, as T. S. Eliot wrote, 'Between the idea/And the reality/Between the motion/And the act/Falls the Shadow'.[5] Lacking foundational reference points, we are inevitably confronted by what Derrida refers to as the 'undecidability of the decision'; and in postmodernity we're made aware of that – made aware, in Keith Jenkins's words again, that 'our chosen ways of seeing things lack foundations', so that ours is 'an era when all the decisions we take – political, ethical, moral, interpretive, representational, etc. – are ultimately undecidable'.

Postmodernism is not, then, simply a 'philosophy', or a part of a subject that everyone knows has little or nothing to do with 'real life'; it's not just a 'theory' that impinges on nothing more substantial than the abstract metaphysical constructions of 'intellectuals'. On the contrary, it impacts upon very practical issues of everyday life as experienced by fellow-travellers on the Clapham omnibus.

In doing that, it contravenes long-lived expectations of what humanities subjects are supposed to be about; and indeed there is (appropriately) a certain paradox that the effects of postmodernism are being most dramatically felt in those very disciplines that have so often been seen as safely confined within the ivory towers of academia, even priding themselves on their intrinsic uselessness and inapplicability to 'real life' situations. Which is to say that postmodernism exposes previously concealed aspects of academic disciplines that other philosophies have seemed unable to reach, or at least unable profoundly to affect. In particular, it has revealed the inevitably rhetorical and ideological dimensions of subjects such as history, where the repudiation of such connotations has previously seemed to constitute a vital part of what comprises that discipline. To be more specific (only briefly here), the supposed modernist ideals of detachment, objectivity, balance and even purposelessness have themselves been revealed as the ideologically freighted shams that, despite their best intentions, they have always been.

It's not surprising, therefore, that a report on the implications of postmodernism should be submitted by advisers to the British Prime Minister. No less than scientific research into aerospace, microchips or DNA, humanist research into postmodernism can *affect* us all, for good or ill.

Definition, nevertheless, remains particularly difficult, not least because there is a sense in which postmodernism seems to deconstruct itself. By which I mean that, in postmodernism's own terms, there can be no one given place from which we can finally describe or define it, and – to compound our difficulty – there can be no necessary external referent for any linguistic description or definition that we may try to impose. As with such other notoriously problematic concepts as 'God', it indicates a constantly developing and constantly remodified attempt to describe and theorise our own situation; and as with such other philosophies as Platonism and Epicureanism (and even, of course, 'modernism'), it denotes an evolving body of thought that can embrace what might seem to be inconsistencies and contradictions.

But postmodernism's refusal to be simply categorised and linguistically (and safely) netted does seem further to offend (and even frighten) the modernist. So while we may concede that the essence itself may continue to elude us, we must make a start by at least suggesting some further characteristics that seem essential to the concept; and, before proceeding to the theory, it might be as well to start with some very practical, socio-political issues, which may resonate with some everyday concerns that have been felt – if not always explicitly articulated – by prospective readers.

2.1 Practice

One of the most interesting commentators on the practical, public and political dimensions of postmodernism is Zygmunt Bauman, who has described, in a collection of essays and lectures published as *Postmodernity and its Discontents*, how 'postmodern men and women [have] exchanged a portion of their possibilities of security for a portion of happiness'.[6] The possibilities of security enjoyed by earlier generations consisted in such factors as a 'job for life' – whether that simply represented the security of a job (however menial) in an industry (such as mining, textile manufacture or motor-car production) which appeared to be as permanent as any human institution can be; or whether it more positively provided a career structure, with a steadily ascending progression within a (seemingly, again, permanently established) profession. Such securities, it is clear, have largely evaporated in the white heat of yet another (but this time permanently ongoing) technological revolution, which ensures that skills, no less than products, carry with them their own inbuilt obsolescence. What was once a coal mine has become a theme park; a full-time miner is now a casual tour guide.

As a symbol of the workforce, then, the mass crowd at the factory gate has been replaced by the solitary individual, clutching an immaculate laser-printed curriculum vitae and personal portfolio, and hireable and fireable at whim (or as changing economic circumstances, or even professional fashions, are deemed to demand). Job security and solidarity can be seen as past banalities that used to be enjoyed by boring old men in grey suits, and are now thankfully banished to make way for the greater excitements of individual enterprise and unbounded aspiration. There's no need for an earthbound ladder when a helicopter will so much more quickly and easily take you so very much higher.

The straitjacket of an old-fashioned career structure has, then, been outgrown by a generation that repudiates any such constriction on its own unbounded possibilities; and that's where Zygmunt Bauman's 'portion of happiness' comes into play; for happiness comes with liberation – or so it is assumed. Freed from the constraints of any need for enduring commitment (in matters personal and public), postmodern men and women prefer to keep their options open, finding 'the open-endedness of their situation attractive enough to outweigh the anguish of uncertainty'. And that open-endedness applies, of course, not only to their professional or working lives, but also to their private selves – their own identities. So a definition of self, in the past so closely identified with work (with what one did in life), can now be indefinitely postponed; or rather, with the uncertainties of work's availability, indefinitely postponed it must be.

That implies, in Bauman's analysis, that men and women are liable in practice to 'live perpetually with the "identity problem" unsolved'. Liberated in some senses they may be, but their liberation has been bought at the price of forgoing 'a rightful and secure position in society'. What postmodern people are liable to miss out on is 'a space unquestionably one's own, where one can plan one's life with the minimum of interference, play one's role in a game in which the rules do not change overnight and without notice, act reasonably and hope for the better'. Forced to play in a game where the rules *are* constantly changed, the roles – and hence the identities – adopted by postmodern people are in danger of losing their substantiality. They ebb and flow with the tide of sartorial and 'life-style' fashion; and their transience exemplifies the disposability of goods (both physical and moral goods) in a consumerist society, where *identity* can come to mean, in Max Frisch's formulation quoted by Bauman, 'refusing to be what others want you to be'. It's only by holding out against the conformities implied in other people's expectations (a rare ability), that we can establish any sense of personal identity at all, or retain any sense of personal 'authenticity'; and the resultant variability (even evasiveness) can be construed as a positive virtue, when 'the hub of postmodern life strategy is not making identity stand – but the avoidance of being fixed'.[7]

That shifty oppositional stance may have its virtue, too, in encouraging a generation of Nietzschean fighters '*against* history and the power of the actual'. But confrontation itself can have its problems, especially when witnessed (as it increasingly seems to be) on a mass, rather than individual, scale. So that uncertainties of identity can have implications, not only for the happiness of the individual, but also for the stability and health of the state, or society at large. For lacking a clear and secure sense of personal identity, individuals may come to view with deeper suspicion and feelings of hostility those 'others' by reference to whom they need to define themselves. It's not only images of self that fragment, but images of a host of ill-defined others who similarly defy categorisation, and are therefore potentially threatening, ill-fitting, to be feared and if possible removed.

Certainties, then, are well and truly assigned to a *past*, where the concept of 'life as a pilgrimage' seems still to have made some sense. It's possible, of course, that we, being so conscious of their absence, may assign such certainties to past others, who did not in their own time feel their presence: the historical past contains those others against whom we measure and identify ourselves, and it suits us to assume or to impose some contrasts. But some evidence for difference does exist: Bauman cites the one-word command 'Forward!', engraved with other moral principles by the Victorian embellishers of Leeds Town Hall – for whom that word was evidently meaningful. That is, there were then, presumably, no doubts about what 'forward' implied: there was a shared understanding of what constituted forward *progression* through space and time; so that a purposeful life could still be lived within a moral structure that provided some meaningful sense of direction. However strait the path, there was a gate, however narrow, at the end of it, providing a goal against which movement and success could be measured (and 'forward' defined).

That defining space–time structure is lacking in a postmodern world that has seen both the weft and the warp of that previously close-textured structure relativised out of meaningful existence, so that 'space and time themselves display repeatedly the absence of an orderly, intrinsically differentiated structure', and as Ihab Hassan has observed, 'In a world no longer linear, we must wonder: *which way is forward?*'[8] We shall need, in our concluding chapters, to return to these matters as potentially positive aspects of postmodernity that liberate from modernist constraints, but we can note here already that postmodernist time has had its flow flattened, as Bauman describes, 'into a continuous present', where (or when) any injunction to take thought for the past or the morrow has been superseded by an insistence on the optimum utilisation of an ever-present 'here and now': 'synchrony replaces diachrony, co-presence takes the place of the succession, and the perpetual present *replaces history*'.[9]

Nor is it only history that has been replaced, but the values too that have previously been transmitted through that history – values both moral and aesthetic, which had previously been essentially unquestioned on their route through the generations. The near universal acceptance of such values, within some defining context, provided a cultural skeleton that could be fleshed out in a variety of ways: bodies of whatever kind could at least be assessed in relation to some set standards – to some accepted template. In the general context of culture 'high' could at least be distinguished from 'low', and each be assigned its proper sphere of influence and patronage. Despite some overlap, with the more daring intellectuals deigning (not always without some affectation) to confess to their love of football or the Beatles, people on the whole knew where they stood.

That knowledge is now harder to attain. Withdrawal of cultural absolutes has led to what one music critic has described as a 'seismic shift in cultural definition', when 'the canonic assumptions of music curators are melting in multicultural heat', and when, in the words of a BBC reformer, 'the old categorisations are no longer valid'. In this 'confusion . . . right across culture', Norman Lebrecht writes, 'nothing seems to mean what it used to': culture itself is in the process of being redefined.[10]

So taking a stand on anything is liable to be condemned for being 'élitist', or whatever is the latest term of politically correct abuse. 'Highbrow' and 'lowbrow' have been superseded by 'nobrow' in a postmodern world in which, it has been observed, there is 'a near universal reluctance . . . to make judgments of value'. Zachary Leader is referring in particular to literary academics, but his assessment can surely be generalised in a context in which Hal Foster (in a review of John Seabrook's significantly entitled *Nobrow*) implies that 'the old map of oppositions – high and low culture, Modernist and mass art, uptown and downtown – no longer corresponds to the world', and 'the Arnoldian criterion of "the best that is known and thought" is long gone', replaced by 'the Buzz principle of whatever is hot'. In John Seabrook's quoted words, which themselves defy any such trendy injunction against judgementalism: 'The real and important artists had to compete for attention with every kid with a guitar and an interesting haircut.'[11]

Postmodernism in practice, then, has been experienced, or at the very least observed (and often also feared), by anyone who has lived through the closing decades of the twentieth century. How does that practice relate to (if not derive from) its theory?

2.2 Theory

First, and most obvious, perhaps, to diagnose, is the central characteristic of 'decentredness'. By that I mean that postmodernism in any context – personal, cultural, historical, geographical or whatever – questions the prioritisation of any single centre. Centres have often been simply taken for granted: for the classical Greeks, an 'omphalos' or navel-stone at Delphi marked 'the centre of the entire earth',[12] and subsequent navel-gazers have similarly identified centrality as the point at which they stand; it's just the place from which we ourselves perceive and interpret the external world around us. But postmodernists assert that there is – there can be – no one privileged position from which to view that world, or from which to draw any meaningful conclusions about it. A slight shift of position – a slight adjustment of the centre – and it would all look very different; and who is to deny that shift? Relativity rules.

Postmodernism's 'decentring' can itself be taken, or interpreted, or understood, in many ways. But the essential point is simple: we lack any absolute external point (as sought by Archimedes in his theoretical efforts to move the earth) on which (or from which) to set our lever in such a way as to get a grip on our object of study – whether that study is the earth itself, or the past, or some structure of aesthetic or moral values. Frustrating though it might be, there's no place outside ourselves, or outside whatever it is that we wish to study or move, that can serve as our foundation.

That essential decentring on which postmodernism insists has implications for our perceptions and treatment of both space and time. In modernist mode let's take the former first – the decentring of space. As heirs of the Renaissance recovery of the rules of perspective, we might have assumed that the representation of space is a comparatively straightforward matter: all that's required, surely, is to draw it, or paint it, or define it as it is – 'realistically', as we used to say. Artists have progressively been able to leave us records of past places and people as they were: art historians can trace the development of their ability to master the techniques necessary to represent the external world 'truthfully' – as it exists or existed; so that whereas mediaeval painters may have distorted reality by (for instance) making important figures disproportionately large, their more sophisticated successors from the Renaissance on have progressively solved the problems of realistic representation. And later still, from the nineteenth century, we might have claimed to have evidence of past spatial realities from photographs, taken, we assume, with one of those wonderful cameras that 'never lie'.

But, as most of us have learnt from personal experience, spatial representation proves to be not quite so simple after all. Quite apart from frustrations we may have experienced with pencil or paintbrush, and perennial disappointments with holiday snapshots that fail to record the fullness of our experiences as we remember them, we may (at a yet more banal level) have tried to draw a map. Trying to direct someone, for instance, from the station to the college or to our home or wherever, we've all become aware that maps are (have to be) grossly oversimplified representations of an enormously complex reality. We have needed to simplify deliberately, in order to make our maps intelligible. So while there may be good reason to include the Old Red Lion pub on the corner, since it makes a useful landmark, there's no point at all in showing all the letter-boxes and litter-bins, and all the fifty-seven houses between that pub and our own home. Similarly, the map of the London Underground has no need to show a single road: roads are irrelevant when one's sole concern is a railway system. That's not to say, of course, that the roads are no longer there: it's just that we've chosen another focus, another centre from which some details (that remain important in other contexts) are irrelevant, and would only prove confusing. So we exclude much more data than we could ever include – data that may be central to the concerns of others, but (for the moment) is only peripheral to our own.

Fair enough, we may think, in a personal map or in a plan drawn for a specific purpose. But what about a representation of that same space without any such defined purpose? Then we would have to include everything, because anything might prove relevant; and that is what a 'real' map is. But, of course, no map can be real in that sense: it can never be a total representation of any given space; it must always be drawn from some standpoint, and for some purpose. We simply can't draw it all, as it is, from every possible position. We may, with the interests and motivations of medieval Christians, draw our map of the world with Jerusalem at its centre; or we may take our starting point and central point as Europe. But there will always be innumerable other possibilities and perspectives, from which the world and its pictorial representation would look quite different: the focal and the peripheral are contingent and infinitely interchangeable.

Omissions, too, or 'silences', may reveal as much as what is shown. There's no hint of poverty or squalor in the green and pleasant land indicated by the pretty pastels of Georgian maps of the English counties; nor would one guess at slums from nineteenth-century maps of London. Native American names and settlements are significantly absent from seventeenth-century maps of New England, designed to entice white immigrants; and cycle-routes and footpaths find no place in the latest road map of North Carolina. Maps can never be neutral: even (or perhaps especially) through what they omit as irrelevant, they 'send messages and serve interests'.[13]

So even in that seemingly earth-bound subject of geography, we are left lacking any due north by which to take our bearings; and left with the unsettling conclusion of postmodern geographers, that 'No one is quite sure of the ground on which they stand, which direction they are facing, or where they are going'.[14]

That uncertainty is exacerbated by the postmodern erosion of belief in the possibility of any one *cultural* centre of physical space. Just as Jerusalem may have claimed the central ground in mediaeval maps, so Europe (and later more widely 'the West') long provided a starting-point, both for geographical definitions and representations, and for cultural norms and assessments. Others could then be accounted relatively inferior, less civilised, or more 'primitive', when measured against largely unquestioned Eurocentric standards; so that at least there was a structure in which people, actions and ideas could be located. But late twentieth-century globalisation, together with the radical re-evaluations necessitated by post-colonialism, changed all that; and quite new emphases are now placed, affecting which parts of the world seem worthy of study, and which perspectives they are to be viewed from.

That cultural and spatial decentring and its resultant ambiguities have obvious implications for everyone – but not least for historians, who, after all, must deal in space as well as time. So if the spatial definitions and boundaries of the objects of their study are in doubt, they already have a problem.

But that problem is exacerbated by the *chronological* questionings of postmodernism, and the doubts (and fears) provoked about the seemingly obvious subject of *time*. Time again, for most of the time, is something that we take very much for granted, referring in particular to past, present and future as discrete entities, which can each be defined without any significant problem. In this context of chronology our centre is the present. How otherwise could we ever organise our diaries and our lives? But even our seemingly tight and tidy chronological categories have come under question in the condition of postmodernity: the formerly fixed (as it seemed) centre of our present, from which we could look back and view the past or peer forward to the future, has been dislodged, no less than its spatial counterpart.

For the postmodernist, past, present and future seem to merge. In the words of T. S. Eliot:

Time present and time past
Are both perhaps present in time future,
And time future contained in time past.[15]

So historians are left with their own perennial problem exacerbated, of knowing where to insert their analytic knife into that seamless chronological whole, and of knowing in particular from what assumed standpoint in time they should operate.

This is something we'll need to consider further in Chapter 2, but the problem is far from confined to historians. Everyone is left with the difficulty in practice of viewing themselves (and defining their selves) at an unstable moment in time – a time in which 'the present' is deprived of its absolute centrality, and appears more as a constantly shifting position as it supervenes on what was (just now in the immediate past) 'the future'. Our identities themselves, so dependent as they are on time, take on a form more blurred, and also with greater potential, when, in John Forrester's words, 'the reorganisation of the past and the future go hand in hand . . . the past dissolves in the present, so that the future becomes (once again) an open question, instead of being specified by the fixity of the past'.[16]

That openness is precisely what is so phobia-inducing – or so exciting – about postmodernism; and the doors are not just inched aside, but flung wide open at both personal and public levels. By that I mean that the future of personal and public identities itself becomes an open question; for, decentred again, we are no longer defined and 'specified by the fixity of the past'. We are no longer what we have to be, or what we are expected by others to become, or what we might be in relation to others who are themselves fixed in themselves and in relation to us. We are emancipated from the constraints by which other people (in the form of parents, society, religion or our workplace) would define us, and left free to redefine ourselves.

That freedom of self-definition is not always easy to assume (which is why, again, it can often induce phobia), for it implies a need to find a meaning and a purpose, and even an essence, for ourselves; and, on the moral assumption that our choice for ourselves must be universalisable (so fit for others, too), that has public as well as merely personal implications. In other words, we are involved in defining the sort of society or world we want ourselves and our successors to aim for as the future, and to live in.

That helps, then, in our attempts to define postmodernism, for it is shown importantly as revealing the open possibility (the freedom and indeed the necessity) of defining ourselves and our societies. But there is one other problem, central to any definition, that no less forms a part of postmodernism's own definition. That problem is linguistic. The notorious 'linguistic turn' must be central to any discussion of what postmodernism is, for it raises again the whole question of how we experience ourselves and the world, and of how (if at all) it's possible to communicate such experience. For communication in any language is based on the presupposition that both parties know how their shared language is used. That is, communication is premised on a belief that words refer to 'things', external entities of one sort or another (whether physical or abstract), and that there is a fixed and reliable relationship between the word and its referent. In other words, when I refer to my desk or the sun, I'm confident that you know what I'm talking about.

But the linguistic tributary to postmodernism's current has swamped any such confidence in a sea of doubt (and thence of distress and fear again). For how, it has been asked, can we ever know that our verbal descriptions refer to any external actualities? Is there any correspondence between what we apprehend through the senses and the descriptions that we formulate in language? And how can we ever demonstrate that there is or that there isn't? Always we'll find ourselves needing to base our arguments on something that we cannot prove; we'll have to start by taking something for granted. And while we may seem to get along with that, on the whole, at a practical level, in theoretical terms it seems to leave the whole of language like a net that's cast over the physical world, catching some things and excluding others, and utterly contingent in its process of selection. With another linguistic net, we'd catch another world; and how do we know which one is preferable, or more valid, or more 'true'?

That in turn relates closely to the whole problem of categorisation. For if our experienced world has to be caught in a linguistic net, the component parts of it have to be identified; and that identification is not always as straightforward as it seems. It seems straightforward because of habit – because we see things as we expect to see them, and our expectations have already been defined in language. That is, we've chosen a way of structuring our perceptions, discriminating individual entities; and we see things accordingly – as if that's how they are, rather than how we've made them. On the whole, we can take those delineations and definitions for granted: indeed, we have to, in order to attempt communication. But they could be different.

Thus, for example, when Australian aborigines first saw a horse and rider, they thought that what they were seeing was a single creature. It was only when the rider dismounted that they were able to discriminate between the human and the animal, and so interpret their perceptions, as we would say, correctly. Nothing in their previous experience had enabled them to adopt the categorisations that Europeans had long taken for granted, and so they failed to make the distinctions by which the phenomenon of a 'horse-and-rider' is normally meaningful. In a similar way Europeans (in a now discredited example) were thought to fail to discriminate, and therefore to name, the many different types of snow recognised by the Inuit; and we anyway know that we can be mistaken in our apprehensions, visually mistaking one person for another, tactually misreading skin for plastic, and even finding it hard to distinguish our own corporeal boundaries from those of a partner with whom we are feeling particularly close.

In terms of both space and time, then, and of our descriptions of the world and of ourselves, postmodernism's decentring has profound, and potentially disquieting, implications. Any certainties have been superseded by the opening up of new, and therefore unsettling (and exhilarating), possibilities. (We'll be considering these further in our final chapters.)

That opening up, too, has implications not only at a personal level, but in the public sphere: decentring refers not least to politics. Whereas, then, in the past traditional hierarchies, or orderings of society, have generally been accepted until some crisis has (very rarely) provoked a revolution that instituted an (ultimately) equally orderly alternative, the centres of power and authority are now revealed as being as potentially unstable as those of geography or time. From what standpoint, it can be asked, do we necessarily defer to some other(s)? What justifies allegiance to one set of socio-political institutions and values rather than another? As Tony Blair's advisers noted, unquestioning 'respect for authority' may well be 'in terminal decline', unless authority can be justified in terms of a structure of values that we've agreed to share; and that can be further cause for political concern – another area where theory may well impact on practice.

3 Pomophobia: some symptoms

It is, then, at least in part the loss of personal and public certainties that results in pomophobia. The condition was foreseen by, respectively, T. S. Eliot and Rainer Maria Rilke, when they explained poetically that 'human kind/Cannot bear very much reality', and that we apparently 'don't feel very securely at home' in what is seen to be only an 'interpreted world'.[17] Postmodernism has served to confirm Rilke's perception that the world we inhabit is a world that *we* (not God, nature or some impersonal force) have constructed, or 'interpreted', from a range of possibilities; so that it could be interpreted (and thence experienced) quite differently. That 'reality' of the contingency of ourselves in relation to the world, and of our own responsibility for choosing our own interpretations, is what is hard to bear; and it's at least a part of what induces pomophobia.

Confronted by the crisis of personal insecurity induced by recognition of our situation in postmodernity, we may, like David Hume (some two centuries earlier), escape to the pub for a pint of beer and a game of backgammon, to take our minds off sceptical 'reality', but more likely we stay behind morosely in our studies, lashing out in what is best described as 'fear' – quite literally a 'phobia' in the face of what we can no longer tolerate. Minor outbreaks of such pomophobia have been detected for some decades, but the problem seems now to be reaching, as they say, epidemic proportions. As postmodernism intrudes ever more obviously not only into academic life, but (as Tony Blair's advisers noted) even into the wider public consciousness, so does a fearful resistance build up against it. Forced to take cognisance of what they had assumed and hoped was to prove merely a short-lived intellectual fad, an increasing number of traditionalists now find themselves impelled to get off their fences and take up arms against the barbarian hordes that threaten them – and threaten them not (as is now clear) with just some passing trend, but with the prospect of a permanent *condition*.

'For a time', says a character in Joseph Conrad's *Heart of Darkness*, 'I would feel I belonged still to a world of straightforward facts; but the feeling would not last long';[18] and with those words he expresses well the feelings of those modernists who have long continued to believe that they live in 'a world of straightforward facts', but who have now been challenged by the increasingly insistent questioning of postmodernists. The security of 'belonging' to a world where 'facts' can be ordered in a 'straightforward' way is not to be lightly given up; but there is some consciousness now that that security will 'not last long'. The result is an anxiety, and even fear again, which is often manifested as aggression.

In relation to 'facts', historical study is a discipline that is particularly vulnerable. We'll consider some problems of postmodernism as they relate more specifically to history in the next chapter, but it's worth noting here that one eminent historian, Arnoldo Momigliano, is said to have been 'visibly distressed at the view of his American colleague Hayden White' – the postmodern guru who had notoriously claimed 'that history was a form of rhetoric'. As Momigliano later explained: 'I *fear* the consequences of [White's] approach to historiography because he has eliminated the *research for truth* as the main task of the historian.'[19]

Similar fears have been expressed by others. Richard Evans has published his 'defence of history' against the 'disintegrative attack' of postmodernism, believing, in the words of his blurb, that 'under the onslaught of postmodernist theory, the profession of history is in crisis'. Nor is that crisis safely quarantined in Europe: in the United States history has been similarly perceived as 'under siege'; and 'a new historical society' has 'emerged', with the express object of getting well-minded troops together, and concentrating forces, in order to make a more effective stand against the postmodern invaders.[20] In history, as in academia more generally, and in society and politics, pomophobia is a real issue.

As Momigliano indicated in the quotation above, it is concern with the attainability (at least in principle) of 'truth' that lies at the heart of academic fear of and resistance to postmodernism. Many intellectuals may affect to have come to terms with the death of a religious God, as announced so long ago by Nietzsche, but they are still far from assimilating Nietzsche's associated moral message. His main point, of course, was that, in the absence of God, humans would flounder in a moral vacuum; they might live for a time on the basis of decaying Christian values, but they'd come to realise that, after the death of God, those values were without foundation. A superstructure (in this case an intellectual and moral superstructure) can't last long suspended, as it were, in space, with nothing underneath to hold it up; once faith in it has gone, the whole edifice collapses – unless some substitute foundation is inserted in the place of what's been lost.

In the absence of any such injection or all-sustaining substitute, and rather than risking exposure to any general collapse, academics have lovingly embraced their own, more particular solutions: God may have died, but long live god – our new god, sometimes known, again, as 'Truth'. Siren calls from a multiplicity of 'special interest groups' entice us away from the turbulent waters unleashed by smashed-up disciplinary dams, towards the calm of some freshly revealed inlet (called feminism, postcolonialism or whatever) where we can take shelter and adjust our focus appropriately. That new focus may be narrow, but it enables us to keep our emotional (though not our intellectual) balance. No longer 'overwhelmed by choice', we can at least contrive 'to cope'.

Whether in art or philosophy, then, or history or literature, 'truth' has continued to provide a Holy Grail, the pursuit of which ultimately justifies the study of humanities (as well as sciences). 'It is the search for truth that must guide our labours,' wrote Geoffrey Elton of his history; Keith Windschuttle has reaffirmed that it is the historian's obligation to 'pursue the truth' – an admittedly difficult task, he does concede, but not impossible; and C. Behan McCullagh has yet more recently and more extravagantly asserted that 'Historians must provide, not just the truth, but the whole truth.' Brenda Almond has similarly defined philosophy as 'the pursuit of truth'; and Bernard Williams seems implicitly to agree when he suggests that 'if philosophy, or anything like it, is to have a point, the idea of *"getting it right"* must be in place'.[21]

I shall consider this further in relation specifically to history in Chapter 2, but here we should note that it is, perhaps, above all postmodernism's questioning and relativisation of truth that has provoked the disease of pomophobia.

This should not surprise us. People have seldom shown much enthusiasm for having their most profound beliefs brought into question. Some two and a half millennia ago, Socrates was to learn that lesson to his cost. As the archetypal 'gadfly', he set about provoking his fellow Athenians from their intellectual and moral torpor, questioning the bases of their values and their 'truths'. But although his motives were no doubt of the highest, Socrates was not thanked for that gratuitous irritation. On the contrary, he learnt that his potential pupils preferred to retain their gods, their truths, and lead their lives (however worthless) unexamined.

And that's because examination – a probing questioning of long-accepted fundamentals – must always prove highly unsettling, at both political and personal levels. Politically, postmodernism has (appropriately enough) cut across the traditional divisions between 'left' and 'right', but there is no doubt that, from either perspective, it can seem subversive. It threatens the order and totalities of any ideology, and a conservative fear of such 'opening up' is by no means confined to the political right. Geoffrey Elton, though, does again conveniently express the point that for some people there is something naively irresponsible about being 'ever anxious to promote changes that will make things better', since, for them, 'being adult means being able to accept people and things as they really are'.[22] To Eltonians, postmodernism then represents the childishness of trying to redefine what things and people 'really are', which opens up all sorts of threatening possibilities.

The politically inspired anxiety of Elton and others is paralleled at a more personal level. Barbara Herrnstein Smith has identified a condition of 'cognitive dissonance', experienced when one's most deeply held beliefs are brought into question. Her description may sound melodramatic, but only to those who have not (for whatever reason) yet experienced the phenomenon:

> an impression of inescapable noise or acute disorder, a rush of adrenalin, sensations of alarm, a sense of unbalance or chaos, residual feelings of nausea and anxiety. These are the forms of bodily distress that occur when one's ingrained, taken-for-granted sense of how certain things are – and thus presumably will be and in some sense *should* be – is suddenly or insistently confronted by something very much at odds with it.

Our response to ideas that are incompatible with our own beliefs may, she explains, range 'from perplexed and resentful withdrawal to elaborate condescension, detailed counterargument, virulent attack, or attempted suppression'[23] – and that diagnosis is one that can be confirmed by any exponent of postmodernism. What complicates the matter is that it's not only intellects that are engaged in such issues, but emotions; and the dominating emotion here is fear.

3.1 The fear of chaos

That fear is ultimately of a reversion to primitive chaos. Christian and Greek creation stories recount the triumphant overcoming of the chaotic formlessness of which the world originally consisted. In Genesis 1.2 we read of how 'the earth was without form, and void; and darkness was upon the face of the deep', before God duly created light and distinguished one part of the universe from another, giving the whole enlightenment and structure. In the words of the seventeenth-century believer Thomas Browne, the Christian God is 'the ordainer of order'. And for early Greek thinkers similarly, 'verily first of all did Chaos come into being', from which day and night and the distinct parts of the earth were subsequently formed; or in Plato's later words, 'out of disorder he [God] brought order, considering that this was far better'.[24] Indeed, in his enormously influential work *Timaeus*, Plato goes on to describe how:

> When all things were in disorder God created in each thing, both internally in relation to itself and externally in relation to other things, certain harmonies in which were included all possible harmonies and proportions. For in those days nothing had any order except by accident; nor did any of the things which now have names deserve to be named at all.[25]

Human intellectual history starts with that victory over chaotic form-lessness: order prevailed, with units of the world individuated, defined and described.

But as Max Weber reminds us, that order was not (*pace* Plato and post-Nietzsche) in fact God-given: all systems of ideas represent attempts 'to bring order into the chaos of those facts which we have drawn into the field circumscribed by our *interest*'.[26] So *our interest* determines the centre from which some order can be constructed from what nevertheless remains essentially disordered; and it is, as Hume saw, in our further interest to retain our faith in our chosen foundations, since it's only that that makes any knowledge possible. But in Plato's terms we remain in a pre-creation situation where any order that prevails is only 'by accident' or faith, and can be challenged at any time. And, of course, our interests do change, so that any intellectual victories we win are never final, but only ever provisionally secured. The order imposed (and the language which that order makes possible) remains always in danger of falling apart again, of dis-integration, of dis-appearing to reveal primeval realities once more. So again, as Rilke saw and felt (and as pomophobes recognise but cannot accept), we are never very securely at home in our ordered world, where the order depends on what is only an interpretation, and so is itself contingent and constantly under challenge.

That whole matter is interestingly exemplified in Jenny Diski's novel *Rainforest*.[27] As the central character, Mo is (at least through most of the book, before she becomes a part-time cleaner) an anthropologist. Her researches of the huge rainforest in Borneo necessitate selecting a small (manageable) sample area, which can be divided into a grid, marked off by string into squares of land that she can then study, classify and report on in detail. Over the natural chaos of rampant, essentially uncontrollable nature, she contrives to cast her framework of scientific rationality.

As she realises (and as she comes personally to experience), some people, including most obviously poets and philosophers, can literally be driven mad in the absence of such intellectual definitions, boundaries and constraints. For that imposed structure is what enables her and others to go to the forest (representing nature) and look at it, measure it and collect their data, without any risk of being overwhelmed by it, or of personally becoming a 'part of the natural world'; it's what enables humans to remain deliberately detached, 'unconnected' and 'alien'. Mathematics, recommended by Galileo as the very 'language' in which nature herself is written,[28] is of course the supreme model for facilitating such distancing techniques: as Mo realises, it 'was invented to avoid madness; it's what scientists use to stop themselves going crazy'. And her own characteristic orderliness encourages her too in acceptance of the proper scientific procedures: it suits her normally cool and careful temperament to cast her controlling net over the otherwise unpredictable disorderliness of chaotic nature.

But one day she loses that habitual control of her own emotions and allows herself to be sexually seduced; and that encounter threatens more than just her physical integrity. For her offhand young lover, Joe, also raises fundamental questions relating to her careful (and hitherto unquestioned) scientific procedures:

> 'There's one thing that occurred to me though, about your grids and your search for the ultimate truth about the rainforests.

Supposing they're in the wrong place, your squares? Supposing they're in the one place that doesn't give you a representative sample . . .? Supposing . . . the truth you're searching for is between your squares, or concealed by the lines that make the framework of your grid? All those bits of paper would be meaningless, wouldn't they?'

Her recognition that Joe might indeed be right, that all her careful work might be grounded on false premises and be invalid, and that the ultimate threatening chaos had not after all been satisfactorily circumvented, provokes Mo's mental breakdown. Joe's scepticism seems only to confirm a lesson she had previously learnt about her own past, when the ideal (idealised) construction of her memories relating to her childhood and her father had been similarly (if inadvertently) exposed as invalid by her mother's conflicting account. Newly discovered alternative perspectives on her past left Mo feeling 'cheated. They had stolen the world of her childhood.' Her carefully constructed biographical narrative, all centred on herself, 'turned out to have been no more than a piece in a jigsaw', one interpretation among many possibilities; and her previously firm 'memories' proved to have been 'no more than imaginings'.

Natural science and history are there brought together in biography, and Mo later comes to accept that those who try to make sense, whether of nature or of the past, can do no better than 'come up with interesting and plausible stories . . . [that] are no more than speculation'. Producing a linear narrative of one's life, or of the natural world, is really just a way of coping – a way of narrowing things down, to prevent the need for further thought. And after her breakdown that's how, on a personal level, she continues to cope: 'I get through the time by making one thing follow another. A simple line of events, of time . . . Above all, I don't want speculation'; for speculation is what disrupts, is what reveals anew the underlying chaos, and what results, for Mo and pomophobes, in intolerable anxieties and fears.

3.2 Some problems of identity

You've stirred in me my unacted part.
(Virginia Woolf)[29]

A self-portrait by the artist Glenys Barton is entitled *Lady with Three Faces* (Figure 1). It takes the form of a small sculpted figure of a woman. She is presented in a demure pose, with hands clasped in front of her;

Figure 1 Identity: choosing our mask. Glenys Barton, *Lady with Three Faces*, 1980
Source: Angela Flowers Gallery. Photo: Karen Norquay.

and at her feet lie three masks. The woman herself has no face – no features to indicate a recognisable identity – but she is ready to adopt any one of three possible selfhoods, which lie there ready and waiting, by donning the appropriate mask. She just awaits some stimulus to choose one rather than another, or like Virginia Woolf's character Miss La Trobe (in the quotation above) awaits some provocation for a change in role.

Pomophobes' anxieties and fears relate not only to underlying cosmic chaos, but also (and nearer home) to issues of the self and personal identity. For it's not only the natural external world that threatens to elude the constraints of our tidy but contingent laws and structures, and to disintegrate into chaos, but our own good selves. Remove us from the ordered social frameworks within which we normally operate, or simply adjust the grid that, like Mo, we've attempted to throw over our everyday experience, and then see how we fare. As Miss La Trobe indicates, aspects of our personality can lie repressed, unused, unacted for many years, or even for ever; but they can suddenly be provoked or encouraged to emerge, and we realise what we might have been. 'I might have been – Cleopatra,' as Miss La Trobe suddenly recognises.

Our reliance on external supports for our identities obviously varies: the less ontologically secure might be rendered nervous by the loss of their (specially chosen, self-defining) designer shoes, or by unexpected retimetabling or rerouting of the train that regularly carries them to work; but even the toughest can disintegrate in solitary confinement, where the self can't be confirmed by any place or any other person. And the problem of a potential psychic disintegration (an unravelling of the whole) is an important constituent of pomophobia.

It's a problem that derives from the postmodern insistence on multiple perspectives. That is to say, the self can no longer simply be taken for granted, as a coherent and enduring entity, under a supposedly unitary gaze (whether of self or others or both – for both would presumably conform). Instead, the self fragments, as it is variously observed and defined from various standpoints and perspectives. Just as the supposedly 'objective reality' of *events* is liable to disintegrate, so too does that of *people*; and that can be just as disturbing, or even more so. In the poetic words of Coleridge:

> What is there in thee, Man, that can be known?
> Dark fluxion, all unfixable by thought,
> A phantom dim of past and future wrought.[30]

We may, then, find it impossible to integrate the various, sometimes anomalous, or even self-contradictory descriptions of a person into a single and coherent definition, impossible to fix the 'dark fluxion' of a person's past, present, and future. We may be surprised by how people act, and refer to them as acting 'out of character', but there remains a limit to what we can accept as having been done by them; there comes a point at which credulity is stretched too far. For example, it may be unlike our friend to go out and get drunk and cause mayhem in a bar, but we may be able to 'rationalise' such behaviour on a particular occasion, as a result of some bad news he'd recently received about his wife's infidelity. But we can't believe that, however much provoked, he'd actually kill another person. Our perceptions of his character – his identity – can be modified so far, but no farther.

But the awful truth seems to be that our friend did kill someone that night; so not only is our previous characterisation of him demolished, but also our own perception of ourselves as reasonable judges of other individuals and (yet more unsettling) of what human beings more generally are like. This is one of the problems of the Holocaust, with which we're still struggling to come to terms: how were supposedly 'civilised' and 'cultured' people reduced to behaviour that was utterly 'barbaric'? How do we accommodate such an obvious contradiction and anomaly? We can hardly redefine our terms in such a way as to include barbarism as a characteristic of civilisation; so we are left with the problem of redefining what we believe that it is to be human. And that's something that can't be easily or conclusively defined at all: on the contrary, it is as elusive as the personality or selfhood of Miss La Trobe, who, having chosen another mask, might have been, or might be, Cleopatra.

4 Conclusion

Fears, then, of cosmic chaos and of disintegrating identities have to be included in our diagnosis of pomophobia. Such fears are driving a seemingly increasing number of postmodern people into rapidly reviving 'fundamentalisms' (or extremisms) of various kinds. The theoretically foundationless prove most likely to seek practical foundations; and in a supposedly secular society certainties (however paradoxically, as it might initially seem) are sought not least in religion. There is, in fact, of course no paradox: however apparently inconsistent, fundamentalism can be seen as an obvious outcome of postmodernism. The unlimited freedom of choice, in matters ranging from lifestyle to morals and to the formulation of one's personal identity – that freedom proposed by postmodernism – is no more alluring to many now than it has ever been. Better one leap of faith into a totalitarian ideology, whether political or theological, if that removes the intolerable burden of having to make incessant choices as an individual burdened with (and tortured by) autonomy.

The 'speculation' that Mo feared, with its potential disruption to existing order, has historically (before, that is, the advent of post-modernity itself) appeared most obviously in the period that marks the earlier great transition, from 'mediaevalism' to 'modernity'. We'll examine that previous threat to intellectual and emotional order, together with some responses that parallel contemporary pomophobia, in Chapter 4. First, though (before looking in Chapter 3 at some claimed antecedents), we'll consider postmodernism's relationship more specifically with history.

2

POSTMODERNISM AND HISTORY

1 Introduction

> They [scholars] are like impassioned lovers when one dares to
> suggest to them that the object of their passion has faults.
> (Samuel Auguste Tissot, 1768)[1]

Postmodernism and history have made uneasy partners. Indeed, as we
have already seen, historians have been particularly prone to severe
bouts of pomophobia, behaving in the manner suggested by Tissot in the
quotation above – affronted that the supposedly perfect object of
their passion might be subject to external critique. So when they haven't
gone so far as to attack postmodernism, they've usually contrived to
ignore it, in the belief, presumably, that it's an irritant that will simply
disappear if they keep their heads down and uncontaminated by any such
irrelevant theorising. Professor Norman Davies has described postmodernism as 'a pastime . . . for all those who give precedence to the study
of historians over the study of the past' – implying, among other things,
that even if postmodernism (discounted, significantly, as nothing more
serious than a 'pastime') might have something to do with historians, it
has nothing whatever to do with history, or with what historians do.[2]

That assessment by an historian seems to be borne out by other
commentators. In his wide-ranging examination (and actual historicisation) of the condition of postmodernity in 1989, David Harvey lists
'art, literature, social theory, psychology, and philosophy' as 'other
realms' sharing the postmodern concerns of architecture and urban
design; but no mention there of history itself. Charles Jencks edited *The
Post-Modern Reader* as 'An Anthology of a World Movement' in 1992.
By that publication date, the blurb claimed, postmodernism was already
'embracing all areas of culture', so entries were included on literature, art,
architecture, film, sociology, politics, geography, feminism, science and
religion; but history remained conspicuous through its absence and

27

presumed immunity to the otherwise all-embracing world movement. There has been little movement since. An anthology of texts designed (in 1996) to set postmodernism in its historical context should, the publisher's blurb claims, prove 'an indispensable and multidisciplinary resource in philosophy, literature, cultural studies, social theory, and religious studies'; but despite the historical orientation, history itself can apparently dispense with such theoretical resources. *The Icon Critical Dictionary of Postmodern Thought*, published in 1998, includes a substantial first part devoted to the 'History and Cultural Context' of postmodernism, but while it contains contributions on the relationship of postmodernism with philosophy, critical and cultural theory, politics, art, literature, music and much else, no reference to history is made. History's absence is evident, too, in the context of the important and wide-ranging collection of essays by Zygmunt Bauman, cited in Chapter 1. In *Postmodernity and its Discontents* Bauman discusses theoretical and practical aspects of postmodernism, including matters of time and art and fiction, which can hardly fail to impinge on an informed historical study. But the book, as we read on the cover, will appeal to students of 'sociology, cultural studies, philosophy and anthropology' – but not, it seems by implication, history.[3]

Admittedly (as we shall consider later), there have been notable attempts by some historians to come to terms with the postmodern challenge, and to adapt their work in very positive ways. But, on the whole, historians have retained their traditional and long-lived distrust of philosophy and 'theory', and have seen postmodernism as an alien and hostile force – as something to be feared. Geoffrey Elton considered that it resulted in a 'frivolous nihilism which allows any historian to say whatever he likes', and Gertrude Himmelfarb stresses what she sees as 'the basic incompatibility of postmodernism and historical study'. Postmodernism, she is clear, 'is not so much a revision of modernist history as a repudiation of it'; in the name of 'liberation and creativity', it leads to 'intellectual and moral suicide'. Not so much suicide as murder, in the eyes of Keith Windschuttle. *The Killing of History* (1997) is presented by Windschuttle as a defence of 'the traditional practice of history' against 'a potentially mortal attack'. Postmodernism, he believes, constitutes 'a lethal process [that is] well underway'; and 'if historians allow themselves to be prodded all the way to this theoretical abyss, they will be rendering themselves and their disciples extinct'. For 'theoretical and literary interlopers . . . are now . . . hungrily stalking the corridors', and the discipline of history is in real danger of being 'hunted to extinction'. Arthur Marwick agrees. Referring to postmodernism as 'metaphysical nonsense' and 'pernicious rubbish', he too is convinced of its incompatibility with history. 'I do not believe', he wrote in 2001, 'there can be any accommodation between postmodernist ideas and the approaches of serious professional historians . . . It is open to all young people to adopt postmodern attitudes if they are persuaded by them. But if they are persuaded, they would be best advised to give up the study of history.'[4]

These last examples appear to bear out Robert F. Berkhofer's characterisation of what he describes as 'the *panicky* reactions of those opposing postmodernist trends',[5] and there is indeed some justification for those pomophobic conclusions, in that 'modernist' history's foundations have (as we shall see below) indeed been undermined, irreparably. Such foundational concepts as 'truth', 'fact' and 'objectivity' have been exposed as at worst meaningless, and at best in need of radical redefinition; and some postmodernists have gone so far as to question the point of persisting at all with what can be seen as an effectively outmoded modernist enterprise. But I shall go on to argue that there's no need to be unduly negative: a reconstructed history can incorporate rather than repudiate postmodernist ideas and ideals, and we'll be considering some of the more positive aspects of postmodernism in Chapters 5 and 6. First, though (while remembering the permeability of our own defining borders), in order to assess the force of the postmodern challenge in this context, it's necessary briefly to examine the nature of what is now properly referred to as 'modernist history'.

2 Modernist history

> History, one could argue, has been the essence of the Enlighten-
> ment project.
>
> (Modris Eksteins)[6]

Viewing history, at Modris Eksteins' invitation, as the very core of post-Enlightenment modernism helps to make more comprehensible the fearful reactions on the part of historians to what they believe may be the prospect of their own demise (or radical diminution) under any new postmodern dispensation. The centrality of history derived from its legitimising power – a power, that is, to legitimate and underpin *any* intellectual and ideological position, but in the context of modernity to legitimate the very 'essence' of modernity itself – namely, faith in that progressive development that gave such ample cause for self-congratulation to the Enlightenment thinkers themselves and their successors.

For what (modernist) histories achieved was the imposition of *meaning* on the course of the past. Those fortunate enough to live in the present, it was (and is by many still) believed, could be reasonably seen as enjoying the ripened fruits of a civilisation set on a progressive trajectory, the continuing course of which was guaranteed by the application of those universalisable procedures that had already allowed progression from darkness to light. That light was the beam of reason, and as characterising human beings uniquely, rationality could not only facilitate but also justify human domination of the non-human – whether by science in the case of *sub*-human nature or, in the domain of the *super*-human, by a substitute theology. With the former, we are not directly concerned here, but with the latter we certainly are.

For whereas theology in the past had resort, for its explanations, to gods and spirits (just as pre-scientists relied on beliefs now derided as mystical or superstitious), so now reason could hold universal sway – which implied (or seemed to many to imply) the replacement of theology itself by a more persuasive (a more rational) donor of meaning and direction: namely, *history*. It was history, in modernity, that could be utilised to justify the ways of God to man, showing how we got to where we are, and why. So that unsurprisingly Carlyle, from his lofty vantage-point in the nineteenth century, could claim history as 'the only study', or the only one that truly mattered, resembling as it did nothing less than 'universal Divine Scripture'.[7]

No high priests of such a favoured subject are likely to relinquish their position easily; and modernist historians continue confidently to pontificate, no less than theologians of old, propounding dogma. 'Nowhere in this lengthy book will you come across a single insignificant fact . . . I . . . believed that I understood what he [Marcel Proust] knew, or thought, or felt, and it is my wish to convey this to the reader.' The book will provide 'all that we can know about Proust, everything that is useful to know in order to understand him and his work'.[8] Those claims, made here in relation to a new (2000) biography, exemplify the attitude and aspirations of modernist history more generally. The biographer or historian assumes that he can assemble everything relevant or 'useful' for a complete understanding of his subject, identifying 'facts' as significant or insignificant, and excluding the latter; that he can come to understand what past people have known or thought or even felt; and that it is his professional function to convey that understanding to his reader. As the so-called History Subject Benchmarking Group (a committee of the great and the good drawn from British university history departments in the late 1990s) proclaimed in its initial statement: 'We take it as self-evident that knowledge and understanding of the past is of incalculable value.' That this (unproblematised) 'knowledge and understanding' were attainable seemed not to be in question.

Modernist historians, then, reflected (or, as it seems from the examples above, continue to reflect) the virtues and vices of modernism itself, including not least its confident optimism and its parochial dogmatism. To put the case optimistically in the past tense, both the optimism and the dogmatism of modernist historians derived from their belief that they could ultimately succeed in recovering 'the truth' about what had happened in the past. There was a past out there – namely, what had happened before the now of the present; and if proper professional procedures were followed, the reality – the truth – about that past could be recovered. 'Since Ranke' (in the mid-nineteenth century), writes John H. Arnold in 2000, 'historians of every hue have had first and foremost in their minds the idea of "truth" as something that can be approached or achieved.'[9] So that historians' work was (and again seemingly is) in effect their reconstitution of the past as it had happened, and their re-presentation of that true account to lesser mortals (men and women who were less able or willing to sacrifice themselves for the cause of historical truth). It might, of course, take some time to fill out the whole picture of what the past had been, but individuals could helpfully contribute their jigsaw puzzle pieces to what had to be a communal enterprise of like-minded professionals. They could be hopeful – optimistic – about the ultimate outcome; and they could meanwhile be confident – even dogmatic (in the style of Jean-Yves Tadié) – about their hard-won results.

Fundamental to modernist history's claims and aspirations are two characteristics that I'll go on briefly to consider: first, its claimed status as a 'science'; and second, its presupposed 'centres' in both space and time. Such scientism and centrism have both been subject to post-modernist critique.

2.1 Scientism

> History as 'a science, no more and no less'.
> (J. B. Bury)[10]

Modernist history's claim to scientific status is exemplified in Bury's characterisation of the subject in 1903 as 'a science, no more and no less'. But the underlying assumptions of Bury's modernist position, and the methodologies consequently proposed for historical reconstructions, were parts of an enormously powerful intellectual tradition that stemmed from the very origins of Western thought. As early as the fifth century BC, the great Greek historian Thucydides deferred to science as his model: it's that deference that has made him accounted 'great' by subsequent admirers. A large part of his assumed virtue lies in his specific rejection of the less than scientific approaches of his predecessors, Homer and Herodotus. Those two had admittedly left accounts of what had happened in the past. Indeed, Homer was regrettably the only source available for the earliest period of what (owing to the inadequacy of his poetic approach) had to be slightingly referred to as 'pre-history'; but his evidence couldn't be relied on. As a mere poet, his priority was to 'charm for the moment', rather than (in the manner appropriate to a proper historian) to tell 'the truth'. And Herodotus wasn't much better: though often subsequently acknowledged as the 'father of history', he couldn't really be taken seriously. After all, he often professed himself unable to make up his mind concerning different accounts of the past episodes that he was meant to be recording, and (irresponsibly) left his readers to choose between conflicting versions. So he too is probably best viewed, in the contemptuous words of a much later historian, as just 'an agreeable story-teller, who meant to entertain and nothing more'.[11]

Entertainment on its own has seldom seemed sufficient justification for the weighty matter of historical study, and Thucydides is the first of many historians who have seen themselves as following scientific procedures in order to be, above all, moral teachers. Fleeting 'charm' is not enough: his history is designed to be of *lasting* use – 'a possession for all time'. And that's because, he believes, one may *learn* from the past, so long as it's accurately portrayed: one is, in particular, enabled to see the mistakes that others have made, and so avoid repeating them oneself. It's in that morally didactic context that Thucydides resorts to his model of science – and more particularly to the contemporary medical science of the so-called Hippocratics (followers of the renowned physician Hippocrates).

The Hippocratics believed that, in order to advance medicine, it was necessary to make careful observations and records. Symptoms, prescriptions, and reactions to treatments had to be carefully noted, in order to enable the doctor to predict what would happen in similar situations in the future. The underlying assumption was that, after obviously taking some individual variations into account, human beings generally respond similarly to similar stimuli. So, for example, one person's bodily reaction to hemlock will closely resemble another's; and it's beneficial to have a record of that reaction, so that (unless we greatly dislike our patients) we don't persist in prescribing hemlock for a headache.

It's on that medical approach that Thucydides modelled his own attitude to history: let us get to understand precisely what has happened and ascertain the universal laws that underly that, and then record our findings, to enable people in the future to avoid repeating the mistakes and follies of the past. If we succeed in doing that, our historical records will be of as much practical benefit as our medical records; they will be something of permanent value. But we must be sure, of course, that those records are indeed accurate: we must not be misled by false information; we have to get it right. And Thucydides tells us what lengths he went to, in order to get his record right – personally experiencing some things, selecting reliable witnesses for others, double-checking their accounts, and generally taking all the care about evidence that has enabled so many subsequent historians to claim to have been recording nothing less than 'the truth'.

Thucydides' scientific approach to historical writing was duly applauded when science itself, in its new modernist guise, came emphatically into its own in the seventeenth century. Thomas Hobbes, for example, was so fascinated by the scientific developments of his time that he used them as a model in his own work on psychology and moral and political philosophy; and it's by no means fortuitous that he was also sufficiently impressed by Thucydides to publish his own translation of the *History of the Peloponnesian War*. He appreciated the 'scientific' nature of that early historical work, and David Hume, a little later, similarly contrasts the earlier fabulous works of poets and orators with 'the commencement of *real* history' in the pages of Thucydides.[12]

Scientific history was given a further boost by the highly influential seventeenth-century thinker and philosophical publicist Francis Bacon. In the history of science Bacon is conventionally assigned the role that he claimed for himself – namely, that of a revolutionary thinker who dispensed with the past and pointed a new way forward along the route that leads to us. But that doesn't imply that he renounced any need for historical study. On the contrary, he was well aware of history's power (not least in politics), and followed Thucydides in wanting to keep it free from any imputations of being less than serious and scientific. Again, then, it had to be clearly differentiated from that anarchic charmer poetry, the attraction of which derived from its notorious repudiation of constraints that might have bound it to the laws of nature or to truth. Poetry was the product of irresponsible 'imagination', and that was no contributor to real knowledge. Imagination, indeed, can lead us seriously astray and positively divert us from truth; so the understanding, with which history is associated, should 'not . . . be supplied with [imaginative] wings, but rather hung with weights'.[13] That, he thought, should inhibit any poetic propensity to flightiness on scientific history's part.

The Baconian influence on historiography is soon demonstrated by the comparatively little-known physician and writer Walter Charleton.

Charleton's own relative historical obscurity derives from the fact that his work in natural philosophy and theology was, as it were, overtaken by events, or rather by some more obviously heroic figures, including especially Isaac Newton. But in 1669 he published an essay in which he distinguished between history and poetry on the basis of the different mental characteristics of their respective practitioners. Everyone, he suggested, possesses some reason and some imagination (or, in his terminology, 'Judgment' and 'Phansie') – but in different proportions; and while poets require a predominance of the latter, to ensure their originality, historians need to have the frivolities of their imagination subdued by something more serious. Like the Baconian inductive scientist, the historian is to investigate data 'with an observant but empty mind', and with 'Judgment' (reason) firmly in control.[14]

That anti-imaginative, anti-poetic, scientistic model for history was only reinforced by the continuing successes of the sciences themselves. Enlightenment thought is largely characterised by its confident belief that scientific methods and procedures could be universally applied, so that individual human psychology and societies more collectively could be understood in scientific, mechanistic terms. In the famous introduction to his political treatise, *Leviathan*, Hobbes asks rhetorically: 'What is the Heart, but a Spring; and the Nerves, but so many Strings; and the Joynts, but so many Wheeles, giving motion to the whole Body . . .?' The machine of the human body can be replicated in the machine of society, or political body; and an understanding of their respective workings can only be of benefit. Just as Thucydides had indicated, therefore, a 'scientific' understanding of what had happened in the past could be advantageous for the future, for 'by how much one man has more experience of things past, than another; by so much also he is more Prudent, and his expectations the seldomer faile him'.[15]

History, then, is a scientific subject that enables us to understand the mechanistic (scientifically explicable) events of the past; and the scientific understanding of those general laws that always and invariably operate enables us also to predict what will happen in the future. Emphasising that crucial predictive function of history, the French philosopher Condorcet asks, again rhetorically: 'If man can, with almost complete assurance, predict phenomena when he knows their laws . . . why, then, should it be regarded as a fantastic undertaking to sketch, with some pretence to truth, the future destiny of man on the basis of history?'[16]

That confidence, that 'almost complete assurance', was further enhanced in the nineteenth century, when science (and its implications) became a matter virtually of popular entertainment, and when the renown (or notoriety) in particular of Charles Darwin – another self-confessed Baconian – was widespread. Successful science seemed to provide an example of what could be more generally achieved, and so became, yet more emphatically, a model for universal emulation. It was at this time, significantly, that the word 'scientism' was coined, intended to express the hope (or belief) that the scope of science, and the application of scientific methods, could be indefinitely extended.

Historians weren't slow to appropriate that credibility-inducing formula for their own discipline. Indeed, Darwinian antecedents were specifically claimed by the president of the American Historical Association when he formulated his ideal of a 'genuinely scientific school of history, which shall remorselessly examine the sources and separate the wheat from the chaff; which shall critically balance evidence; which shall dispassionately and moderately set forth results'.[17] Balance, lack of passion, moderation – these moral characteristics supposedly displayed by the Victorian scientist – were widely applauded in public, and were appropriately adopted by approval-seekers elsewhere; and if remorse-lessness was a less obviously desirable human quality, it could properly be shown towards something that was as seemingly inanimate and untouched by human contact as historical evidence. At all events, the qualities ascribed to scientists were to be emulated by historians, who then, no less than their illustrious models, would be enabled to separate the gold from the dross, the wheat from the chaff, and with due humility convey the truth to lesser mortals.

It was no wonder, then, that in Britain Lord Acton could optimistically envisage the perfection or *end* of history, 'now that all information is within reach, and every problem has become capable of solution'. And it was only right that the justification for that optimism should be attributed, as it was by Bury, to the divorce of history from her traditional humanities partners, in favour of entering 'into closer relations with the sciences, which deal objectively with the facts of the universe'.[18]

The prestige of science persisted through much of the twentieth century, and continued to encourage a perceived need to maintain professional respectability and academic credibility by re-emphasising what were supposedly 'scientific' virtues. Historians were expected to eliminate all traces of themselves – their own partialities and prejudices, their own 'subjectivity'; remaining detached from their objects of study, they were to let the evidence speak for itself; and they would then be able to produce a 'balanced' and 'objective' account of the past, which as closely as possible resembled (if it didn't yet quite equate with) 'truth'. This depended, of course, on the existence of a real entity out there – a (single) past with its attendant (real) objects left as evidence – which it was the historian's duty to reach and get to know; and as recently as 1975 the respected historian Peter Gay was reaffirming belief in just such an entity. Thus, the 'pressure toward objectivity is realistic because the objects of the historian's inquiry are precisely that, objects, out there in a real and a single past'.[19] Historians then could reasonably remain insistent that they were tracking down the truth about the past, and that, just like scientists again, they were revealing only what was already there awaiting their discovery; they were penetrating to the reality of the past, to what was the case, to the truth.

The scientistic aspirations of history can thus be seen to be a part of the much wider, and hugely optimistic, modernist enterprise. A belief in a directing God, making appropriate interventions to ensure a moral progression through time, may, from the eighteenth century on, have been largely eroded; but all was not lost, when a ready replacement could be seen in the form of a more specifically *human* progress. That human progress could be effected through the application of human reason (or what came to be thought of as scientific procedures) to natural and human problems; and that included a knowledge of the truth about the past. Modernist, scientistic history was, as Modris Eksteins claims, at the core of the whole modernist project, revealing the foundational base and the subsequent trajectory of a supposedly indefinite human progress. It's no wonder that postmodernist challenges to that function have been the cause of great concern.

2.2 Centrism

Here I stand.
(Martin Luther)

In making the location of his (intellectual/theological/political) stand explicit, Martin Luther was unusual. On the whole, we stand where we are without even ourselves being very aware of where that is; we are barely and only rarely conscious of our own egocentricity – of the fact that we are viewing the outside world from our own particular and limited perspective, from 'here' rather than 'there', or 'there', or 'there', *ad infinitum*. And that psychological point has serious implications for historical study. If 'scientism' in the context of history implies a belief that historians need to emulate scientists (to adopt their professional procedures and even their assumed moral characteristics), 'centrism' (our other main modernist ingredient) can be defined as the related *presupposition* that it is possible to adopt one single (central) position (standpoint) – both geographical and chronological – from which science or history (or theology or anything else) may be properly done.

Centrism, in other words, implies the acceptance of a uniquely privileged position and perspective; and it has the enormous advantage of enabling us to make some sense of the past – to impose some structure, meaning and direction on it, in accordance with our own requirements. Thus, the nineteenth-century historian of philosophy Johann Eduard Erdmann explained (with commendable self-consciousness) that his own ambitious work had been unified by his 'unswerving adherence to a single point of view'. That quasi-theological stance had enabled him to achieve his primary aim – which was 'to show that, not chance and planlessness, but strict coherence, rules the history of philosophy'.[20]

Belief in the validity of our own 'single point of view' – our own stand, here and now – is something that most of us probably (in our egocentric, self-centred way) subscribe to for most of the time, however unconsciously, choosing on the whole to forget that, in T.S. Eliot's words, 'what is actual is actual only for one time/And only for one place'.[21] From what other standpoint than ourselves, it might be asked, can we possibly be expected to assess actuality – to view either the natural phenomena of the 'external' world (the world outside ourselves), or the historical evidence that's left as traces of other people's past (again external to ourselves)? No less than Luther, after all, we've got to stand somewhere, and here and now is where and when we are; we can hardly extricate ourselves from those defining constraints.

It's the acceptance of such positioning (of such self-centring) as uncontentious that makes possible any optimism and dogmatism that modernist history enjoys (or has enjoyed), for it's that that makes the past negotiable, coherent even, and potentially meaningful. It's only from the privileged position of some uncontroversial centre that historians can make their judgements – about who and what and where are important. The only way that a certain and comprehensive history can be achieved is through the adoption of a single spatial and temporal point from which to view that history. Modernist history, then, has to be mono-perspectival – 'centrist' – in relation to both space and time. We'll look at these two elements in turn.

First, then, the *spatial* centre or perspective most 'naturally' and unselfconsciously adopted is obviously that of history's 'winners'. Indeed, as has often been noted, it's usually only those winners who are in a position to write history at all, and it's they who then contrive to represent themselves as history's agents – as the important people who have *made* history. In the Western tradition that has usually meant the adoption of what has come to be seen as an essentially Eurocentric position: for centuries, Europe was seen as the spatial, geographical centre, from which other parts of the world and their peoples could be judged.

From that perspective, historians' research could and should, as the nineteenth-century positivist philosopher Auguste Comte explained, be confined 'to the élite vanguard of humanity comprising the greater part of the white race or the European nations', or confined 'to the development of the most advanced peoples', while avoiding 'every digression to the other centres of civilisation, whose evolution has so far been, for some cause or other, arrested at a more imperfect stage'. Such places as India and China had not, after all, ever 'exercised any real influence on our past'; so study of them could be safely characterised as a 'puerile and inept display of sterile, ill-directed erudition'.[22] 'Better fifty years of Europe than a cycle of Cathay', agreed the intellectual historian J. T. Merz at the end of the century, citing the well-worked poetic words of Tennyson. In relation to other cultures Europe could be viewed as the supreme achievement of civilisation – a standard against which others could be judged, towards which they could and should be encouraged, and towards which they themselves would naturally aspire. Expressing that Eurocentric self-confidence (now seen as arrogance), Merz conceded that:

> The savage tribes of Africa have a history: but this history is all known when the order of the day, the year, at most a genera-tion, is known. Even the highly complicated but stagnant life of China would have a short historical record – many thousands of years taking up no more space than as many days of modern European history.[23]

In 1927 historians were still claiming that European civilisation '(as developed on both sides of the Atlantic) sets the standard for all the peoples of the earth'; and as recently as 1995 John Vincent could still complacently assert that 'We do not understand Asia and will not need to'.[24]

Such Eurocentric presuppositions had (as we shall see in Chapter 3) been challenged centuries earlier, and they have more recently been effectively reversed by postcolonial revisionists, with their own anti-imperialist and nationalist agendas. But any history seeking (however unrealistically) to establish a single reliable reconstruction of what happened in the past will need to locate some geographical, spatial point – whether nation state or Europe, or the West or East, or wherever – on which can be planted the telescope through which the past can (supposedly) be clearly viewed. It's the blurring of sight-lines, through incessant questioning of the validity of the telescope's position, for which postmodernism is responsible.

To turn, then, from telescopes to *time*, it was not only 'here' that Luther located himself, but also in the present tense. In times past or in the future he might have been, or might be, somewhere (geographically or intellectually) different; but he had chosen a moment in time – the present – at which to make his statement of commitment. That location of self and subject in a framework of time is another prerequisite for modernist history, and the postmodern questioning of such a core constituent has presented further problems and possibly provoked further fears.

In relation to historical study time has usually seemed uncontentious enough. It consists, as everyone knows, of past, present and future; and it is of course the first of those with which historians are professionally concerned. That's their ever-enlarging territory, long since assigned to them by Aristotle in a generous disciplinary dispensation that has seldom been subsequently questioned. The present hardly exists: little patience is required to await its transformation into the historian's legitimate arena of the past. And while some few may have cast an envious eye on that more poetic domain of 'what might be' in the future, most have had their energies consumed in defending their more mundane birthright of 'what has been' in the past.

Just in case, though, there might be some temptation to transgress those chronological boundaries, an elaborate modernist stockade has been constructed to prevent any possibility of seepage. The future could generally be discounted and ignored as being quite beyond the pale: it's obvious from the very definition of their discipline that no historians should concern themselves with that. But the present has sometimes threatened some incursions, and was identified by Herbert Butterfield, for instance, in 1931 as being a major problem. An intrusive, infiltrating present, he believed, was bound to distort any image of the past; it provided an inappropriate perspective from which to view the evidence, and would divert historians from their proper quest for uncontaminated truth. 'The study of the past with one eye, so to speak, on the present is the source of all sins and sophistries in history . . . It is the essence of what we mean by the word "unhistorical".'[25]

Many contortions have subsequently been effected and affected, in hopes of avoiding any such awful imputations. One American historian in the middle of the twentieth century boasted of his total immersion in the past, even though it seemed that that had entailed some sacrifice of life in the present. While then, he explained, he had carefully read the Elizabethan Poor Law and the theological works of Calvin, he had only 'rather haphazard notions' about his own Social Security arrangements and contemporary philosophy.[26] We have probably all met his counterparts (and sometimes in the mirror), who in varying degrees live in, and even for, the past.

This may have something to do with the need for roots of personal identity. We need to fix a past, from which we can be seen to have come – a past that will provide some framework within which we may locate ourselves and ascribe some direction (and even meaning) to our lives. It's only by confining the past within a rigid chronological structure that we can impose on it some manageable form. So it's significant that early historians and chroniclers seem invariably to start their works by locating themselves in time – by sketching a coherent and orderly past that provides a framework into which their story can be slotted.

Thus, Nennius, as the assumed earliest historian of Britain and first recorder of the feats of King Arthur, starts decisively (if somewhat ponderously) as follows:

> From Adam to the flood are two thousand and forty-one years. From the flood to Abraham nine hundred and forty-two. From Abraham to Moses, six hundred. From Moses to Solomon, and the first building of the temple, four hundred and forty-eight. From Solomon to the re-building of the temple, which was under Darius, King of the Persians, six hundred and twelve years are computed. From Darius to the ministry of our Lord Jesus Christ, and to the fifteenth year of the Emperor Tiberius, are five hundred and forty-eight years. So that from Adam to the ministry of Christ, and the fifteenth year of the Emperor Tiberius, are five thousand, two hundred and twenty-eight years.[27]

That conclusion may seem to lack much excitement, but it has the important effect of enabling Nennius to locate his subsequent narratives in a comprehensive chronology in relation to what he believes is the key event of Christ's ministry. Just as we like to arrange our family photographs in some sort of chronological sequence, and thus provide some parameters for our own histories, so chroniclers such as Nennius took care initially to order the important figures and events from the past, to provide a secure frame in which to locate their own historical accounts.

That frame, in the case of Nennius, is obviously Christian; and his history goes on to emphasise the role of Providence in human affairs, with King Arthur, for example, being enabled to kill 940 of his enemies, 'no one but the Lord affording him assistance'.[28] And that Christian and providential framework has subsequently served historians well, providing them not only with a chronological framework and consistent mode of dating, but also with a motive force that drives historical events through time. As some ideologically committed Christians proclaimed in South Africa in 1948: 'We believe that . . . the life of Jesus Christ is the great turning-point in the history of the world' – a moment in time, as T. S. Eliot wrote, 'transecting, bisecting the world of time . . . and that moment of time gave meaning'.[29]

Any such tidiness, or attempt to shackle the Protean past, is challenged by postmodernism, and the revealed elusiveness of time itself is not the least cause of modernist historians' anxieties. One of the related problems is that, postmodernism apart, we personally experience time as something other than a straightforward flow, or simple line from past to present to future. Those seemingly obvious and clear-cut categories become blurred and indistinct, even in everyday life, when the past merges with the present, in which the future sometimes seems to be already contained. But its literary representation is problematic, and has thus far been attempted by novelists and poets (and visually by film-makers), rather than by historians. Thus, at the end of Joseph Conrad's novel *Heart of Darkness*, the narrator Marlow goes to see the 'intended' of the mysterious and now dead Kurtz, to return her portrait and some letters. When the two meet, Marlow perceives that she is

> one of those creatures that are not the playthings of Time. For her he had died only yesterday. And, by Jove! the impression was so powerful that for me too he seemed to have died only yesterday – nay, this very minute. I saw her and him in the same instant of time – his death and her sorrow – I saw her sorrow in the very moment of his death . . . I saw them together – I heard them together.[30]

That experience of seeing and hearing 'together', at the same time, what is nominally 'past' and 'present', that collation of memory and current perception, is not uncommon; indeed, such blurring is more or less constant, as one thing reminds us of another in an endless chain or series.

Another, earlier literary example is in Shakespeare's *All's Well that Ends Well*, when Bertram, the Count of Rousillon, is introduced to the King of France. Instead of acting as the present required, and greeting Bertram himself appropriately, the King is taken over by memories of his past friend, Bertram's father: 'Youth, thou bear'st thy father's face', he observes, and then, virtually ignoring the youthful son, starts off on a long reminiscence of his own youth and the absent (and now dead) father:

I would I had that corporal soundness now,
As when thy father and myself in friendship
First tried our soldiership! He did look far
Into the service of the time and was
Discipled of the bravest.[31]

And so, despite some polite interjections from Bertram, the King rambles on with his own memories for some forty further lines. The 'great artist Memory' – she 'of the many tongues, the myriad eyes', as another poet puts it[32] – comes all unbidden, so that his past is effectively his present, and that experienced intermingling of tenses defies the rigidly distinguished past that modernist history conventionally assumes.

3 Postmodernist underminings

If the conventions of modernist history have long been challenged by the more poetically inclined, they have recently been further and more radically undermined by postmodernism. Earlier work on that undermining – the undermining of an assumed ability to produce a true account of the past as it had been – will be considered in Chapter 4, but it's worth noting here that history inadvertently became one of postmodernism's first collateral casualties. For history was inevitably implicated in the development of architecture, where the earliest usages of the term 'postmodernism' have been identified – referring in particular to the self-conscious plundering of earlier styles, and their ornamental application to modernist buildings (Figure 2). In doing that, postmodern architects have often been seen as frivolous players in some cultural game, resuscitating defunct aspects of the past in order to reapply them, however incongruously, in the present – humorously imposing classical motifs and decoration, for example, on otherwise seriously brutalist modern constructions.

But the playfulness ascribed to postmodern architects (as to other artists and writers) can often have a serious purpose; irony is a precondition for satire. And the purpose of retrieving some aspects of the architectural *past* is precisely to question the direction of the architectural *present*. In other words the past (or some bits of it) are being deliberately *used*, and not just unthinkingly recycled, in order to challenge the widely accepted 'march of progress' narrative, in terms of which modernist architecture is seen as a natural and necessary (and desirable and progressive) outcome of previous development. It is the course of history – that seemingly inevitable progression – that is under question, and the *meaning* that has been imposed upon the past. The

Figure 2 Uses of the past in postmodern architecture: classically derived frieze on
        James Stirling's No. 1 Poultry, London
Photo: Ben Southgate

architect Will Alsop, for example, has deliberately set out to challenge
the principles of order and form that underpin modernist buildings, and
to replace them with something that (for him) better expresses the
complexities of human experience, with all the unpredictability that
that entails. In his own work, therefore, imagination works alongside
reason as a tool: some of his first sketches for new developments bear no
resemblance to technical drawings, but look instead like imaginative
abstract paintings.

Such thinking clearly has ramifications well outside the field of
architecture, where the early seeds of doubt about progressive modernism
were sown, or first observed as physically manifest; and the discipline
of history itself, with its shared interest in space and time, and its
own potentiality for imaginative reconstructions, lies adjacent. Small
wonder, then, that historians themselves are at last becoming aware of
the subversive potentialities of their subject, as the most obvious site for
demolition and rebuilding of a past that can't fail but impact upon the
present and the future.

I don't want here to rehearse once more the arguments that post-modern theorists have brought to bear on history,[33] but in modernist mode, and in conformity with the previous section's structure, let's just consider briefly postmodernism's impact on our two selected characteristics of traditional history – scientism and centrism.

3.1 Scientism

A major problem with scientism in history, or with claims like that of Bury that history is a science, is that it fails to take into account the historicity of science itself or the historical nature of those goals and methods that are set up as models to be emulated. For science, like time and everything else, moves on; and it's often an outdated model on which historians have set their sights – the model associated in particular with claims to such detachment and objectivity as supposedly enable a direct knowledge of external reality (whether nature or the past). In that tradition, the scientist or historian – or the historian as scientist – can access the truth by remaining strictly apart from the object of study.

Any pretensions to such splendid isolation can now be seen as hopelessly outmoded, both in science and in history: few any longer believe in the possibility of somehow removing ourselves, or our influence, from what we are doing (whether we're looking at nature or the past); we are not (as had been hoped) simply mirrors that can be so cleaned as directly to reflect what's there; however seemingly desirable as a moral aspiration, self-effacement's just not possible.

Nor indeed is it necessarily desirable anyway: 'I can't stand these lustful eunuchs', Nietzsche wrote of those who affect to adopt 'an objective point of view', and likened them to religious ascetics in their quest for self-denial. Claims to be operating simply as 'a mirror' and to be tastefully (objectively) describing without any personal input or presuming 'to play the judge' must, Nietzsche believed, be exposed for what they are – a part of the self-indulgence so characteristic of what he called 'modern historiography'. He went on to express his contempt for 'these weary and played-out people who wrap themselves in wisdom and look "objective"': 'I know of nothing that excites such disgust as this kind of "objective" armchair scholar'.[34]

Nietzsche's distaste for the scientistic pretensions of historians has more recently been shared by many others, including Michel Foucault, who takes a similarly sceptical approach to any aspiration 'to adopt a faceless anonymity'. Historians, he argues, are simply misguided in their belief in 'objectivity, the accuracy of facts, and the permanence of the past' (those old presumptions of a scientistic history). They aim, as good scientists were once (and by some, of course, still are) believed to aim, at the effacement of their own individuality and values, in order to replace their particular perspective with 'the fiction of a universal geometry'. But fiction, of course, is all it can ever be: no one in practice can erase all personal input from their historical (or any other) productions. And the very attempt to remove one's own perspectival traces in the interest of disciplinary authority is itself highly revealing, for it indicates an ideological commitment – an implicit alignment with what's already accepted and acceptable, an alignment, that is, with prevailing power. In terms of that, everything can (and must) be reduced to a readily comprehensible common denominator: there's nothing that can't be calmly assimilated into a respectable historical narrative. And what that indicates further, Foucault suggests, is an inhumane indifference – an 'insensitivity to the most disgusting things'.[35] It might, in other words, instead be time for historians to abandon the scientistically derived pretence of god-like detachment and concede their own inevitable involvement and commitments. Which leads conveniently to our next section.

3.2 Centrism

For just as the questioning of scientistic pretensions has eroded confidence in the claims of traditional modernist history, so too has that 'decentring' that (as indicated in Chapter 1) constitutes one major aspect of postmodernism in general. When applied to historical study more specifically, 'decentring' alone can be seen to have dramatic effects on what seems possible. For once we have removed any possibility of a single and uniquely privileged position in time and space – one here and now – from which historians can view the past, we are left with the alternative inevitability of multiple perspectives from an infinity of centres. And with all of those perspectives claiming equal validity, who is to choose between them? The choice of any one must inevitably itself be partial, both in the sense that it can represent only a part of the potential whole, and in the sense that it will have been chosen as a result of an individual's own interests and agenda.

The recognition of that problem, as we shall go on to see in Chapter 3, is hardly new; but it has become exacerbated by two further strands of postmodern thought – namely feminism and post-colonialism. Though obviously coming from quite different angles, and each having its own history and agenda, both of these have conspired to question history's previous centres, and have made significant contributions to the destabilised state of historical study in postmodernity. Thus early feminists claimed that historians, from their conventionally adopted standpoint, often failed to take sufficient account of women in the past: most historians were men, who presupposed patriarchy and male pre-dominance; and so they had simply ignored what women did, and had left them out of histories as being unimportant or irrelevant. Still within the modernist tradition, then, it could be argued that more attention needed to be given to women and their roles, so that a fuller, truer picture of the past could emerge. And similarly in the case of post-colonialism it was clear that histories had almost always been written from an imperialist perspective: the voices of indigenous peoples had been ignored, if not suppressed; and the result was again a lopsided account, the 'balance' of which needed to be redressed. In both cases it could be seen that complementary centres could and should be added, if only in the interest of completing the historical task of presenting a properly rounded picture of what had happened in the past.

Initially, then, neither feminism nor post-colonialism seemed to constitute much of a threat to historical practice: 'inclusivity' had already become a virtue in the case of 'ordinary people', who had claimed and won their place in the face of an earlier more aristocratic ('drum and trumpet') tradition; and that virtuous inclusivity could now be extended, and room provided for those previously excluded on grounds of sex and race. The club rules surely required only slight modification.

But the implications proved in the event to be rather more radical. First, in the case of feminism, it wasn't just a question of unearthing and utilising a few more texts by women authors, and disinterring further evidence of women's contributions to existing narratives. Feminism, rather, came to imply a complete rethinking of the past – of the stories that had supposedly represented that past, and of the structure, form and manner in which those stories were themselves presented. Traditional chronologies, for instance, were questioned by those who doubted that such key events as the Italian 'Renaissance' had proved a positive experi-ence for women after all: far from it being a time of rebirth, it proved to be a period when women's fortunes had declined. And the early modern 'scientific revolution' also needed re-evaluation: long considered as another intellectual success in triumphalist accounts of modernity's progression, it was subjected to a feminist reinterpretation that forced fundamental reassessments. As we shall go on to consider further in Chapter 4, modernist success in 'mechanising' nature could be viewed not so much as progress as a potentially fatal regression; and that was not just a matter of historical interpretation, but also importantly had to do with ecological concerns about the future.

Such fundamental reassessments of previously accepted periodisations and narrative structures went hand in hand with an invitation to reconsider the very language in which histories are written. For feminists could argue that male centrality affected not only the structures of historical narratives but even the language in which stories were told; male dominance extended yet more widely and more deeply. The masculine emphasis shown in standard interpretations of the scientific revolution was confirmed by the very language officially advocated and developed at that time – a language that eschewed the poetic and embraced simplicity and univocality. As the ideal language of science, mathematics provided the model; and while clarity and unambiguous meaning have been generally applauded as virtues, they can be seen too as imposing an excessive rigidity – advocating the sort of 'closure' against which feminists and postmodernists rebel. Feminist writers, then, have conversely emphasised the fluidity of meanings to which experience must be subject, and the creative potential of leaving definitions open.

That openness extends to definitions of femininity (and masculinity) itself. For femininity (and gender) can themselves be historicised, and seen to be products of specific historical situations; which implies that they change over time – that they are contingent and could (and will) be different from what they now appear to be. So too can 'history' itself: it too can be historicised – considered as a developing study through time – and found to be, as Bonnie G. Smith in particular has shown,[36] a 'gendered' activity, with the female and feminine often by various means excluded, devalued and discounted. An important part of feminism's contribution, therefore, is its demonstration that constant redefinition is necessary of the central components of historical narratives and of the very language and procedures of historical study itself; and if that has tended to destabilise the subject, it has also served to open it (and life itself) up in potentially exciting ways.

Any decentring that feminism might have provoked has been supplemented by post-colonial inputs to historiography. Again the movement originated with recognition that accepted histories were less than 'full': they were obviously incomplete in the sense that they conveyed a one-sided impression of events that could (at least in theory) be viewed from a number of alternative perspectives. Again that recognition was by no means new. But as was the case with feminism, history had continued to be written with largely unquestioned assumptions of dominance: just as male historians presupposed patriarchy, so on the larger scale did European, and later more generally Western, historians assume the superiority of their own centre. It came naturally for ancient Greek historians to write their histories from a presupposed Hellenic centre from which non-Greek-speaking 'others' were 'barbarians'; or for Romans similarly to view world events from an imperial centre whose frontiers bounded the civilised world. And there remained, in the case of later Western histories, a similarly seldom-questioned set of standards and values by which others could be judged.

Unsurprisingly, therefore, the histories of colonies had been written from an imperial perspective – from the standpoint of a privileged metropolitan centre; and if a first step was to realise that alternative centres (and viewpoints) did exist and could be incorporated – rounding out, as might readily be conceded, the picture of the whole – the realisation next occurred (as with feminism) that something more radical might be required, or was at least implied. For again, a whole set of values and a whole language were put in question – indeed, the whole civilisation that had constituted history's centre. So it wasn't just a question of politely letting others speak and be heard – of adding voices to an existing monologue – but rather of instituting a complete historical upheaval. It wasn't just the presence and the contribution of the 'other' that required acknowledgement, but also a total reappraisal of the centre itself.

That reappraisal might include, for instance, consideration of such Western Enlightenment virtues as technological progress and scientific rationality – two major concepts that might well be questioned and viewed afresh in the light of Eastern cultures with very different values and priorities. It might include some new analysis of Christianity as a longstanding central constituent (and direction-giver) of histories, and even of secularism as its more recent replacement, in relation to what have lately come to be seen once more as possibly competing faiths. It might, as in the case of feminism, necessitate revisions to periodisations and chronologies, in the light of alternative time-scales presented by a multiplicity of other (hitherto unconsidered or ignored) cultures. And it might further imply a need to examine how imperial actors had themselves been affected (acted on, however unconsciously) by their contact with others whose passivity had previously been assumed.

At which point post-colonial and feminist thought can be seen to come together again in their requirements, and the once seemingly solid core of traditional historiography fragment. Even the central roles – whether of male/female or imperialist/colonist – need to be historicised, and their contingency and heterogeneity recognised. For just as definitions of men and women have been applied, or imposed, in relation to each other and in accordance with prevailing power structures, so too have identities in the context of colonial and post-colonial historical narratives. As the supposed fixity of such identities is questioned, so the centres of our histories are once more destabilised.

So too, once more, is history's very terminology. Countries change their names in order to express the interests and histories of indigenous populations; statues are replaced and textbooks rewritten as newly rediscovered heroic figures take precedence over old; terrorists are redefined as freedom-fighters (and vice versa), and mutinies as wars of independence. And history thus recedes from being a truthful representation of a single reality to being a problematic, multi-layered, palimpsest-like textuality, having at best a tenuous connection with the elusive actuality that it purports to describe.

That redefinition of history's nature, with implications for its proper aspirations, may open new doors of possibility, as we shall see in our concluding chapters; but they may be doors that some modernist historians would prefer to have kept firmly closed, and through which they have no wish to be invited. For open doors, in a construction that lacks its previous rigidity, might let in unwanted guests, and invite the sort of disciplinary trespass that historians have long resisted – invite an overstepping of that threshold that has marked the centrality of the historical discipline itself. For while lip-service may sometimes have been paid in theory to the educational ideal of interdisciplinarity, many historians have in practice been more concerned to maintain their own subject's purity; and that has involved ring-fencing against any possible intrusions from inappropriate neighbours.

Literature, philosophy and psychology (to say nothing of politics and ethics) were to be viewed not as allies in any search for understanding, but as potentially threatening competitors and distractions from the truth. According to the influential Geoffrey Elton, for example, theorists are once again displaying their essentially reprehensible adolescent attitude when they propose bringing 'history and non-historical studies under one roof'. A discipline is a discipline, after all: it implies rules, and the sacrifice of extraneous frivolities; and in the case of history, it requires the sort of professional training that sets initiates apart from mere amateurs. Real historical work 'has to rest upon the sort of inside understanding which only professional attitudes and training can supply'.[37]

Although perpetuated in Arthur Marwick's updated *The New Nature of History* (2001), where we are advised that 'any contamination with the faith' is still to be resisted,[38] that sort of Eltonian approach begins to sound seriously dated. And in short it's clear that in a number of important respects postmodernism has undermined modernist history's claims and aspirations. Its scientistic pretensions, its spatial and temporal centrism, and the claimed inviolability of its own exclusive disciplinary centrality, have all been assaulted – to such effect that even diehards have been forced to reconsider the tenability of their positions.

4 Attempted reconstructions

Responses to the postmodern challenge have been varied, but can (again in modernist mode) be conveniently grouped under three main, but inevitably overlapping, categories. These categories, as surely befits what must designate very personal responses, can be described in terms of rejection, ambivalence and embrace. All three can be viewed as deriving from a concern to retain some sort of historical study in the context of a postmodernity that has been taken by some as threatening its actual termination.

First, then, there has been the ultra-pomophobic response of historians who remain determined to retain their subject totally unsullied by any threatening postmodern insurgents. They feel well justified in dismissing theorists – and above all postmodernist theorists – as potentially destructive but ultimately irrelevant to their essentially practical concerns. These number the self-appointed guardians of Western civilisation, who are determined to fight off the barbarian invaders, selflessly manning the barricades on behalf of future generations. For them, postmodernism is a passing intellectual fad which, like such earlier affectations as existentialism, can and must be quickly seen off, to enable proper historical work to go on as it has ever done (or at least has done since the nineteenth century). Concern here, then, is to retain the status quo, or where that seems dented to restore it.

We have already seen how, for example, Geoffrey Elton, Gertrude Himmelfarb, Felipe Fernández-Armesto, Keith Windschuttle and Arthur Marwick have vehemently repudiated postmodernism, and reaffirmed the conventions of traditional modernist history. These have been particularly outspoken in their reaffirmations, but behind them many supporters are lined up – including not only the members of the 'more than two dozen leading historians' in the USA, committed to reconstructing history as members of an emergent 'new historical society',[39] but also those numerous sympathisers who simply (if tacitly) take for granted the assumed virtues of 'proper' modernist history.

If that first group perceives the immediate prospect of a Manichaean conflict between the forces of absolutely good traditional modernism and absolutely bad revolutionary postmodernism, and explicitly rejects the latter as the devil's work, the second group adopts a somewhat subtler approach. Historians falling into this second category deliberately assume the characteristics of 'balance' and 'reason' that befit their professional role. So they purport to concede the weight of certain postmodernist arguments, which (it's claimed) are anyway nothing new but have been long since accepted and integrated within the model of conventional history. Thus, for example, the essentially hypothetical nature of historical explanation is stressed, and the acceptance that no final truth is attainable; the desirability of a multiplicity of different histories (from the previously overlooked) is readily conceded; and the positive contributions that can derive from other disciplines are welcomed. Any appearance of a storm, we are assured, can be safely contained within the confines of an old-fashioned teacup, or at least within the slightly less pretentious mug by which it's been replaced.

However, claims to have incorporated the most important, and often far from novel, aspects of postmodernism are not always easily substantiated, and they often go hand in hand with denigration of such other aspects as can be presented as dangerously extremist. These latter are identified as potentially disruptive, not only of history itself, but more widely of morality and culture; and so, from the moral high ground, it's made clear that they have to be resisted. As an example here we might take Richard Evans, the title of whose work, *In Defence of History*, clarifies his position at the outset. While conceding that postmodernism has brought many benefits to historical study, he is concerned to defend what is essentially modernist history – and not least because the fundamentals of such history directly impinge on society more widely. That is to say, the issues by which historians are confronted symbolise 'the much bigger problem of how far society can ever attain the kind of objective certainty about the great issues of our time that can serve as a reliable basis for taking vital decisions for our future'.[40] So, having acknowledged the force of postmodernism, Richard Evans continues to write against it and in defiance of it. Thus, for instance, in the face of postmodernist critiques that would rebut him, he continues to insist that there really are numerous 'rules for assessing the *factual reliability* of the traces left by the past'; he claims that 'the study of historians' writings as linguistic texts is almost [sic] bound to be of secondary importance'; he asserts emphatically that 'it *is* possible to reconstruct the meanings which past language had', so that historians can distinguish a 'true' from a 'false' reading; and, in further modernist mode, he writes of the 'shackles that normally bind historians to the facts', of the need 'to be objective' through the adoption of 'a detached mode of cognition', and of the requirement to avoid any manipulation of 'the reality of the past'.

These aspirations and assertions would not necessarily be accepted by our third category of historians, comprising those who take a much more positive approach to postmodernism, and who have engaged more deeply with the issues raised. From that engagement, a productive marriage has evolved, and new forms of historical writing have been produced. Simon Schama, for example, claims openly to have blurred the traditional (and for proper historians fundamental) distinction between 'fact' and 'fiction' – between the 'truth' supposedly derived from documents in archives, and those inadmissible imaginative reconstructions indulged in by such lesser breeds as novelists and poets. Natalie Zemon Davis, similarly, has proclaimed (or, as some would have it, confessed) that her presentation of the story of Martin Guerre (a fifteenth-century French peasant who left his family and property, and then returned to reclaim them from another man who had impersonated him for several years) was 'in part my invention' – though admittedly 'held tightly in check by the voices of the past'. Modris Eksteins, in his compelling evocation of 'the Great War and the Birth of the Modern Age', has advocated that we 'retreat from the restrictive world of linear causality and think in terms of context and confluence rather than cause'; and, in another search for compromise between history and fiction, he has (to enormous effect) organised his work 'in the form of a drama, with acts and scenes'. Greg Dening's account of the mutiny on *The Bounty* is a self-consciously postmodernist treatment, organised as a drama again (with prologue, three acts, two entr'actes, and epilogue), and including 'multiple viewpoints of the actors and those who interpreted them then and now'. Annabel Patterson has no doubt shocked many by disdaining to write in the dispassionate manner approved of and affected by proper historians, but rather admitting to having a mission, and an aspiration through her historical work to have some practical moral effect. So, for example, by tracing the 'secret histories' (sometimes long repressed) of those who resisted authoritarian pressures, she hopes to enhance awareness of a liberal tradition that still needs determinedly defending. And in his studies of Eastern thought, John Clarke makes no attempt 'to disguise my own partiality to Daoism', but sees his work 'not just as an exercise in the history of ideas but also a contribution to the expansion of the philosophical and spiritual imagination'. He has, he explains, set out explicitly to challenge 'the Eurocentric narrowness of intellectual historiography'.[41]

Their remarkable admissions do, of course, expose such historians to charges of nothing less than heresy, from those who continue adamantly to deny the propriety of any personal intrusions into historical writing from historians themselves, whether in the form of imaginative input or ideological involvement. But they are not alone, and there is increasing recognition that postmodernism might indeed serve to open up, rather than simply terminate, historical study. We shall return to this point in our concluding chapters, but can already note that new forms of narrative have been proposed, revealing a variety of perspectives and a less than definitive conclusion. Alternative modes of presentation, too, have been attempted, challenging conventional representations of linear time and space. Historical events, in short, together with the various possibilities of their re-presentation, have increasingly been recognised as far too complex to admit of any tidy (let alone unique) 'closure'. Their constituent fragments can, for various purposes (aesthetic, moral, ideological), be provisionally bound together in various ways; but, like the fragments in a kaleidoscope, they must always await being shaken once again, for an alternative image to come into focus.

5 Continuing fears

I can do anything I want!
(Anon)

As portrayed in Homer and Virgil,[42] Proteus was part historian, part prophet: he had knowledge of both past and future, so that naturally people sought him out for his advice. The problem, however, was to pin him down: he had to be caught and manacled before he would divulge any information or disclose the truths he knew; and to escape capture he would assume any number of different forms – whether of lion or boar or snake, or fire or running water. It's the Protean elusiveness of historical knowledge that is finally revealed by postmodernism: as soon as you think you've caught it, it changes to another shape, and constantly eludes you; the tighter you grip, the more insubstantial it becomes. That can be disturbing – and even a cause of fear.

It's linked to another major and highly problematic fear: that postmodernism is essentially amoral, encouraging a selfish irresponsibility that can impinge, with highly deleterious consequences, on everyday life and more particularly on historical study. In an article on the perceived decline of Britain into (postmodern) barbarism, Janet Daley recorded how a woman holding a protracted conversation on the telephone had successfully prevented a lift (elevator) full of prospective shoppers from getting off the ground floor.[43] Each time the lift doors nearly closed, she pressed the button once again in order to reopen them; and she was obviously determined to keep the lift immobilised and available for her own use until she'd concluded her telephone call. On being reproached by an aspiring ascender to the upper floors with the words 'You can't do that!', she had replied (as quoted above), 'I can do anything I want!'

Whether the persistent telephone-caller had successfully graduated from one of the fashionable and seemingly ubiquitous courses on 'assertiveness' was not revealed; nor whether she had read and absorbed the latest primer on postmodern culture. But her attitude was taken as typical of an increasing number of people, and her blatant self-interest as exemplary of the amorality of our contemporary (postmodern) society. For the historian, her prevention of closure – or refusal to allow closure – is, perhaps, particularly symbolic; for pomophobia in the context of history includes the fear that there can indeed be no 'closures' or final conclusions, to serve as firm bases for subsequent ascent to higher realms. Postmodernism, as Gertrude Himmelfarb fears, 'recognises no reality principle, only the pleasure principle – history at the pleasure of the historian'.[44] Such irresponsible hedonism would clearly have no end.

I scribbled the above paragraph on Hampstead Heath, and on my way home passed some small shops. Outside one stood a tower of plastic containers, and a delivery driver inadvertently knocked part of it over. His companion reassured him: 'They shouldn't f***ing be there.' Thus was human responsibility for the minor accident conveniently removed: any morality – as denoted by the word 'should' – was to be ascribed to some inanimate and instantly dispensable principle rather than to any human agency.

Each of those cases, then – exemplifying the refusal to accept personal responsibility for others; the affirmation of self, if necessary at the expense of any others; the belief that the individual is free to do anything without accruing blame, regardless of any evidence to the contrary – might well justify continuing fears about what is assumed to be the amorality of 'postmodern' life. And they relate not only to the practicalities of everyday living, but also to historical study itself, where it is assumed that the implication is a situation in which 'anything goes' – or in which we can have the past, not 'as it was', but as we want it.

The freedom that can be (and recently has been) taken with history is shown in many ways – in so-called 'docudrama', for example, where documentary 'fact' is blended with dramatic 'fiction', often for political purposes; in films, which purport to be historical, but which (more or less blatantly) present their history in such a way as to foment or pander to parochial patriotisms and national pride; and even in sites of 'heritage', where archaeological remains are (sometimes imperceptibly) restored and sanitised in the interests of our burgeoning tourist industries. In all these cases, the fundamental modernist distinction between 'fact' and 'fiction', already undermined by postmodern theorists, is ignored and further eroded.

But that erosion, and the fears engendered by it, can be most clearly seen in the context of Holocaust denial. While there is nothing new or unique about the denial of a past we'd rather be without, the example of the Holocaust is, for obvious reasons, particularly emotive – stirring emotions not least in those who still have personal memories of the events that are denied.

These issues have become a matter of general public concern as a result of the David Irving libel trial and related commentary; and one thing that needs to be clarified at the outset is that Clio, as the muse of history, may have a well-deserved reputation for promiscuity, but certainly not for being self-effacing. That is, it has long been recognised that history (as the past) will, in Keith Jenkins' words, 'go with anyone': she can be used (or abused) by virtually anyone for virtually any purpose at all – whether personal, moral, political, ideological or whatever. But that doesn't imply that the past in general – or even particular aspects of it – can simply be eliminated. Parts of the past are inevitably ignored or excised in the interests of any historical narrative, since a narrative is only a story that we've chosen to impose upon that past, in order to make some sense of it. By 'emplotting' the traces of the past, we necessarily choose what fits and what doesn't fit our story – what we are going to remember and what forget, what we are going to include and what exclude. But to exclude does not imply denial of the *reality* of what's excluded; it implies only denial of its immediate *relevance* for present purposes.

So it would have been conceivable in the 1940s to write a history of the Second World War that excluded reference to the Holocaust. For 'the Holocaust' as an entity didn't exist at the time, or until well after the end of the war. 'There was', as Hans Kellner has written, 'no Holocaust for anyone to experience or witness; it was an imaginative creation, like all historical events.'[45] That is to say that 'Holocaust' was a word that became a shorthand, or collective noun, to denote numerous actions and events that took place during the German Third Reich, and which were subsequently narrativised under that head. But that doesn't by any means imply any scepticism about the singular events that later came to constitute that 'imaginative creation' ('the Holocaust') having actually happened. It is possible to view them, and describe them, and force them into narrative form, in many different ways (however inadequately); but it is not possible, without denying the standards of evidence by which we live as both historians and human beings, to deny that something (that we can now refer to as the Holocaust) did happen. It is, again, possible to question such matters as the numbers of individuals who died, and when, and how; and these remain matters of empirical investigation. But no postmodernist, by virtue of postmodernism, would be bound to deny that something (now referred to as the Holocaust) did take place.

But although Holocaust denial is by no means necessarily an outcome of postmodernism, there remains some continuing fear that it might be.

The often related theories of relativism and deconstruction have, for example, been described as 'a seedbed for pseudohistory and Holocaust denial' by Michael Shermer and Alex Grobman. And Saul Friedlander has written of how 'The extermination of the Jews of Europe, as the most extreme case of mass criminality, must challenge theoreticians of historical relativism to face up to the corollaries of positions otherwise too easily dealt with on an abstract level.'[46] However unjustifiably, then, these matters might remain of continuing concern and fear to those with a particularly virulent form of pomophobia.

6 Conclusion

It may not be inappropriate to conclude a chapter on postmodernism and history with some reference to history's own supposedly impending conclusion – or an end for history that has been proposed by at least one postmodernist. For Keith Jenkins has gone further than most in questioning why we should any longer bother with the past at all. The discipline of history, as we have seen, constituted a vital core of modernity by contriving to justify and underpin modernism's own credentials. Modernism, that is, could be (and was) shown to be the culmination of an historical (and progressive) trajectory. But now that both the methodology of the discipline and the validity of the whole modernist enterprise have been undermined, what, Jenkins asks, is the point of going on – or of going on at least with history? We might as well recognise historical study for what it is: an outdated modernist activity that we're better off without.

So let's just forget it! History, it's claimed, has already been renounced by some leading postmodernists: they've shown the way, and all we have to do is follow. 'My argument', Keith Jenkins explains, 'is that if Derrida and Rorty *et al.* can do without history . . . – then we all can . . . The idea of the historical past can . . . be considered as just one more example of the many imaginaries we have fabricated to help us make some sense of the apparent senselessness of existence'; and if other tough-minded postmodernists have managed to dispense with it, then why can't we all?[47]

The answer is surely that it's unrealistic to expect everyone to have the capacity to become Nietzschean supermen, who are able to live without the escapes and refuges that others find so necessary. And it's hardly surprising that Jenkins has personally provoked serious bouts of pomophobia, from those unwilling or unable to envisage the elimination of their pasts (as well as their professions). Indeed, he himself suggests an answer to his question 'Why?' when he significantly attributes to postmodernism 'the *deeply disturbing* removal of those protective covers, those fictive shelters that modernist historians have constructed to help keep us away from the *abyss* of the interminable, interpretative, relativistic flux'.[48] In other words, history has served the vitally important function of protecting us from the need to confront the stark reality of existential meaninglessness. For as Arthur Danto much earlier concluded, 'Our actions lose their point and, in dramatic cases, our lives their purpose', when our belief in real history is shattered:

> For when the past is in doubt, a question mark blurs the present, and, since we cannot will falsehood, our lives persist unclearly until history-as-science has had its say. The present is clear just when the relevant past is known.[49]

Better, we might think, to have lived and lied than never to have lived at all; but some postmodernists are uncompromising in their belief that the present (and the future) is better left unclear – that a blurring question mark is preferable to clear definition, and that reliance on history-as-science is a cop-out. Jacques Derrida, for instance, is quoted by Keith Jenkins as insisting that 'it is endlessly necessary to renew transcendental questioning'.[50] Far from aspiring to the stability that secure knowledge of the past might provide, Derrida makes a virtue of instability, of repudiating peace and relaxation and the comfort of old habits. Like Socrates, he believes that we should endlessly question the most fundamental aspects of our lives – and thereby, it might be noted, act in accordance with the original meaning of both 'historia' and 'scepticism', both of which implied not any imminent attainment of the end, but rather the need for continuing, even endless, search and enquiry.

Similarly, Baudrillard's 'absolute rule of thought is to give back the world as it was given to us – *unintelligible*. And, if possible, to render it a little *more unintelligible*' – which uncompromising aim hardly needs further commentary: no possibility of any cosy evasions there. Nor yet with Lyotard, who writes of postmodernism overcoming 'chronophobia' – that fear which impels us to attempt 'to plot or master the course of time'. For Lyotard we would be better liberated from the constraints of linear time, even though that implies forgoing its security; and we are required, in that and other respects, to be 'prepared to receive what thought is not *prepared to think*'.[51]

That challenge is taken up in a very practical way by Elizabeth Deeds Ermarth, who presents herself as willing and able 'to think what seems unthinkable'; and applying herself specifically to the issue of time, she seeks to establish 'an alternative temporality', with a new rhythmic, 'swinging' concept of time. That newly theorised time, significantly, 'subverts the metaphysics that posits essences like stable, self-identical, nondiscursive identities', and 'destroys the historical unity of the world by destroying its temporal common denominator'. So it's no wonder that Frank Ankersmit goes on to claim to be witnessing (perhaps) 'the definitive farewell . . . of all the essential aspirations which have actually dominated historical writing as long as it has existed'.[52]

Rather, then, than providing the comfort and emotional reassurance with which it has previously been identified, postmodern history's function becomes to *destabilise* – endlessly to question certainties, reveal alternatives, and provoke reassessments. History becomes, as it was envisaged by the Czech philosopher Jan Patočka, 'nothing other than the *shaken* certitude of pre-given meaning'. In a situation where the certainties of meaning are deliberately 'shaken', and where that 'shaking' itself is seen as a positive virtue and as a legitimate aim for history, there can be no going back to Keith Windschuttle's confident modernist belief in history as 'a search for *truth* and the construction of *knowledge* about the past', built on a core of 'factual information'. The prospect of such finalities and closures has been lost in postmodernity.[53]

It's not hard to see why the postmodernist undermining of such modernist beliefs has provoked (not least in historians) distress, anxiety and *fear*. But after trying in the following two chapters to contextualise these issues, I shall go on to emphasise the more positive corollary of *freedom*.

Part 2

CONTEXTUALISATION
(THE PAST)

3

POSTMODERN PERSPECTIVES

Some antecedents

1 Introduction

Soon the postmodern category will include Homer.
(Umberto Eco)[1]

Gods and goddesses often defy the natural laws of birth and parenthood: in religious history virgin births such as that of Jesus Christ are not uncommon, and the Greek goddess Athene was believed to have leapt from the head of Zeus already fully formed, armour-clad and shouting war-cries. But intellectual movements, however revolutionary they sometimes seem to be (or are claimed by their proponents to be, or are viewed in retrospect as having been), invariably lack such melodramatic origins, and can usually be seen to have enjoyed both respectable parentage and a relatively conventional upbringing. This may be some cause of consolation – not least for pomophobes. For even postmodernism is no Athene. However loud its war-cries against traditional historians, it comes clad with its own history, in both meanings of that word: no virginal construction, it has a past, and a dubious development through time, of which historians can attempt to make some sense. Or, to put it another way, we can look back and pick out earlier intellectual developments, which can retrospectively be identified as postmodernism's 'antecedents'. We can construct a narrative that will show that postmodernism itself seems to be a natural (if not inevitable) outcome from, or culmination of, a number of previous ideas. In that sense, then, I'll try in this chapter to put postmodernism into some historical context – to see postmodernism *in* history (the past) – and show that the force of its present flood has been supplied by a number of long-established tributary streams.

It may seem to be not so much paradoxical as logically inconsistent for a deracinated postmodernist to seek roots in the past – for one who purports to accept the reality of chaos, to strive to identify a more or less orderly line of succession through history, in the assumed (but otherwise repudiated) form of a coherent (and even teleological) narrative. But that is to presuppose that the human mind works within the confining structure of a single matrix. Which is precisely what the modern mind was induced to accept: a form of tunnel-vision, in terms of which the multiple opportunities of childhood were renounced in the name of 'growing-up' into an adulthood where logical inconsistencies can (must) be no sooner diagnosed than responsibly discarded. The adoption of that single matrix is now as much under challenge as any other aspect of modernity; and the proposal here is to enjoy the game of historical construction, while remaining aware of the self-imposed rules of that game. So let's fulfil Umberto Eco's prophecy and go back more or less to Homer.

2 Scepticism

> Postmodern philosophy is to be defined as an updated version of scepticism.
>
> (Stuart Sim)[2]

Stuart Sim's claim may be oversimplified, but is not without some justification. Certainly scepticism is the philosophy with which postmodernism is most closely associated, and we can at least concede that the length of scepticism's history gives a good indication of the depth of postmodernism's roots.

One person's knowledge claim is another's cause for doubt, so that the rise and development of scepticism run in tandem with the rise and development of philosophy itself. When one presocratic thinker in the sixth century BC comes forward with a theory, another is immediately provoked to question it; for all the faculties and means by which fellow humans lay claim to knowledge can be counter-claimed to be defective. If Thales postulates water as the underlying substance of all matter, his reasoning – however well justified in terms of his own experience – can quickly be challenged by Anaximander, who believes he can make a better case for air. And he in turn is no less immune to the criticism of his successors. For can we ever trust our senses or our powers of reasoning? Of course we can't: we've all been taken in by defective messages received from our eyes and ears and sense of touch; time and again, we've made mistaken identifications and drawn faulty conclusions. So that our confidence becomes eroded: can we ever be sure on any occasion that we haven't been deceived once more? Can we be absolutely certain even that a material world exists out there, outside of us and independent of our minds? How could we ever prove that? For isn't any reasoning we might apply to the problem dependent on axioms that we simply have to take for granted – dependent, that is, on foundations that we have deliberately undertaken not to question?

Early Greek epistemological probings, or questions about the empirical and intellectual bases of our beliefs and claims to knowledge, culminate in the full-blown philosophy of scepticism attributed to Pyrrho of Elis (c. 360–c. 270 BC). That philosophy was recorded and transmitted to posterity much later by Sextus Empiricus, in a work now entitled *Outlines of Pyrrhonism* (c. AD 200). In this, Sextus describes how (at least in one tradition, though there were, appropriately, others) Pyrrho, for all his sceptically induced doubts, contrived in practice to live like other men. He chose to assume that there was indeed a world outside himself – a world that he was reasonably well equipped to get around in; and working on that assumption, he didn't need to impose on his friends for continual help (as he did in an alternative account). But as a philosopher, he remained aware, of course, that it was possible to be proved wrong at any moment.

As far as history specifically is concerned, Pyrrho is represented as being a true proto-postmodernist. He realised that, just as natural philosophers lacked any means for determining which of competing claims for knowledge about the natural world was true, so too historians inevitably lacked any criterion for distinguishing between true and false accounts of the past. So that, he concluded, it must always be in such matters (to put it no more strongly) 'a hard task to try to discover the truth'.[3] That task remains hard, and it's only much later that we can pick up our own historiographical thread, with Dio Chrysostom in the first century AD. By then, though, we can claim that proto-postmodernity has traces of Foucault, inasmuch as history is already recognised as a source of power, with historical narratives adaptable, and adapted, for ideologically motivated purposes. Thus, Dio questions the whole basis of his contemporaries' supposed historical knowledge of that major conflagration of antiquity known as the Trojan War. Surviving evidence, such as it was, lay encapsulated in the poetic record of Homer – a notoriously suspect authority anyway, whose colourful descriptions referred to an event that had supposedly taken place centuries earlier, and so themselves relied on a protracted oral tradition. By anyone's judgement, then, there was plenty of scope for the intrusion of inaccuracies and failures of memory, but Dio was concerned with something rather less obvious and innocent: Homer, he believed, was guilty of deliberate and politically motivated historical distortion – a far graver charge that came to be paralleled some two millennia later in the case of those who denied the comparatively recent events of another major war.

Dio himself, significantly, was an orator; so he was no doubt well aware of rhetorical exercises, as well as actual courts of law, in which alternative versions of an event were routinely presented and proposed as true. From the time of the fifth-century BC Sophists, rhetoric had formed an essential part of political education for Athenian citizens, preparing them (as debating societies continue to do) to play their part in the cut-and-thrust of democratic debate. That training, like so many other aspects of Greek culture, was later exported to the Romans, and in 155 BC the Greek Carneades shocked his Roman audience by delivering two seemingly incompatible speeches on consecutive days – the first arguing in favour of just actions, and the second against them.[4] The whole point of rhetoric, then as now, was to present a cogent argument, regardless of any moral rights or wrongs in the case being argued; and working within that tradition Dio would quickly realise that historical claims and accounts could be similarly construed: they too could be deliberately moulded, and used for purposes of persuasion or (as we might say in a political context) propaganda. It would, then, be quite natural, he concluded, that the Persian king should encourage the broadcast of 'a false account' of his war with the Greeks: it would hardly do to provoke his people by news of an ignominious defeat; so he'd modify the story, 'in order to keep them quiet'. And Homer similarly had engaged in a deliberate and politically motivated distortion in his historical account of the Trojan War. Indeed, he had gone so far as 'to represent the opposite of what actually occurred'.

To justify his scepticism, Dio pointed out that Homer's veracity as a historian was obviously questionable for a variety of reasons. How, for example, could the poet possibly have been privy to the intimate conversations that he purported to report between Zeus and his wife Hera? 'It is unlikely even in human affairs that any outsider knows of the occasional scenes where husbands and wives fall out and abuse one another'; but claims to have such knowledge of the gods assuredly reveal Homer as nothing less than 'the boldest liar in existence'. And as far as the reporting of the war itself is concerned, its poetically recorded origin and conclusion may have been dramatically effective, but as far as Dio was concerned they were both well beyond the bounds of belief. The notorious abduction of Helen was supposed to have set the whole thing off, but that was all a myth – a poetic fabrication: Helen had gone off with her lover quite voluntarily, and with her family's full approval. And the melodramatic ending of the war, with its famous story of the Greeks finally entering Troy concealed in the belly of their wooden horse, was no less obviously another poetic fiction: it was ludicrous to believe that 'a whole army was hidden in a horse, and yet not a single Trojan noticed it or even surmised it' – and that too 'in spite of the fact that they had an unerring prophetess among them'. Altogether, then, Dio believed, it was high time to realise that Homer's whole account was totally unreliable, and to accept that the Greeks, far from winning the war as he had claimed, had lost it.[5]

That sceptical approach towards the conventionally accepted records of past military glories became prevalent again in the early modern period, when the rediscovery of Sextus Empiricus's text on *The Outlines of Pyrrhonism* served to underpin a developing sceptical philosophy that had ramifications in the whole field of history. Sextus' account was widely utilised, and when the sceptical arguments were applied to claims to have knowledge of the past, what resulted came, by the end of the seventeenth century, to be known as 'historical pyrrhonism'. That could be described as proto-postmodern doubting of any claims to know 'the truth' about the past.

Foreshadowing twentieth- and twenty-first-century debates, then, the French sceptic La Mothe Le Vayer pointed out in relation to Roman history that a hypothetical commentary by the defeated leader Vercingetorix would look very different from the surviving account by the victorious Julius Caesar – an early example of history having been written by the winner. In more recent times La Mothe noted that the Battle of Pavia had been described in very different ways by the participants: French, Spanish, Italians, Germans – all had their various national interests, perspectives and emphases; so, with their different criteria, all produced quite different narratives. It could only be concluded that there is indeed 'generally speaking, little certainty in Histories'.[6]

La Mothe's fellow countryman, the Jesuit Father Pierre Le Moyne, is similarly aware of those hazards of partiality and prejudice that confront any historian, but he sounds at his most 'postmodern' when lamenting the impossibility of penetrating to the inner workings of events. Just like scientists in their dealings with nature, historians may of course describe appearances, or what seems to them to have been the case, but they can never reach the essence of what has gone on, or know 'the truth' about it. They may see 'the Bark and Coverings of things', the outer case for instance of a watch, but what they need is sight of 'the Springs and Movements', which of course remain invisible.[7]

La Mothe's almost exact contemporary in England, the renowned philosopher Thomas Hobbes, for all his admiration of Thucydides as an early aspirant to 'scientific' history, expresses similar reservations concerning historiography. At his own most 'postmodern', Hobbes emphasises difficulties that stem from the complexities of language and the literary conveyance of historical data. In one of his earliest works, he discusses what he calls the 'equivocation' of language (or ambiguities of meaning): words, he accepts, are 'signs we have of one another's opinions', but interpretation of those signs can be highly problematic. As we all seem to recognise in practical everyday life, the meaning of a word depends not least upon the context in which it's used, so that interpretation is facilitated when we can physically see the speaker, guess his intentions, and observe how he acts. But these advantages are necessarily denied us in the case of history: people from the past have left us only their writings.[8]

The meaning of those writings, then, can be retrieved only by recovering the original contexts in which they were written – and it's the reconstitution of those contexts that becomes the function of history. That function was particularly important for those early modern theologians who competed with each other in their attempts to establish secure grounds for Christian faith. Inevitably their search took them back in time to the very origins of their religion, for what Catholics and Protestants sought was some certain link between those origins and their own uniquely favoured selves. Sceptical questioning of the historical validity of the scriptural writings lies at the centre of these theological debates, and it extends to a sceptical approach towards historiography more generally.

Thus, Hobbes's attention to language is taken up by the Catholic champion John Sergeant. Ideally, thought Sergeant, there would be no linguistic ambiguities; but in practice the problem of 'the equivocation of words' does have to be confronted – a problem that is exacerbated in the case of history, with its reliance on the words of people long since dead. In the normal way we need, as Hobbes had indicated, to take account of the context in which words are used, and the intention of the author. So, as Sergeant writes: 'the Context may help much to give us the right Notion [meaning] of the Words'; and 'the Intention of the Author, and the Argument and Scope of the Book, avail much to direct us to the right sense of those words in it which are most Material and Significant'.[9] But those tests obviously remain problematic in the case of writings from the past, or history.

Such historiographical problems, argues Sergeant, relate even to what are taken by Protestants to be the most reliable of historical writings – the scriptures themselves. One needs a more secure basis of faith than that – a basis that he finds, for Catholics, in oral tradition. But the irony remains that the fervently anti-sceptical Sergeant is himself driven (as his Protestant adversaries note) to an extreme form of historical pyrrhonism, for if the validity of the scriptures is undermined, so too (*a fortiori*) must be the validity of all other historical writings. 'Pyrrho himself', therefore, as one of Sergeant's main Protestant adversaries exclaimed, 'never advanced any Principle of Scepticism beyond this.'[10]

Historical pyrrhonism, or the application of sceptical philosophy to historiography, was thus a well-established intellectual position by the turn of the eighteenth century. 'Would it not be correct to say that the age of historical pyrrhonism began in our time?' asked the Jesuit Father Paulian in 1689. With an implied affirmative, Jacob Perizonius lectured on that very subject in 1702: indeed, in his inaugural address at the University of Leyden, he drew attention to the grave crisis by which historical study was then confronted, in the form of trendy sceptical theorists who denied it any validity. His own conclusion foreshadowed that of later pomophobes in both its manner and its content: 'To hell with Pyrrhonism!' But his more philosophically orientated contemporary Pierre Bayle was none the less prepared to take the risk of making frequent references to the infernal subject in his *Historical and Critical Dictionary*. Having, then, conceded in relation to science that 'nature is an *impenetrable* abyss . . . [so that] it is enough for us that we employ ourselves in looking for *probable* hypotheses', Bayle went on to apply a similarly critical approach to the problem of penetrating to any knowledge of the past; and 'in many Cases', he concludes, 'Historical Truths are no less impenetrable than Physical ones'.[11]

From Bayle, this sceptical – or realistic, or even proto-postmodern – view of history passes to England in the philosophical luggage of Henry St John, Lord Bolingbroke. As a practical man of affairs who, as secretary of state under Queen Anne, had played an important part in the negotiations that culminated in the Treaty of Utrecht, Bolingbroke was well aware of the political uses to which history could be put; and to his practical insights some theoretical sophistication was added after his dismissal from political office on the accession of George I. Then, as an exile in France from 1715–23, he came into contact with such continental thinkers as Le Moyne, Bayle and Voltaire; and their influence is indicated not least by Bolingbroke's self-reflexive writing on historiography. He himself was accused, like so many other retired politicians, of writing his histories as a self-justificatory exercise – 'to vindicate', in John Leland's words, 'the conduct of the ministry that made the peace of Utrecht'.[12] And certainly he shows himself well aware of contemporary (and continuing) historiographical issues in his own so-called *Letters on the Study and Use of History*, which were finally published posthumously in 1752.

Those *Letters* now serve to put Bolingbroke in the forefront of our claimed antecedents of postmodernist historiography. In the context of historical pyrrhonism he writes explicitly of contemporaries who are 'ready to insist that all history is fabulous [fictional/made up]'. Aware of the long-lived tradition of rhetoric and of the linguistic issues raised by earlier thinkers, such men believe (with their twentieth-century successor Hayden White) that the very best history is just a mixture of fact and fiction, a well-presented and persuasive account of what might have happened – or, in Bolingbroke's own words, 'nothing better than a probable tale, artfully contrived, and plausibly told, wherein truth and falsehood are indistinguishably blended together'. It's possible, after all, to claim more or less anything: either that Julius Caesar conquered England or that he was defeated by the Britons. As in the case of Helen of Troy, a case can be made either way, so that 'historical facts' come to be seen as 'in some sense arbitrary'. And the solution is not, as sometimes claimed, to refer to primary sources, or the evidence of actual participants, since (as, again, he knows from experience) such people are particularly prone to partiality as having been personally affected by the events they describe.[13]

Despite all his sceptical reservations, Bolingbroke himself draws back from the most extreme form of historical pyrrhonism – a position he describes as 'folly'. Instead, he seeks a middle way, for 'There is', he concludes, 'no reason to establish Pyrrhonism, that we may avoid the ridicule of credulity'. It doesn't have to be one extreme or another: some compromise is surely preferable and possible. And taking his cue from earlier theologians and natural philosophers, he finds that compromise in the acceptance of degrees of probability. We may never attain that highest degree of infallible certainty that provides (in Joseph Glanvill's earlier words) 'an absolute Assurance, that things are as we conceive and affirm, and not possible to be otherwise'. That ideal situation is reserved for God alone. But as mere mortals we can still get along pragmatically, and enjoy a high enough degree of probability to enable us to live and continue doing history. While never 100 per cent certain, we can critically apply our common sense, and if our evidence stands up to empirical scrutiny and is corroborated by seemingly reliable witnesses, it takes on a high degree of probability:

> An historical fact, which contains nothing that contradicts general experience, and our own observation, has already the appearance of probability; and, if it be supported by the testimony of proper witnesses, it acquires all the appearance of truth: that is, it becomes really probable in the highest degree.

As in everyday life, or any other professional context, the historian will have a reason 'for examining and comparing authorities, and for preferring some'; and so he will be able to present his hypotheses about the past with a reasonable degree of confidence.[14]

Bolingbroke himself, as an historian, was probably as torn as the rest of us about the impact of scepticism upon his subject. On the one (perhaps emotional) hand (if that is physiologically possible), he wanted to retain some confidence in history; but his other (intellectual) side forced him to concede the insuperable problems pertaining to historical evidence and any claims to knowledge of the past, with the result that inevitably even 'the best [historians] are defective'. One's historical explanations of the past may sound plausible enough, and they may even correspond with what happened (for at least he retains some concept of that); but equally, an alternative chain of causation might have been in operation – and how then can the historian ever choose between those two competing possibilities? As Bolingbroke feels forced to conclude, historians 'may account for events after they have happened, by a system of causes and conduct that did not really produce them, tho it might possibly or even probably have produced them';[15] so that absolute certainty about the past must forever continue to elude them. He personally may have continued to work pragmatically and write history on his own account, but it was in defiance of a theoretical position that qualifies him, in a historiographical context, as a remarkable eighteenth-century proto-postmodernist.

Then as now, that theoretical stance exposed him to what Voltaire refers to as 'gross insults' and 'virulent attacks'. Voltaire himself was a great admirer of Bolingbroke, and did his best to defend his posthumous reputation; while the poet Alexander Pope openly acknowledges an intellectual debt to his 'guide, philosopher, and friend', particularly in the composition of his 'An Essay on Man' (originally published as separate Epistles in 1732, 1733, 1734). But Bolingbroke's acceptance of Richard Simon's earlier critique of the Bible's historical validity, and his description of the scriptural writings as nothing better than 'holy romances . . . broken and confused, full of additions, interpolations, and transpositions, made we neither know when, nor by whom',[16] provoked hostility especially on religious and moral grounds. Not without some justification, one critic accused him of having entirely subverted 'the Foundation of Protestantism', since Protestants, of course, had always referred to the scriptures as their essential 'rule of faith', or reliable connecting link with the origins of Christianity. By destroying Protestantism's foundation, Bolingbroke had effectively provided 'the surest way to bring Men back to Popery [i.e. Catholicism]'; and so, from a Protestant standpoint, he had 'effectually . . . laid his Axe to the Root . . . of Christianity itself'.[17]

Other critics, too, see Bolingbroke's critique of scriptural history as destructive of all Christianity. Robert Clayton tries to retrieve that situation by arguing on a theoretical level for the authenticity of the Bible. Such books as Kings and Chronicles, he insists, enjoyed contemporary and respectable corroboration, having been accepted as genuine records 'by the most learned and holy Persons who lived nearest to those times, in which they were written'. And the gospels similarly met the criteria for assent proposed by Locke, with regard to the number of witnesses, their integrity and skill, the consistency of their accounts, and the validity of contrary testimonies.[18] John Leland, similarly concerned that Bolingbroke had 'unworthily insulted . . . the honour of Christianity', tries to bolster biblical authority; but he does concede the sceptical point that historiographical certainty may sometimes have to be replaced with probability: 'where absolute certainty cannot be attained to, an happy conjecture may be both pleasing and useful'. And he further notes with approval that Bolingbroke himself had not been reduced to the extreme historical pyrrhonism purveyed by some of his contemporaries: 'His lordship had too much sense to deny (as some have been willing to do) the certainty of all historical evidence as to past facts.'[19]

That compromise, attributed to Bolingbroke in the face of the sceptical challenge, has generally been retained, even up to our own postmodern times. When the sceptical philosophy has periodically returned to fashion, its effects on historical study have been duly noted. Leslie Stephen in the nineteenth century, for example, recognised the significance for his own work of Hume's sceptical approach to causation; for how, he asked, are we to make any sense of a past in which anything might be the cause of anything else? For him the implication to be drawn is that the past is intrinsically chaotic, and indeed that 'the world is a chaos, not an organised whole'. And Froude, for similar reasons (at the end of the same century), referred to that potentially chaotic history as 'a child's box of letters with which we can spell any word we please'. Even where there has been that awareness of the theoretical effects of scepticism, it has not been allowed overly to disrupt historical practice, but such sceptical spokesmen may surely be seen as important precursors of our own postmodern position.[20]

3 Relativism

Man is the measure of all things.
(Protagoras)

Relativism often runs in parallel with scepticism, and again sports roots deep in classical antiquity. But while scepticism, in everyday speech, is widely applauded as 'healthy', relativism is almost as often (and sometimes by the same people) denounced as 'vicious'. Assertions concerning the relativity of truth, implicit even in the quotation from Protagoras above, have proved particularly contentious. 'Truth' (as we've considered in Chapter 1) has been thought to lie at the centre of many human aspirations – whether theological, scientific, philosophical or historical. So the challenge of the early Greek philosopher, reported by Aristotle as having 'said that man is the measure of all things, meaning simply and solely that what *appears* to each man assuredly also *is*',[21] has stirred strong emotions through the ages. Far from being an absolute, claims Protagoras, far from being eternally the same for everyone (as his near contemporary Plato always insisted), truth no less than beauty lies simply in the eye of the beholder, looking different to different people, from different places, and at different times.

That belief in the relativity of truth, deriving as it did from a more general moral and cultural relativism to which the fifth-century BC Sophists notoriously subscribed, had obvious implications for historiography; and those implications are well drawn out by the man most often cited as the 'father of history', Herodotus. Having travelled widely in his search for historical material and evidence, Herodotus was well placed to note how customs and values varied widely between different peoples, all of whom thought their own ways more right and proper than anybody else's. He recorded the story of the Persian king Darius, who appalled some Greeks by suggesting that they might eat the bodies of their dead fathers, and who then horrified some Indians, whose custom it was to eat their fathers, with talk of the Greek method of disposal – namely, cremation. Our beliefs and customs, in other words, are culturally determined. They may seem to be natural and may be assumed to be universal; but they only seem so because we've been brought up with them since birth, and we've never so much as considered the possibility of any alternatives. As Herodotus astutely comments:

> If one were to offer men to choose out of all the customs in the world such as seemed to them the best, they would examine the whole number, and end by preferring their own; so convinced are they that their own usages far surpass those of all others.[22]

That was a point that the sceptical Pyrrho also made. Having enjoyed foreign travels in the entourage of that early internationalist Alexander the Great, Pyrrho was in a position to note again the relativism of customs and moral standards. Travellers could see that the Ethiopians, for instance, tattoo their children, that the Persians like to wear brightly coloured long dresses, and that the Indians have intercourse with their women in public – though none of these customs was approved back home in Greece.[23] It was, then, only parochialism that allowed a belief in the absolutism of one's own customs to persist: travel broadened the mind and induced an acknowledgement of cultural relativism.

That point relates, too, to the writing of history, where there has often been a tendency to narrow nationalism – treating one's own country as the centre of the world, or as the only place that really matters. As early as the first century BC, the historian Diodorus Siculus noted that his predecessors had often been guilty of such narrowness and of geographically based partiality. They wrote, as he accused, 'the history *only of a single nation*'; and they were thereby 'writing not history, but only a certain *disconnected piece* of history'.[24] Their histories told only a part of the story – the part that related to themselves.

That complaint of historiographical relativism was taken up again in the early modern period, when once more new explorations and discoveries were opening eyes to alternative possibilities, and when as one consequence the inevitability of such relativism and partiality from historians became increasingly recognised. So in the mid-sixteenth century Juan Luis Vives followed Diodorus in noting the nationalistic emphases of different historians – with the French writing about France, the Italians about Italy, the Spanish about Spain, the Germans about Germany, the English about England, 'and others likewise, for the sake of some specific nation'.[25]

The resultant lopsidedness was recognised also in the following century by the antiquary Thomas Baker, who took a highly cynical view of nationalistic Spanish reports of their South American conquests. They were obviously written from a Spanish point of view, with the Amazons (in relation to the Spanish) described as 'monsters'. The force of such rhetoric was realised by Baker, who foreshadowed later post-colonial perceptions, in his explication that the description 'monsters' was nothing but a convenient ploy – an assessment that had to be evaluated in relation to its European and Eurocentric origin. From another viewpoint, it became quite clear that the Conquistadors were simply after the Amazons' gold, and that, by representing their victims as monsters, they hoped to justify their own murderous activities.[26] An appreciation of the relativism inherent in the historical writing enabled

Thomas Baker to have a 'healthy' scepticism about the motivations of nationalistic historians.

Eurocentrism was similarly questioned in the context of philosophy and science. As one of Pyrrho's sceptical followers in the seventeenth century, the intellectually aspiring Joseph Glanvill noted the relativism of what were often taken as philosophical truths. Those presumed truths, too, he realised, might be relative to the cultures in which they were pronounced: what seems true or reasonable in one place may seem the reverse elsewhere; and 'It may be', he concludes, that 'the grossest absurdities to the Philosophies of *Europe*, may be Justifiable assertions to that of *China*'. One such example was duly provided by Fontenelle in the context of science. For the Chinese, he explained, regularly witnessed celestial phenomena (such as stars falling into the sea, or moving eastward and bursting noisily) that refuted the Aristotelian beliefs, still maintained by European astronomers, concerning the incorruptibility and unchangeableness of the heavens.[27]

Despite such proto-postcolonial insights by some, persisting parochialism (as we have seen in Chapter 2) allowed absolutism for the most part to persist as an ingredient of modernist history until the late twentieth century. But that is not to say that it wasn't subject to periodic challenges along the way, as the path to postmodernity can be seen to have been prepared. Importantly, for instance, in the eighteenth century, Johann Gottfried Herder specifically rejected the absolutism that resulted from a narrowly Eurocentric stance:

> There is no such thing as a specially favoured nation on earth
> . . . there cannot, therefore, be any order of rank . . . The Negro
> is as much entitled to think the white man degenerate as the
> white man is to think of the Negro as a black beast . . . Least of
> all must we think of European culture as a universal standard
> of human values . . . Only a real misanthrope could regard
> European culture as the universal condition of our species. The
> culture of *man* is not the culture of the *European*; it manifests
> itself according to place and time in *every* people.[28]

That extraordinary and explicit repudiation of Eurocentrism and proclamation of cultural relativism by Herder in Germany was paralleled in England in the writings of Jonathan Richardson. As an historian, Richardson reflected seriously 'on the moral nature of man', and his reflections inspired him to survey a great range of customs in earlier times and in various places. He was then provoked to ask how all such customs were to be assessed, how they were all to be evaluated in relation to each other. And sounding in this context like a reincarnation of Herodotus, Richardson concludes that 'we can have no decision; but every one must go on, as they have done from the beginning, each abounding in his own sense and very sure that he is right, and all the rest wrong'.[29]

He feels forced to that relativistic position by the historical record of customs that he finds morally repugnant, but which had obviously been taken for granted in earlier (but supposedly no less civilised) times. The exposure (or, as we would say, murder) of newly born babies, for example, seems to have been widely accepted, even by 'cultured' people, in classical Greece; and there is historical evidence that gladiatorial contests were hugely popular for many centuries in Rome, however much they may offend our modern sensibilities:

> The combats of gladiators were a darling diversion of the Romans, for six hundred years; but they are so horrid and offensive to our manners, and so repugnant, one would think, to human nature, that such a practice, so long continued, would be utterly incredible, if all history did not testify the truth of it. But, as it is undeniable that it appeared otherwise to a noble and polite people, it is almost presumptuous to pronounce in our own cause, and from whence there is now no appeal, that our sense is better than their sense.[30]

Richardson is obviously torn between his instinctive disgust at hearing of certain customs that had been considered acceptable by past genera-tions and his determination to refrain from making moral judgements; and that ambiguity has remained as virtually a defining characteristic of subsequent historians. On the one hand, their studies reveal activities that they themselves consider inhumane; but on the other hand, those same studies encourage the adoption of a relativistic position that asserts the infinite variety of human nature and denies the propriety of taking any absolutist stand. All that can be safely concluded is that relativism rules – and that includes the relativity even of truth and rationality. For as Richardson is forced to concede, 'That which is a self-evident truth in one nation, and one age, is the very reverse, diametrically contrary in another!'; and 'what we call our reason, is little else than the customs we have always been used to'.[31] At such points he confirms once again that many postmodernist concerns for history – and not least those concerning relativism – are by no means new.

4 Linguistic prison houses

Language is central to the concerns of postmodernists, and has, no less than scepticism and relativism, been at the centre of philosophy from its earliest days. It's through their language that humans impose a structure on the world – on the natural universe and on themselves; it's only through language that we can get any grip on our experience, or even on our thoughts. Our language enables us to make sense, and to convey that sense to others; and no (or little) sense can be conveyed to others who do not share our language. The trouble is that what has been an *enabler* – what has enabled us to get around in the world, and make sense of it, and communicate about it – can become a captor, a restrainer, something that confines and limits. For having once accepted (or having had imposed upon us) the linguistic framework within which we can negotiate our way, we are unwilling, or even unable, to apprehend anything that lies beyond or outside that structure. Our language then no longer facilitates but circumscribes and *determines* our experience; it becomes, in the words of Fredric Jameson, a veritable 'prison house'[32] (of which it's essential to know who holds the key).

This is particularly obvious in the case of such supposedly *ideal* languages as logic and mathematics. Logic is a manifestation of the human desire to tame life – to confine it within tight constraints, in such a way that particulars can be identified, classified and related to one another in a formal and necessary way. Within a closed logical system, causal connections can be established, contradictions noted and avoided, progression and certainties assured. Logic presupposes and confirms the establishment of order – an order that is imposed on the recalcitrant disorder of 'real' life, but that sometimes comes to be seen as an ideal representation of that 'reality' itself.[33]

When viewed in that latter way, logic and its close relation mathematics perform a quasi-mystical, religious function, seeming to confirm the inherent order of the universe itself, and to justify a correspondingly ordered explanation of it. This is exemplified in early modern science, when Galileo insists on mathematics as the ideal language for representing the essentially mathematical structures of nature. The book of nature has to be carefully distinguished from books of poetry, which are works of fiction and 'the least important thing is whether what is written . . . is true'. To read the book of nature, and ascertain scientific truth, one has to learn the language in which that book has been written; and that language is 'the language of mathematics'.[34] So, as for Plato, mathematics becomes for Galileo the idealised language of the creator God, who writes his creation accordingly, and whose creation must then be understood and appropriately described in similarly mathematical terms.

Mathematics thus appears as the ideal language that enables human beings unambiguously to communicate, not only with each other but also directly with their divine creator.

But, of course, that idealised communication – whether in mathematics or in a logically constructed language – might *limit* the range of what is accepted as communicable, or what is able to be experienced, or even what is real. The development of such formal languages in the interest of science in the early modern period was quickly seen to have its limitations; for, as the Cambridge Platonist philosopher Ralph Cudworth observed at the time, such scientifically orientated language takes no account of experience that lies outside science's own (inevitably limited) purview. There are some things that just cannot be expressed or described in terms of such language, and religious or spiritual concepts are particularly evasive: we are not 'able to inclose in words and letters, the Life, Soul, and Essence of any Spirituall truths'.[35]

Cudworth's essential point has been picked up by late twentieth-century postmodernist thinkers, including feminist historians who have identified the early modern scientific revolution as involving a 'masculinisation' of culture. The linguistic conventions established at that time may have suited the development of science, but their emphasis, it has been claimed, is unduly constraining for the more feminine aspects of humanity. 'The logic of reason' cannot comprehend those aspects of experience that don't conform to its own rules, which seem to be less than clearly defined or even self-contradictory, or which are not of the right size, shape and type to be caught within its 'ready-made grids'. So Luce Irigaray has gone on to write of a woman's language 'in which "she" goes off in all directions and in which "he" is unable to discern the coherence of any meaning'.[36] One might question Irigaray's distinction here in terms of sex, but she confirms the point that we are all constrained within the prison house of some language or other; and that of mathematics and logic may have cells smaller than most.

Even in the case of less idealised forms of language, though, problems have plagued human beings since the time when God punished the hubristic builders of what came to be known as the Tower of Babel. Aspiring to construct a city and a tower 'whose top may reach unto heaven', the people were suspected by God of potentially lacking any restraint in their pursuit of imaginative projects. They had to be brought down to a more banal level of reality, and their nemesis could be most easily achieved through the confusion that inevitably resulted from the imposition on them of a multiplicity of different languages. Unable to communicate, they lacked the socio-political cohesion needed for achievement; and so they gave up their plans, and were scattered abroad 'upon the face of all the earth'.[37]

If the sudden and providentially imposed profusion of languages had such negative effects for those aspiring tower-builders, linguistic relativism and related issues have subsequently had dire consequences for the architecture of historical narrative. When (as noted above) the Conquistadors defined their indigenous Amazonian competitors as 'monsters', they exemplified the wider power that can be wielded by those controlling language. It's a power that comforts us, both in relation to the natural world and in relation to other people. For by linguistically categorising, we exercise control: we not only describe by means of language, but also, within our own scheme of values, put in its place whatever is described; and without an ability to do that, we are in danger of reverting to a potentially fearful chaos where such description, categorisation and control are lacking.

Anyone who has been to a country without being able to speak its language, or even to decipher its alphabetic symbols, will have experienced feelings of that sort of helplessness, and will have enjoyed a corresponding upsurge of power on return to a more familiar linguistic environment. Once having been temporarily deprived of the effective use of language (as a result of foreign travel or amnesia, for instance), we can sympathise with George Eliot's character in her historically orientated novel *Romola*, who regains his memory and his ability to decipher written marks, and so feels once more 'the keen delight of holding all things in the grasp of language'.[38] Descriptions, then, such as that of the Conquistadors, are not just found, but imposed; and they are always imposed for a reason. Words are never neutral: as constituents of rhetoric, they carry not only meaning, but purpose; and that's why historical narratives enjoy such power.

That is also why language is modified especially at times of cultural crisis – in times of war or political or intellectual upheaval; and recognition of such ideologically motivated linguistic fluidity goes back again at least to the fifth century BC. Thus, Thucydides observed how, in a political crisis during the war whose history he was writing, words were made to change their ordinary peacetime meanings:

> Reckless audacity came to be considered the courage of a loyal ally; prudent hesitation, specious cowardice; moderation was held to be a cloak for unmanliness; ability to see all sides of a question, inaptness to act on any. Frantic violence became the attribute of manliness; cautious plotting, a justifiable means of self-defence.[39]

That analysis by Thucydides was most notably followed in the twentieth century by George Orwell's warnings of politically motivated 'newspeak', the convolutions of which have become a regular part of our own daily lives.

That language is important, then, not only for the articulation and transmission of ideas, but for political and ideological purposes, is no new postmodern discovery. Nor is recognition that we are confined by language within the conceptual limits that have been previously articulated and transmitted to us. Some nineteenth-century intellectual historians were particularly conscious of such matters, realising that language encapsulates those aspects of the thought of earlier times that are considered (by whomsoever and for whatever reason) appropriate to pass on to the next generation. It is, then, inevitably in some sense conservative, and even restricting, or a 'prison house'. For as Leslie Stephen (echoing Francis Bacon) puts it, 'Old conceptions are preserved to us in the very structure of language'; and so they are passed down through the generations, without ever being consciously recognised or questioned. Or, as Richard Rorty has more recently put it, we continue 'to use the language of our ancestors, to worship the corpses of their metaphors'.[40]

This highlights another important function for history. To recognise and question the unrecognised and unquestioned foundations of our own thoughts, we need to examine those of the past – to assess origins, modifications, continuities, discontinuities. And so historical study becomes, to a great extent, a study of language – of what people *meant* and *intended*. 'To understand the past we must in the first place understand the words used by those who made it,' wrote Isaiah Berlin in his study of the eighteenth-century German philosopher Johann Georg Hamann, who himself, in postmodernist vein, observed: 'The history of a people is in its language.'[41]

As John Locke had long since pointed out, we accept linguistic structures as if they were reliable indicators of the *natural* structures they purport to represent: 'Because men would not be thought to talk barely of their own imaginations, but of things as they really are; therefore they often suppose their words to stand also for the reality of things.'[42] Under that misapprehension, we refrain from questioning our language, until some major anomaly has intruded on us as something that just won't fit the descriptive framework that we've traditionally used. It's only then that we reassess our language and our vision, when, in Richard Rorty's words again, we come to recognise 'a contest between an entrenched vocabulary which has become a nuisance and a half-formed new vocabulary which vaguely promises great things'.[43] These perceptions are central to postmodernism, but are, again, not without much earlier antecedents.

5 Romanticisms

Another group of proto-postmodernists needs to be briefly mentioned in this context: those we might term 'Romantics'. So many diverse meanings have been ascribed to the term 'Romanticism' that it was already considered virtually unusable by intellectual historians in the 1940s, and I am deliberately using the plural form to indicate the generality of my approach here. In crude historical terms, though, Romantics can be seen as the antithesis of 'Enlightenment'-style advocates of rationalism, scientism and the objectification of nature. Their best-known incarnation took place in the late eighteenth and early nineteenth centuries, as a response to the scientistic attitudes provoked by the early modern scientific revolution, but as with sceptics and relativists, they recur through history as a perennial type – expressing that side of humanity which, in the quest for scientific knowledge and control, is periodically denied or overlooked or undervalued. As such, they can be seen as forerunners of postmodernism in a number of important respects.

Most importantly, Romantics deny the absolute validity of any *order* – order being seen as something that can be only arbitrarily imposed on what is an essentially chaotic nature (and human nature). Whereas the Enlightenment ideal is to reduce the universe, or our experience of it, to something manageable and controllable, explicable and predictable, Romanticisms reassert the potentiality for alternative realities. Any order we see derives from our own eyes, rather than from the external world itself. Far from being inherent in the world, order depends on nothing more substantial than our own interest or even arbitrary whim. Thus, for example, we may claim to identify particulate parts of an entity or event, to facilitate analysis; but the incisions that we necessarily make into the whole only deform and obscure the reality that it is hoped to explain. And far from being written in the language of mathematics, as Galileo had claimed, the truths of nature are expressible only in a *poetic* form that evades any such control. God, as Hamann put it, was not a geometer after all, but a poet; so that the universe is never cut and dried, but always spontaneous, full of surprises and inexhaustible possibilities that can be realised at any moment. 'To the Eyes of the Man of Imagination', wrote William Blake, 'Nature is Imagination itself.'[44]

We cannot, of course, however imaginative, realise all potentialities simultaneously; but we can remain aware that they exist. Rather than just accepting the losses necessarily incurred through the adoption of any single theory or vision, we can contrive to remain aware of those losses and aware of their potential value – so that their retrieval remains an ever present possibility. The world thus remains not in static form, but in a perpetual *process* of re-creation, and experience becomes a matter of individual responsibility. That is, our universe becomes what we let it be. Just as Luther had replaced intrusive external authority with individual conscience in matters of theology, so Romantics (such as Hamann) extended that responsibility to life itself. One historian in the 1940s noted the anti-authoritarian (even anarchic) connotations, and effectively described (or prophesied) some of the social, political and theological implications of contemporary postmodernism, as described above in Chapter 1: 'Romanticism spells anarchy in every domain . . . a systematic hostility to everyone invested with any particle of social authority – husband or "paterfamilias", policeman or magistrate, priest or Cabinet-minister.'[45] In these general terms, then, Romantics can be seen as further precursors of that postmodernism to which Prime Minister Blair has more recently been alerted.

So far as historical study more specifically is concerned, it's significant in the first place that Romantics characteristically question conventional categorisations, and not least those neatly defined disciplinary boundaries with which academics are so often obsessed, and on which (as we have seen in Chapter 2) some modernist historians have continued to insist. Of particular relevance in this respect is the categorical distinction traditionally insisted on between 'history' and 'literature' (and especially poetry). It's this distinction, with its origins in classical antiquity and its reaffirmation by many subsequent historians, that is questioned by 'Romantic' historians such as Carlyle, Macaulay and Trevelyan. Thus Carlyle, for example, notes how the popular historical novels of Sir Walter Scott had revealed a historical 'truth' that had often been obscured by historians themselves – the simple truth 'that the bygone ages of the world were actually filled . . . not by protocols, state papers, controversies and abstractions, [but] by living men'.[46] To many, that will now seem so obvious as to be hardly worth saying; but Carlyle was provoked to make his point amid the prevalent constitutional and diplomatic histories that were fashionable in his time. His aim was obviously to counterbalance that tendency with a reminder of the essential humanity of ordinary 'living men' in the past, and his point was that that aspect of history had best been captured not by historians at all, but by a novelist. Carlyle's 'romanticism' thus serves as an antecedent for postmodernism inasmuch as – writing as a historian himself – he erodes the disciplinary boundary between history and literature, and so threatens to blur any supposed distinction between historical 'fact' and novelistic 'fiction'.

His proto-postmodernist romanticism appears also in relation to historical narratives. For he is aware that any such narratives are not found in the past but are imposed upon it, and that any linear narrative we may construct must in some sense violate the organic unity or *solidity* of the past – a solidity that ultimately renders any scientific search for supposedly isolated lines of causation hopeless. In seeking to impose tidy structures on the past, historians are attempting the impossible:

> Alas for our 'chains' or chainlets of 'causes and effects', which we so assiduously track through certain handsbreadths of years and square miles, when the whole is a broad, deep Immensity, and each atom is 'chained' and complected with all.[47]

Carlyle's recognition of the impenetrable complexity of the past, and of the impossibility of historians doing anything more than carving an arbitrary route through that complexity in their attempts to impose some meaningful narrative upon it, marks him again as a forerunner of postmodernism.

As a contemporary of Carlyle, Thomas Babington Macaulay appears as another nineteenth-century 'romantic' disciplinary renegade, with whom postmodernists might feel some sympathy. His heresy lay in arguing that Enlightenment-influenced historians such as David Hume and Edward Gibbon, far from being helped in their enterprises by adopting respectably 'scientific' procedures, had been 'seduced from truth, not by their imagination, but by their reason'.[48] And with an even more decisive emphasis, Houston Stewart Chamberlain – described critically by Modris Eksteins as 'another intriguing wayfarer in the modern odyssey into irrationalism' – repudiated any pretence to objectivity on the part of historians as 'academic barbarism'. By modernist standards, that remains an ironic inversion, but in the Romantic tradition Chamberlain felt justified in his belief that history had no objective reality, and that its spirit could be accessed, if at all, not by the critical methods professed by his disciplinary peers, but by intuition.[49]

That point was reiterated by another professionally maligned, but nevertheless popular social historian, G. M. Trevelyan, when he provocatively claimed that 'Generations of *dispassionate* historians . . . unerringly missed the point'. Their very attempt to be dispassionate, he insisted, was bound to prove counter-productive, since it was precisely their own affected *lack* of passion that effectively cut them off from a past that was itself '*full* of passion'. Properly to understand the past, then, Trevelyan believed, 'Clio [as the muse of history] should *not* always be cold, aloof, impartial'. What history requires, rather, is an imaginative, even poetic input.[50]

That remains heretical talk: ask Simon Schama, who has more recently been accused of allowing imagination to intrude into history's supposedly rational domain. But the overall message here from 'Romanticisms' is that history is not, after all and in defiance of tradition, a 'science'. The nature of the past, that is, can never hope to be apprehended by scientific means (involving objectification and detachment), but rather by an imaginative assimilation into the object of study, such as is more usually associated with poetry, or with the 'Orientalisms' that provide the subject of our next section.

6 Orientalisms

In many respects orientalism appears to be in league with post-modernism.

(J. J. Clarke)[51]

Like Romanticism, 'Orientalism' is subject to such numerous and diverse definitions that I'll try to expose fewer hostages to fortune by again using the plural for the title of this section. 'Orientalism' in the singular has suffered from a bad press, at least from the time of Edward Said's diagnosis (in the 1970s) of what he concluded was a self-seeking and self-serving Western imperialist imposition of cultural 'otherness' on an alien and supposedly less civilised region of the world. Said and others have argued that the 'Orient' doesn't even exist on its own account, but only as a construction of Westerners, who use it as a convenient 'other' on which to project their own deficiencies. But for present purposes we shall assume at least that 'Orientalisms' (in the plural) do exist, as modes of Eastern thought – whether those are considered as somehow intrinsic to the East or as merely a Western construct; and we shall indicate further the close connection between these and the 'Romanticisms' just considered. It should follow that forms of Orientalism itself can be seen as precursors of, or (as in the quotation from John Clarke above) at the very least 'in league with', postmodernism; and we might note here that, as a comparative philosopher, David Hall similarly has gone so far as to suggest that 'classical China is in a very real sense *postmodern*'.[52]

To claim a connection between Orientalism and Romanticism may already seem perverse to those who recall that Voltaire – that paragon exemplar of the Enlightenment (against which the Romantics rebelled) – himself was a leading enthusiast for Eastern thought. But the apparent paradox can quickly be resolved by recognising the complexity of the concepts involved here. The Orientalism of which Voltaire and some of his Enlightenment successors so approved is essentially that Confucian strain that has always seemed to fit most easily with Western ways. In China itself Confucianism has often been claimed as the mainstream philosophy, and for progressive thinkers in eighteenth-century Europe, it seemed to offer a model, both for a rational and personal religion without the supernatural and institutional accretions of Christianity, and for a well-ordered and enviably stable political Utopia.

Even within Chinese classical philosophy itself, however, there was an alternative tradition that appealed, to others, for altogether different reasons. With its repudiation of conventional values, and its aspiration towards personal union with the world-spirit, Taoism is more mystical, more personalised and more potentially subversive; and it is with this alternative tradition, embracing thought and art, as well as spirituality and even garden landscapes, that Western Romantics became (and remain) enamoured. At the high point of European Romanticism, Taoism represented a welcome and supportive reassertion of alternative values, emphasising as it did the primacy of spirituality and the validity of an organic and holistic model of the cosmos, against the pervasive materialism that seemed increasingly to characterise modernity. And that Taoist strand of Orientalism went on to confirm the Romantic inclinations of Emerson and Thoreau, and their band of American transcendentalists, some of whose views remain congenial in the context of postmodernity.

Narrowing the field of Orientalism to Taoism more specifically, then, John Clarke (to whom I am indebted for much of this section) has indicated some respects in which the notoriously fluid – not to say ineffable – theories (or, rather, modes of perception) ascribed to Taoism can be seen as further precursors of postmodernism. Of course, the very vagueness, or lack of clear definition in its teachings, already marks out Taoism as likely to appeal to postmodernists, predisposed as they are to question the imposed structures that characterise modern Western thought, and to question also the competence of language to encapsulate any truth about the world. A blurring of conceptual edges, and a denial of the possibility of any precision in communication, when (as conceded by Tao Te Ching) 'the name that can be named is not the constant name', and when (in the admittedly paradoxical words of Laozi) 'Those who know do not speak; those who speak do not know'[53] – such aspects of Taoism commend themselves to the more 'romantically' inclined, for whom language can often be more of a barrier than bridge to understanding.

Questioning the very basis of linguistically defined categories goes, too, with that ready acceptance of chaos that we have already seen to be one of the defining characteristics of postmodernism. Thus, whereas Western philosophers have long seen their role as imposing some sort of order on to an otherwise terrifyingly chaotic world, Taoists rest more content with acceptance of experience 'as it's given'. That implies, in defiance of the West's tendency to abstract and universalise such concepts as 'Truth' with a capital 'T', an insistence on the concrete and particular manifestations of (lower-case) truth as experienced. In terms of response to nature, then, the formal and geometrical order of Western garden design, representing a nature that has (like Mo's rainforest) been subdued and tidied up, contrasts with the 'orderly chaos' of its Chinese counterpart. Furthermore, aspirations to control, dominate and exploit the external world are replaced by recognition of the self as an integral part of that world, and a desire only to experience one's essential unity with it. An assumption of that unity presupposes those blurred and permeable boundaries that characterise an organic and holistic, rather than mechanistic and analytic, model – such as that adopted, again, by Romantics and (at least in certain respects) by postmodernists. And that has implications, as has been widely recognised, for our modes of apprehending the external world (as well as the past): a more intuitive grasp replaces attempted detachment, when we ourselves, as aspirants to knowledge, can no longer be clearly defined and categorised, or distinguished from the objects of our study.

That essential lack of fixity in the Taoist perception of people and the natural universe opens the way to those repeated transformations of vision that we see applauded by such European thinkers as Blake (as Romantic) and Lyotard (as postmodernist). More or less 'final' theories that seem to conform to natural 'reality' hold little credence for those for whom 'reality' is ever changing, and awaiting personal apprehension in an infinite variety of ways. Those various ways, further, must obviously lack any absolute validity of their own, when viewed as links in a chain that represents a progressive path towards enlightenment; so that the linearity and singularity of the Western intellectual tradition curve, for the Taoist, into a cyclical process, accessible through a multiplicity of equally valid perceptions. Any notion of an 'end' is repudiated in favour of the possibility and potentiality for constant re-creation.

Such processes include not least the possibility of cyclical re-creations of the self. Re-visions, or new perceptions of ourselves (as of the external world), are facilitated by recognition of the complementarity of seeming opposites – by recognition, in Taoist terms, of the principles of 'yin' and 'yang', which represent not (as in the Western tradition) polarised opposites that are forever mutually exclusive and ultimately irreconcilable, but complementary parts that can be creatively interwoven into a harmonious whole. That, in personal terms, might imply recognition of the complementary nature of those 'masculine' and 'feminine' qualities that each of us has in varying degrees. Instead of repressing or denying those qualities that seem to be inconsistent or incompatible with our assumed identities and roles (as men and women), each can be allowed to play its part in a formation, the ingredients of which are susceptible to ongoing renegotiation.

That sort of self-creation has been advocated by the Romantically inclined from the Renaissance on, and is but one (important) example of the Taoist denial of absolutes that would be embraced also by post-modernists. For Pico della Mirandola in the Renaissance, for twentieth-century existentialists, and for contemporary postmodernists, the unstable nature of the self is to be welcomed, as offering the potential for never-ending redefinitions; so that the function of life becomes an exhilarating process of spontaneous self-creation. Whether in Taoism, existentialism or postmodernism, this imposes responsibility on the individual – responsibility to choose. For in the absence of absolutes, moral and political goals have to be individually (and self-consciously) chosen and embraced – and that is a part of the reason that Taoism (no less than postmodernism) has been feared by some as potentially subversive. There is (as Tony Blair's advisers reluctantly realised) no final or 'clear' template out there, only awaiting recognition and adoption; rather, it is left to individuals to work out their own salvation – which, for the Taoist as for any Romantic or postmodernist, means allowing them to espouse those values that imply their own self-actualisation.

Taoism, though, is not the only Oriental influence that can be detected in Romanticism and postmodernism: the thought of India, too, has played its part in challenging the West. As John Clarke explains:

> Just as the philosophes projected onto Confucian China their concept of an ideal polity governed by wise and philosophically educated rulers, so the Romantics projected onto India their idea of a more fully realised human existence and a more holistic and spiritually driven culture.[54]

From the late eighteenth century, such well-known Romantically inclined thinkers as Herder, Goethe, Hegel and Schopenhauer all took an interest in Indian thought, seeing it as an alternative, again, to the materialistic and mechanistic mainstream that had flowed in the West from the seventeenth-century scientific revolution; and the well-known Romantic poets – Shelley, Byron, Coleridge and others – all provide evidence of Oriental influence. And the more spiritual and transcendental approaches of both Hinduism and, later, Buddhism were adopted and passed on, through the works of Nietzsche in particular, to late twentieth- and early twenty-first-century postmodernism.

Martin Heidegger's studies of Zen Buddhism, for example, confirmed him in his antipathy to Western logocentrism and scientism, and in his proto-postmodern 'life-long attempt to free us from the prison-house of Western philosophical categories'. More generally Buddhism has been seen as promoting an emphasis on change and 'process' rather than on the typically Western preoccupation with 'substance', and as possessing a 'self-corrective methodology' that is well suited to assist in what we have seen to be a postmodern programme – namely that of liberation from the 'hypnotic grip of mental habits, or parochial patterns and social convention'. It can thus, in N. P. Jacobson's words, be seen as constituting 'one of the major resources . . . in the struggle of the contemporary world to free itself from the culture-bound astigmatisms of the past'.[55]

Orientalisms thus impinge, in a number of ways, on our past and on our historical re-presentations of that past. Above all, they provide a range of alternatives that inevitably highlights the relativity of Western concepts and positions. Orientalisms, in other words, have contributed and continue to contribute significantly to the decentring that we have seen to be an important aspect of postmodernism. They have shown that there are quite other perspectives from which to view the world, or of course to view the past, with quite other priorities and values; and there are other routes to understanding and to what is taken to be knowledge. These have been paralleled by and intermingled with characteristics of Romanticisms as presented in the preceding section; and, not least through the whole movement of post-colonialism, they continue to give support to postmodernist attitudes and historiography.

7 Conclusion

In a number of important respects, then, twenty-first-century post-modernist evaluations of history can be seen (or can be shown) to have had their own historical antecedents – going back in some cases, as Umberto Eco predicted, almost as far as Homer. Postmodernism itself, as we have seen, is a slippery concept that defies instant or facile definition; but I have tried here to identify at least some important characteristics – a sceptical attitude not least to truth, an acceptance of cultural relativism, an emphasis on the centrality of language, and the reaffirmation of qualities associated with Romanticisms and Orientalisms – which recur perennially through the history of thought. That is not to say that postmodernism is not itself a unique amalgamation and manifestation – a cultural phenomenon in its own right, in its own time and place, a condition for us here and now. But it is to claim that,

if only in the interests of self-knowledge, we need to view the phenomenon by which we are confronted, and of which we form a part, with
some awareness of some of its antecedents – to view, that is, again,
postmodernism *in* history.

4

POSTMODERN PARALLELS

The transition to modernity

1 Introduction

> But if Aristotle is to be abandoned, whom shall we have for a
> guide in philosophy?[1]

We've been here before! That's easy to say, and increasingly tempting
as age and cynicism take over, with a recognition of the many cycles
to which human life seems prone. So while it's a truism that the condition of postmodernity is something new (as, by definition, coming
chronologically after what's been known as modernity), it's still arguable
that that condition (as well as responses to that condition) have their
parallels in earlier historical transitions. Having considered some of
postmodernism's antecedents (or having categorised certain intellectual
movements so that they can be defined as such) in Chapter 3, I want to
claim now that pomophobia, too (as a fearful response to alternative
ideas), does have its parallels, during the transition from what we might
call 'medievalism' to the 'modernity' that is now in turn, and in our own
time is being superseded.

These terms, 'mediaevalism' and 'modernity', are of course, no less
than 'postmodernity' itself, highly problematic – and not least in the
context of postmodernism. For it is only by assembling what we choose
to consider 'key' elements that we can presume to universalise about such
concepts, and present any definitions at all. And it goes against the
grain of postmodernity to do just that. 'Let us wage war against totality',
proclaimed Lyotard,[2] and there can be few enterprises that aspire to
greater 'totality' than the attempt to characterise a Europe-wide world-
view (whether 'medievalism' or 'modernity') supposedly subscribed to
through several hundred years.

The problem is compounded in the case of such 'intellectual' history,
since there's always the danger of ascribing thoughts – on the universe
and other such abstruse concepts – to people who may well have had

more pressing and practical matters (such as where to get their next meal) on their minds. Philosophising has never been everybody's cup of tea, or interest, and isn't now; so we're necessarily dealing here primarily with an 'élite' – those few for whom ideas mattered, or those, perhaps fewer still, who may have been (or may be) even unconsciously subject to intellectual influences. Just, then, as it may make some sense to claim (as in the quotation with which I opened Chapter 1) that 'Britain is dominated by "postmodern" attitudes', so there may be some justification for the universalising claims implied by such phrases as 'the mediaeval world picture'. At least, some confirmatory evidence can be adduced from contemporary cultural artefacts – poetry, drama, paintings – though not, perhaps, from any man or woman in the street.

We have to concede, at all events, the underlying irony of what we're doing here, or trying to do – which is to put postmodernism into a form of historical narrative, the validity of which seems to be denied by post-modernism itself. As Robert Berkhofer observes, 'The very notion of postmodernism presumes a Great Story at the same time as it denies the credibility of metanarratives in today's world'.[3] Yet to make any sense of where we are, we seem still to need to know where it is (or was) that we have come from. And that leaves us with a need to resort to historical practices – reducing the unmanageable to fit our tidy boxes, and imposing causal patterns on otherwise chaotic developments. That is surely a paradox that postmodernists of all people, with their readiness to accept inconsistencies, might be expected to be able to accept with equanimity; and I hope to clear myself of hypocrisy by openly confessing the contingency of the interpretation that I've chosen here.

So the well-worn net of meaning that I'm tentatively casting essentially entails the replacement of the coherent cosmos bequeathed by the thirteenth-century scholastic synthesisers of Aristotelian philosophy and Christian theology – a cosmos that was coherent in the sense of being finite, circumscribed by an outer rim embedded with fixed stars, and being, within that finitude, perfectly ordered in a harmonious all-embracing pattern. Within that tidy frame human beings were particularly favoured, sited as they were at the very centre of a universe that had been purposefully constructed for their benefit. If the stars shone, that was to give pleasure to the human inhabitants of earth, just as minerals were to be used by them for their arts and crafts, and food provided for them from animals and vegetation. And the purpose of humans themselves in turn was to serve the creator, God: their very lives were the expression, the fulfilment of God's creative providence.

The replacement of such a human-centred model by that of an imper-sonal machine, which lacked any human characteristics or orientation, was bound to prove traumatic; and if pomophobia represents a fear that is being expressed in our current transition from modernity to post-modernity, it may be consoling or illuminating, or at the very least interesting, to detect parallels in that earlier transition. Then, as now, there were those who excitedly embraced the new universe revealed by the new thought, and by the new science in particular. But there were others who were more hostile to that change, who saw the developments of their day as regressive rather than progressive, and who continued to resist the new, and perhaps, like pomophobes today, to fear it. As Galileo's representative of the old thought indicates in the quotation above, there was concern that, if once the traditional foundations of Aristotelianism were removed, it would be difficult (if not impossible) to find a replacement – and that would leave humankind without the guidance (or foundation) that it needs.

Even in the seventeenth century itself, then, two distinct categories of response to the new thought were identified: the terms 'Ancients' and 'Moderns' were widely used to describe respectively the 'reactionaries' and the 'revolutionaries'; and those terms have been subsequently (though ever more hesitantly) applied in intellectual histories of the period. To categorise in that way (or indeed in any other) is of course inevitably to oversimplify: the more closely one tries to peer at the past, the more one's focus blurs and the assumed sharpness of black and white fades into many shades of grey. People insistently reveal themselves as frustratingly elusive human beings, and then as now the majority might best be represented by the more ambivalent term of 'Janus-face'; which reminds us of the god who looked both ways at once, a face in each direction, not needing to, or able to, decide between two visions, but assimilating both.

As mere humans, we may not be able in that godlike way to get the best of both worlds concurrently, or have our cake and eat it; and there is always some danger of ending up as something of a contortionist, sitting on the proverbial fence, with a modicum of indecision and a foot in each camp. But at least that intermediary (if potentially uncomfort-able) position enables us to assess our gains and losses. And gains and losses there have always been in the replacement of one world-view (or, less grandiosely, one perception) by another. In Wittgenstein's much-cited example, we may gain a duck's beak only at the cost of the rabbit's ears; we can't see, or have, them both at once, but inevitably sacrifice one in order to possess the other (see Figure 3).

So the wonders of that modernity, in which we've luxuriated for some three hundred years, were bought at a price. New freedoms enjoyed by individuals were counterbalanced by new anxieties pertaining to personal responsibility; exhilaration at the prospect of infinity only

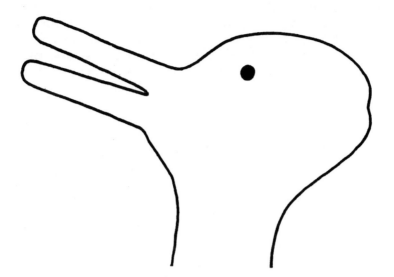

Figure 3 Gains and losses: duck or rabbit?

sometimes (and for some) outweighed a sense of lost security; and the huge explanatory advantages of a mechanistic conception of nature may have seemed (if only for a time) to render obsolete many more mystical experiences and approaches. Underneath the surface of the whole progressive, and often presumptuous, and seemingly unstoppable wave of modernism lurked a disquietude that has periodically resurfaced – and currently with greater insistence. Canute may have been swamped by the incoming waters, but the reality of his immersion couldn't wash away all traces of human aspiration to stem the tide, and to retain the possibility of alternatives.

The transition to modernism, then, like the transition to postmodernism, can be shown to reveal both gains and losses; and it's on the ambivalence of responses on the part of those who lived through the former period that I want to focus here, since it's that that may be seen to resonate with our own predicament.

2 A new individualism

He [God] . . . took man as a creature *of indeterminate nature.*
(Pico della Mirandola)

The Italian Renaissance philosopher Pico della Mirandola is well known for his early assertion of humans' responsibility for determining their own nature. God the creator had left them 'of indeterminate nature', without any 'fixed abode, nor a form that is thine alone, nor any function peculiar to thyself'. They could sink to the level of animals, or aspire to the condition of angels; but the main point is that it's up to them to find their place and function and themselves. 'As though *the maker and moulder of thyself*', Pico concludes, 'thou mayest fashion thyself in whatever shape thou shalt prefer.'[4]

In the context of the gradual emergence from medieval thought, Pico's was a revolutionary vision, but his anti-authoritarian emphasis in philosophy was soon to be confirmed in very practical terms by another great revolutionary. Conveniently for the coherence of our narrative, Martin Luther was born only three years before Pico's Oration was composed, and his own challenge to the longstanding authority of the Roman Church was to have implications that extended far more widely than theology. As Erasmus complained to Justus Jonus in 1521, Luther succeeded in 'making even cobblers aware of things which used to be discussed only amongst the learned, as mysteries and forbidden knowledge'. It was not surprising, then, that in the face of such potentially general disruption Jonus should go on emphatically to 'urge that one *avoid disorder*'.[5] But *how* to avoid it was the question. Individuals came to see that, once authority was questioned, they were freed from not only theological but also social constraints of earlier times. An important part of Luther's message was, like that of Pico, that people are not necessarily constrained by traditional institutional bonds: they are (at least in some respects) free to seek their own salvation as individuals.

That individual freedom, articulated as an ideal by such thinkers as Pico and Luther at the time of the Renaissance and Reformation, became an essential ingredient of 'modernity'. As one of the acknowledged founders of modernity, Descartes insisted on the ability of humans to act freely, and on their consequent responsibility for what they do. 'It is a supreme perfection in man that he acts voluntarily, that is, *freely*; this makes him in a special way the author of his actions and deserving of praise [or presumably blame] for what he does.' That freedom of our wills must, he asserts, be innate in us: it's an essential, inborn, defining characteristic of the individual modern human being; so that Kant can later claim that it is the acceptance of individual responsibility for self – having 'the courage to use your own understanding' – that is the core (the 'watchword') of 'Enlightenment'. 'Human reality' henceforth, as Sartre was even later to agree, implies the need 'to *choose oneself*'.[6]

Now it's no doubt all too easy to overemphasise (or idealise) the homogeneity of mediaeval society and the social and psychological stability of pre-modern people, but a case can be made that, as the structures of medieval society broke down, people found themselves deprived of a security that feudal hierarchies had previously provided. Feudalism implied that, unlike Pico's, Descartes's, Kant's and Sartre's liberated self-defining individual, people were born into a specific station in life that would largely determine how that life would be lived. In existential terms the essence of a person was evident from the outset: to a great extent, the course of a life would be programmed from its start; there would be few choices about where and how to live, or about what sort of person to be, in a situation where the nature of one's work virtually determined *who* one was.

Thus, the great historian of the Middle Ages, Johan Huizinga, recorded how the Carthusian monk Denis produced a series of treatises, which were intended to show the ideal form of their professional and social duties to bishops, canons, priests, scholars, princes, nobles, knights, merchants, widows and so on. It was perfectly feasible, that is, to provide a definitive blueprint for different classes of professional and personal behaviour: individuality was not a matter of personal invention but of professional prescription. So even as late as 1577 William Harrison could confirm the existence of a clearly stratified society, with his *Description of England* incorporating a chapter on what he refers to as 'the degrees of people'. Again, an ideal form of life is assumed for the members of each class – an ideal way of living and being that should be aspired to, a general model for specific individuals to imitate, and a template by which to measure failure and success.[7] Naturally, then, Chaucer's pilgrims in the *Canterbury Tales* could be assigned, as it were, ready-made characters to fit their station in life, whether as Knight or Pardoner or Host; and it's noteworthy that they generally keep their respective places in a social hierarchy that is recognised and accepted by all.[8]

That hierarchy determines their place in relation not only to each other, but also to the external and central authority of God; and for members of a society in which a chain of command (and of mutual responsibility) ran from the divine apex through strictly stratified ranks down to the humblest peasant, choice, and the attendant responsibility for exercising choice, was seldom an issue or a practical problem. So far as we can tell, existential angst and ontological insecurity were luxuries well out of the reach of most mediaeval men and women. There were, after all, good theological reasons too provided for the class structure. Theirs was not to reason why, or how, or who, when the situations of the rich man in his castle and the poor man at his gate were ordered by the almighty creator himself. Servitude, for instance, according to the eleventh-century saint Anselm, 'is ordained by God, either because of the sins of those who become serfs, or as a trial, in order that those who are thus humbled may be made better'; and since servitude prompts the great virtue of humility, 'it would seem to be pride for anyone to wish to change that condition which has been given him for good reason by the divine ordinance'.[9]

When that ordering was challenged, or when those stratifications of society were questioned (as of course they sometimes were by those who could exploit a backward-looking vision to a Golden Age, when 'gentlemen' had not been distinguished from their neighbours), then a reversion to chaos was often expected to ensue. 'Take but degree away, untune that string,/And hark! what discord follows', as Ulysses warns in Shakespeare's *Troilus and Cressida*.[10] And on the whole the maintenance of an ordered society must have seemed to all ranks to be preferable to a reversion to a chaotic 'state of nature', in which gentlemen were seldom likely to be seen. It's not for nothing that the greatest English political philosopher of the seventeenth century prescribed strong authoritarian government as an antidote to individualistic libertarian anarchy, and not for nothing that, in practical political terms, the English Commonwealth should soon have been superseded by the restoration of the monarchy.

That theoretical and practical flight from the potentially anarchic consequences of the new individualism serve to confirm the hypothesis of Erich Fromm – a psychologist working in the 1940s and so naturally interested in the perennially intriguing question of why individuals give themselves up to dominating ideologies (such as, in his time, Nazism). He concluded in short that it was the *fear* induced by their own freedom from external constraints that precipitated people into what was effectively another form of captivity – but this time self-imposed. The voluntary submission to some form of authority – whether manifested in theological, political or ideological forms, as Calvinism, authoritarian government or even a conscience that expresses social pressures – conveniently removes from liberated individuals the fear they feel at having destiny placed squarely in their own hands. 'The development of modern thinking', he concludes, 'can be characterised as the substitution of internalised authority for an external one';[11] and without needing here to consider in detail the nature of particular escape-routes, I shall argue that the fear which, according to Fromm's diagnosis, was provoked through the emergence of a new 'individualism' in the early modern period can be seen in some interesting respects to parallel current pomophobia. In the transition from mediaevalism to modernism, and in that from modernism to postmodernism, the removal of traditional constraints is far from welcomed, as might have been expected; on the contrary, it results in the disquieting recognition of a need to assume personal responsibility. Once someone stops telling us what to do, we're left with open choices, and as often as not we react by taking headlong flight into some self-imposed (often internalised) subservience.

One escape-route might be found in religion, and the growth of sectarianism in the mid-seventeenth century foreshadows the increase of fundamentalist religions reported in the late twentieth and early twenty-first. Thomas Edwards in 1645 identified no fewer than sixteen recognisably different sects in England, sharing 176 heresies;[12] and sectarian enthusiasts, such as Thomas Venner in 1661, could threaten such social disruption as to necessitate the imposition of martial law in London. Venner himself, together with twelve of his followers, was executed, but my point about him here is that religious enthusiasm such as his marks the sort of ideological commitment in which men and women (then and now) take refuge during times of intellectual upheaval.

Later ideological refuges have included (and in some cases continue to include) such theologico-political movements as Nazism and Marxism, nationalism and capitalism. But the main point here is that the removal of traditional constraints, whether in early modern times or the present, seems initially to offer liberation, but can also serve to unsettle. Early modern individuals found that they could no longer take refuge in the comforting feudal hierarchies that had for so long predetermined their place and function (and so their very identity): they were forced, as newly constituted 'moderns', to confront their own responsibility for choosing what to do, and who to be. Their resultant fear, as diagnosed by Fromm, is paralleled in the early twenty-first century, when, on the brink of postmodernity, people find themselves similarly confronted by the dissolution of the old order, and by the need to define themselves anew.

3 A new universe

Engulfed in the infinite immensity of spaces of which I am ignorant, and which know me not, I am frightened.
(Blaise Pascal)[13]

The fear of postmodernism, particularly as it relates to history (and by implication to psychology and politics), is analogous to the fear expressed by Pascal (and experienced perhaps more widely) in the face of that impersonal and unknown immensity of spaces that had been opened up by the early modern cosmological revolution initiated by Copernicus. Pascal himself is now best known, perhaps, for his famous wager – his conclusion, as a betting man, that it's expedient to retain belief in God, since nothing is lost if proved wrong, while if God does turn out to exist, it's better to have hedged one's bets in that direction.

The thinking behind that practical advice brings together Pascal's diverse interests as theologian and mathematician; and he personally exemplifies the difficulty that historians face in categorising early modern thinkers (or indeed those of any other period). As a natural philosopher, or scientist, he carried out experiments on atmospheric pressure and applied himself to the mathematics of probability theory; but on the other hand, he might seem to fit our criteria for appearing as another Romantic, or even as another proto-postmodernist. At all events, aware of the emotional consequences of scientific developments in his time, he notes some of the losses incurred by the dissolution of the mediaeval cosmos, and concludes in words that clearly resonate today:

> Man does not know in what rank to place himself. He has plainly gone astray, and fallen from his true place without being able to find it again. He seeks it anxiously and unsuccessfully everywhere in impenetrable darkness.[14]

Believing, like other Romantics, that the universe is a unified whole, Pascal repudiates the validity of analytic slicing; for, as he explains, 'the parts of the world are so related and linked to one another, that I believe it impossible to know one without the other and without the whole'; and that whole includes man himself, who is not therefore (as proposed in the new Cartesian formulation) detachable from the objects of his observation, but 'is related to all he knows'. What he knows, though, or what he is ever capable of knowing, itself remains highly problematic, for 'all the sciences are infinite in the extent of their researches', and all the premises we select as the foundations of our knowledge, or as our ultimate unquestionable starting-points, are themselves 'not self-supporting' at all, 'but are based on others which, again having others for their support, do not permit of finality'. Deprived of any sure foundations for knowledge, then, and confronted by a universe that's infinite in extent, we can only realise the hopelessness of aspiring to any certainty and stability:

> We sail within a vast sphere, ever drifting in uncertainty, driven from end to end. When we think to attach ourselves to any point and to fasten to it, it wavers and leaves us; and if we follow it, it eludes our grasp, slips past us, and vanishes for ever. Nothing stays for ever . . . We burn with desire to find solid ground and an ultimate sure foundation whereon to build a tower reaching to the Infinite. But our whole groundwork cracks, and the earth opens to abysses.[15]

Pascal is well aware, then, that he and his contemporaries were being precipitated from the cosy, closed world of the mediaeval cosmos into a potentially infinite and coldly indifferent universe. In *Ignatius His Conclave* of 1611 John Donne represents Copernicus as claiming to 'have turned the whole frame of the world', and to have become 'thereby almost a new creator'; and although in real life Copernicus himself would have been too diffident or judicious to say such a thing, some sixty years on that claim put into his mouth could be seen by Pascal to have been well justified. Donne himself, quick to realise the wider significance of Copernicus's new world, went on elsewhere to conclude that, with the very cosmic centre replaced, everything else in the universe had been brought into doubt. With the removal of humans from their long-favoured position at the centre, the old certainties were lost: 'Tis all in pieces, all coherence gone.' As Nietzsche was to put it later: 'Since Copernicus, man seems to have got himself on an inclined plane – now he is slipping faster and faster away from the centre into – what? into nothingness?'[16]

To Copernicus, then, can be ascribed the first move towards that decentring that we have seen to characterise postmodernism. The geo-centric cosmology bequeathed from classical antiquity had enjoyed the enormous benefit of having embraced the whole of creation (as it was then known) and having made of it an orderly and harmonious whole – a satisfyingly coherent cosmos. With the earth at the centre of a spatially finite universe bounded by a sphere of fixed stars, human beings knew their place – knew where they were (and who they were) in relation to the rest of nature. In what has been described as 'the great chain of being' all things were linked and interdependent. God, angels, humans, animals, vegetation, minerals: there was nothing that was not, in the words of Sir John Fortescue in the fifteenth century, bound together 'in most harmonious concord'.[17] And if that was true in place, it was also true in time. Humans, that is, knew that they had their place in history. They were bounded in finite time – a time circumscribed by the Christian narrative of creation, fall and subsequent salvation; and they could see their own lives (as well as history more generally) as a progression – as the working out of a previously prepared providential plan. It's hardly surprising that the emotional satisfaction to be derived from that model, which so conveniently provided for both socio-political security and cosmic meaningfulness, ensured the prolongation of its acceptance through some two millennia.

That long acceptance itself made replacement more difficult, and the effects of replacement, when finally achieved, more traumatic. As early as 1606 the astronomer Johannes Kepler, who was himself to play a major part in the replacement of the old model, referred with some apprehension to what was to become the crucial outcome of the new cosmological theorising – namely the decentring and universal displacement that was to be the inevitable consequence of the newly postulated infinity of space: 'That thought bears with it I know not what secret, hidden horror: we feel lost in that immensity to which limits and the centre are denied, to which every determinate place is consequently denied.'[18] Without a centre, that is, the whole concept of place – the location of an object in relation to a centre – becomes meaningless. Milton refers to space as 'a dark/Illimitable ocean, without bound,/Without dimension; where length, breadth, and highth,/And time, and place, are lost';[19] and it was again that loss of time and place in a decentred universe that disquieted Pascal.

By the end of the century the 'horror' envisaged by Kepler was more popularly seen as one outcome of the cosmological revolution that had by then been completed. Thus, for example, the Marchioness in Fontenelle's early attempt to popularise science (presented in the form of reported conversations on the plurality of worlds), having been instructed in the novelties of Copernicanism, understands well the central point of cosmic space and decentring. Her instructor may feel that he can 'begin to breathe with more freedom' in the enlarged cosmological environment, but her own reaction is less enthusiastic:

> 'You have made the Universe so large', said she, 'that I know not where I am, or what will become of me . . . the very Idea of it confounds and overwhelms me . . . We ourselves . . . must confess, that we scarce know where we are . . .; [and] for my own part, I begin to see the Earth so fearfully little, that I believe from henceforward I shall never be concern'd at all for any thing.'[20]

Three hundred years on, we've become more or less accustomed to that modern Copernican universe, and have learnt to feel tolerably secure, not bothering any longer to question what we now take for granted. But today we're challenged by something new – by another proposed revision of our conceptual schema, another intellectual revolution. The wider implications of scientific developments take time, even now, to filter through to the public consciousness, and it's already some thirty years since the Nobel Prize-winning scientist Jacques Monod presented his vision of a universe, once more deprived by science of any *intrinsic* values. 'In the uncaring emptiness of the universe', he believed, 'man must at last wake out of his millenary dream and discover his total solitude, his fundamental isolation.' As any existentialist – or postmodernist – would agree, it is, Monod believed, up to human beings themselves to impose their own structure of values: they are (as Fromm had diagnosed in another context) liberated from previous constraints, but additionally burdened by responsibility. For:

> The ancient covenant is in pieces; man at last knows that he is alone in the unfeeling immensity of the universe, out of which he emerged only by chance. Neither his destiny nor his duty [has] been written down. The kingdom above or the darkness below: it is for him to choose.[21]

More recently Stephen Jay Gould, from a different scientific starting-point, has reached a strikingly similar conclusion. Gould's research on the fossil remains in the Burgess Shale (in British Columbia) led him to conclude that the development of nature and of human life itself has not been governed by any law, but has rather been contingent and altogether unpredictable. And so he too concludes, like Monod, by stressing humans' own responsibility to choose:

> We are the offspring of history, and must establish our own paths in this most diverse and interesting of conceivable universes – one indifferent to our suffering, and therefore offering us maximal freedom to thrive, or to fail, in our chosen way.[22]

These provide further foretastes of the postmodern predicament. Once again we're forced to rethink this and that – and ultimately to rethink everything; to abandon our habits, and to start afresh. No wonder we feel insecure, unstable, lacking in foundations and (rather like those Aristotelians, who couldn't believe that anything could ever replace their own Aristotelian foundations) lacking even in any belief that there can be any foundations at all. No wonder that there's fear.

4 A new nature

In these last hundred years . . . almost a *New Nature* has been reveal'd to us.

(John Dryden, 1668)[23]

It seemed to John Dryden that the early modern intellectual revolution had resulted in the revelation of what was effectively a 'new nature', and there is some evidence that, in the transition from mediaevalism to modernity natural philosophers (and ultimately other thinking people) did indeed come to view nature in an altogether different way. Fontenelle's Marchioness is presented by her tutor with a helpful illustration (Figure 4): she is to imagine herself at the opera, where the

Figure 4 Explanation: mystery or mechanics? Fontenelle's chariot
Drawings: Anne Duke

character Phaethon appears to fly in his solar chariot above the stage. Phaethon's aerial flight seems to be miraculous – achieved somehow by magic. But hidden from the audience's sight are the scene-shifters' ropes, pulleys and counterweights that make the illusion possible: beneath the appearances are hidden mechanisms; and these provide the explanation for any seeming theatrical mystery. And just so in the universe at large (to put the matter in its most simplistic terms), what in the Aristotelian vision had been an organism, full of mysteries, came to be seen rather as a great machine, rationally explicable.

For Leonardo da Vinci, then, as Renaissance polymath, the earth remains a living organism – an animal writ large:

> We can say that the earth has a vegetative soul, and that its flesh is the land, its bones are the structure of the rocks . . . its blood is the pools of water . . . its breathing and its pulse are the ebb and flow of the sea.

But for the new philosophers that animistic model was to be explicitly rejected. As an astronomer, for instance, Kepler's aim became 'to show that the Celestial machine is to be likened *not* to a divine organism but rather to clockwork'; and as a physician, Friedrich Hoffmann could insist by 1695 that 'medicine is the art of properly utilising *physico-mechanical* principles'. No wonder, then, that Fontenelle's astute Marchioness observes that 'Philosophy is now become very mechanical'. And that whole fundamental transition – that switch in perception to 'a new nature' – has been well described by one intellectual historian as 'the *mechanisation* of the world picture'.[24]

The new mechanistic model derived from a much earlier tradition of atomism that had defied empiricists and religious mystics since the sixth century BC. That tradition was recorded in the Roman poet Lucretius' enthusiastic work, *On the Nature of the Universe*. As a convert to Epicurean philosophy, Lucretius (paradoxically, as it may now seem) advocated atomism as a very positive antidote to the fears and anxieties with which most people seemed to him to lead their lives. Worries about offending the gods and being punished in an after-life – these negative preoccupations, he came to see, could be instantly dispelled by the knowledge of how nature worked. For scientific knowledge would make clear that there was no need for any gods to intervene in a universe that ran in accordance with strictly mechanical principles; and there was no after-life to fear for bodies whose death constituted no more nor less than a final dissolution of their constituent atoms (and so their individual identities).

Epicurean atomism never suited any but the tough-minded, and for Christians, with their belief in divine creation and a God who subsequently intervened in the necessary maintenance of natural and moral order, it long remained anathema. But the ability to construct syntheses has always been a prerequisite for Christian theologians as they confront what initially seem heterodox ideas: adaptability is the hallmark of a religion that has, over the centuries, survived encounters with such major challenges as Aristotelianism, Copernicanism, and Darwinism; and even atomism could, in the end, be safely accommodated within its pragmatically flexible house of many mansions.

So by the middle decades of the seventeenth century the so-called 'mechanical philosophy', for all its basis in pagan and atheistic atomism, could be safely embraced by Christian natural philosophers, or 'virtuosi'. Robert Boyle, for example, as the most devout of men, could claim not only the compatibility of the new science with Christianity, but even that the new science positively contributed to Christian faith. His major work on science and religion was designed to show, in the words of its subtitle, 'That by being addicted to experimental philosophy [i.e. the new science], a man is rather assisted than indisposed to be a good Christian'; for by gaining a clearer insight into the workings of nature, the new philosophers would be less likely 'to ascribe such admirable effects to so incompetent and pitiful a cause as blind chance, or the tumultuous justlings of atomical portions of senseless matter', and be more likely to be drawn to God as the creator of such a beautiful and complex natural world.[25]

As Boyle himself explained, too, the new philosophy was so clear and simple that it could be comprehended by the meanest intelligence, and it was so comprehensive – indeed universal in its application – that it could subsume all other hypotheses, and itself explain potentially everything.[26] As Descartes had previously announced, his principles, as universally applicable, eliminated any need to resort to such 'mediaeval' (and now obsolete) terms as 'sympathies' and 'occult qualities' – terms that meant no more than that they were, at the time and within the existing intellectual paradigm, inexplicable:

> There are no powers in stones or plants so occult, no sympathies or antipathies so miraculous and stupendous, in short, nothing in nature . . . that its reason cannot be deduced from these [i.e. mechanical] principles.[27]

For this simple and all-embracing model, the analogy of the clock or watch is often used. As Fontenelle's tutor explains, the new philosophers 'will have the World to be in great, what a Watch is in little, which is very regular, and depends only upon the just disposing of the several parts of the Movement'.[28] Phenomena can appear very complex, but, like the complicated movements of the famous clock in Strasbourg, they can be understood as simply caused by (possibly invisible) mechanical operations. The functioning of even the human body could be explicated in these terms, for, as Descartes proposed in a work completed by 1632 but judiciously withheld from publication in his lifetime, 'all these functions follow naturally in this machine [of the body] simply from the arrangements of its parts, no more and no less than do the movements of a clock'.[29]

Such unitary explanatory schemes, with their inclusion (or alternatively exclusion from 'reality') of anything that had previously defied explanation, are bound to prove alluring to those for whom the uncertainty of the unknown (and unknowable) is disconcerting; and by 1664 Henry Power could extravagantly proclaim that the mechanical philosophy was indeed coming in 'with a Spring-tide', overwhelming any vestiges of earlier models of nature. What humans are finally to be favoured with is 'a true and permanent Philosophy . . . a more magnificent Philosophy, never to be overthrown'; and its success is ultimately guaranteed by the fact that, in its explanations of nature, it utilises the very principles with which God had originally constructed the natural world.[30]

By the following century the great German philosopher Johann Gottfried Herder, however critical and ironical he might have been about the new mechanical philosophy, described how 'It has forced its way into the sciences, the arts, customs and ways of living, and is considered the sap and blossom of our century'. And that mechanistic trend persisted through the next two hundred years, affecting, as Herder indicated for his own time, not only the sciences themselves, but every aspect of human life and culture. The world became, in Hume's words, 'nothing but one great machine'.[31]

That might, as Max Weber was to complain, amount to nothing less than the modernist 'disenchantment of the world'. Nature had had its magic – its mystery and divinity – removed: what had once been a wondrous rainbow, a miraculous sign from God, could now be simply explained in terms of Newtonian optics and the mechanical laws of physics; what had previously been awe inspiring had been reduced (in the Romantic Keats's words) to 'the dull catalogue of common things'.[32] And that symbolic 'unweaving' of the rainbow had come at a price. The innumerable material advantages derived from the mechanical model were inevitably counterbalanced by losses; and a recognition of those losses provoked charges of arrogance and hubris on the part of those who so confidently proclaimed the need for 'no other wisdom'. That will be the subject of our next section.

5 'No other wisdom'

God forbid that Truth should be Confined to Mathematical Demonstration!

(William Blake)[33]

Blake, in the quotation above, was only reiterating a concern that had been expressed as early as the seventeenth century by those 'Romantically' minded thinkers for whom the universalising tendencies of the new mechanical philosophy were anathema. The new philosophy, they saw, was being presented not just as another alternative hypothesis, to contend in rivalry with Aristotelianism and other traditional philosophies. Rather, in the style of a new religion, it was to be seen as incorporating the final revelation of the truth, or at least of the procedures that would enable that truth to be reached. It was, as we have seen, that very unitary vision, with its all-embracing character, that endeared it to its followers, such as Boyle and the fashionable young Fellows of the newly instituted Royal Society. But others decried the presumptuousness of those who seemed to think that science alone (as redefined) could potentially provide a solution to every human problem, and lay claim to territories with which it was ill-equipped to deal. There surely must, they continued to insist, be something that lies forever beyond the reach of 'Mathematical Demonstration'.

One of Blake's early modern predecessors was Méric Casaubon, who similarly railed – and, as the following quotation shows, in very similar terms – against the imperialistic pretensions of the new philosophy:

I hope it will not be required, that *Divinity* [i.e. theology] shall be tried by [i.e. answerable to] the *Mathematicks*, and made subservient to them; which yet the temper of some men of this age doth seem to threaten, which scarce will allow anything else worth a man's study.[34]

In his defence of traditional Christianity and of humane learning, Casaubon was far from being hostile to science *per se*. He claims to have studied mathematics, and to have taken every opportunity to further his appreciation of experimental philosophy: he had, for example, personally consulted the works of Bacon, attempted some experiments (albeit unsuccessfully), and interviewed practitioners. But for all its virtues and benefits, the new philosophy was, he concluded, 'a violent pursuit, that will not keep within its bounds, but ... doth aspire to an absolute Sovereignty over all'. The new philosophers themselves seem to think that theirs is the only way, and 'so magnifie this study [of the new science], as though there were no other wisdom in the world to be thought of, or pursued after'. They seem to think, he went on, that they are opening a completely new chapter in the history of thought, and they assume that whatever came before them is quite valueless, fit only to be unceremoniously discarded. Hobbes in particular 'doth take upon him to be the Oracle of the world; who would make the world believe noe such thing was in the world, truly and really, as art, or science, or philosophie, till he was borne and began to wryte'. And Descartes is no less hubristic, requiring as he does total allegiance to his own all-embracing system: his disciples, Casaubon notes, have to 'adhere to him tooth and nayle', and are encouraged to believe that 'all other bookes and learning should be layd asyde, as needless'.[35]

There was justification in Casaubon's complaints. The enthusiastic proponents of the new mechanical philosophy clearly liked to be seen as at the forefront of ideas – as revolutionary intellectuals who had no time for anything that smacked of the conventional and past. Newton, in one of his humbler moments, may have given public recognition to the earlier giants on whose shoulders he had been privileged to stand, but for the most part such intellectual debts remained unpaid. Bacon, Descartes, Galileo, Boyle – many, if not most, of the founding-fathers of modernity – presented themselves as wholly original, owing nothing of consequence to any predecessor.

Thus, Bacon himself aspired to present something 'quite new, totally new', and 'to commence a total reconstruction of sciences, arts, and all human knowledge'; so that his *New Organon* was deliberately named to imply its replacement of Aristotle's earlier, and now outdated, work. Descartes, too, confidently proclaimed his own novelty – to such an extent that he felt forced to 'conclude that those who have learned least about what has hitherto been called philosophy are most capable of apprehending the true [i.e. his own, new] philosophy'. Nor was it for nothing that Galileo in his dialogues named his representative Aristotelian 'Simplicio'. The forward-looking Sagredo was 'a man of noble extraction and trenchant wit', and his side-kick Salviati too had 'a sublime intellect' that persuaded him to accept the new ways. But the simple Simplicio, alas, had a vested interest in the past, and his own reputation as an interpreter of Aristotle was to prove the 'greatest obstacle in apprehending the truth'.[36]

105

For Galileo, then, any lingering nostalgia for the safe havens of the past was to be dismissed; and Boyle similarly was typical of his own time, in the latter half of the century, in his determination to confront intellectual problems with a mind kept pristine and clear of any obfuscating rubbish from the past. It was that terror of succumbing (or being seen to succumb) to any intrusions from the past (including reliance on literary texts) that led to his professed refusal to read the books of any predecessor: better to study nature herself, with a clear and open mind. So 'I could', he boasted, 'be very well content to be thought to have scarce look'd upon any other Book than that of Nature'.[37]

As another self-presenting fashionable intellectual, the flamboyant feminist Margaret Cavendish similarly claimed that she had deliberately repudiated the old scholarly convention of studying the views of earlier writers. Her own work, she was clear, was to be independent of any previous authorities: far from being derivative, it was to be truly original; and a commissioned portrait makes that clear. Shown standing in a shelf-lined study, Margaret's shelves themselves remain significantly bereft of any books. As a verse, penned probably by her approving husband, explains:

> Her library on which she looks,
> It is her head; her thoughts her books:
> Scorning dead ashes without fire,
> For her own flames do her inspire.[38]

Modernist repudiation of the past, then, went with a confident belief in modernism's claims to comprehensiveness; and just as postmodernism now seems, to some people, to be invading every aspect of life, so in its day did modernism, and modern science in particular. Relics of former times – the more 'mystical' aspects of life as hitherto experienced – were revealed as the fanciful products of a naive mind: if they weren't susceptible to analysis and explanation in modern terms, or to 'Mathematical Demonstration', then they couldn't really exist at all. So that one writer observed how fairies, for example, once ubiquitous, had simply disappeared from the world during the latter half of the century – a disappearance that was confirmed and explained by Thomas Sprat, as historian of the Royal Society. In the past, he recalled, 'an infinit number of Fairies haunted every house', but under the new dispensation – and not least the new way of defining 'reality' – they had been properly eliminated: 'from the time in which the Real [sic] Philosophy has appear'd, there is scarce any whisper remaining of such horrors'. The poet John Sheffield, for whom the new philosophy was represented by Hobbes, was another who saw the eviction of fairies, ghosts and similarly insubstantial entities from the realm of 'reality' as an indication of modernist progress: 'While in dark ignorance we lay, afraid/Of fancies, ghosts and ev'ry empty shade,/ Great Hobbes appear'd and by plain reason's light/ Put such fantastic forms to shameful flight.' In the brave new mechanistic world, there was to be no place for anything not subject to 'Mathematical Demonstration'.[39]

It was, however, not long before such complacency was challenged, and people, 'grown weary of rational romances . . . become fond again of the tales of fairies!'[40] And even at the time, fairies, and other manifestations of the non-mechanically explicable, continued to have their supporters:

> I never yet read of any Anthems composed from the Contemplation of Atoms. Who can Spell the Divine Wisdom, Power, and Goodness out of the Principles of Descartes, where he gives us the Origin of all things in a Puppet-play, interprets all the works of God according to the bruit Laws of Mechanism, and allows no other Operations in Vital Nature, than what he finds parallel'd in German Clockwork?[41]

Counterbalancing the enthusiasts for modernism, then, were the equivalent of contemporary pomophobes who, for whatever reasons, remained determinedly and securely anchored in those calm waters to which they had grown accustomed, refusing to venture out unnecessarily into the stormy and uncharted seas beyond. Then as now, some were no doubt simply frightened to expose themselves to any novelty, and preferred to stay with what they knew; for them the undermining of Aristotelian foundations meant nothing less than a ruinous reversion to intellectual chaos. 'Who would there be to settle our controversies if Aristotle were to be deposed? . . . Ought we to desert that structure under which so many travellers have recuperated? Should we destroy that haven . . .?' Those words, attributed by Sagredo to Simplicio in Galileo's *Dialogue* of 1632,[42] were effectively reiterated by the traditionalist Alexander Ross some two decades later, by which time Aristotle's deposition was well under way: 'These new Philosophers, as if they were wiser then all the world besides, have like fantastick travellers, left the old beaten and known path . . . and have reduced his [Aristotle's] comely order into the old chaos.'[43] Others more deliberately weighed the pros and cons, and concluded none the less that the older was the better way: Aristotle continued to have his supporters until the century's end.

It's a pity, of course, that one can't have it both ways, for by going in one direction we deprive ourselves of the possibility of going in another; so we can never know which in the end would have proved preferable. The need to choose inevitably results in deprivation of one sort or another: by selecting one focus, we necessarily forgo others. So while modern theories may account for some things better, and may seem to bring us nearer to the truth, that gain may be – must be – at the expense of other things that had been better handled by the old. The inevitability of compromise was recognised by Sir William Temple, who, in a long-running debate on these issues, observed in 1692:

> The abilities of man must fall short on one side or other, like too scanty a blanket when you are a-bed: if you pull it upon your shoulders, you leave your feet bare; if you thrust it down upon your feet, your shoulders are uncovered.[44]

That homely example made the point, which was to be more widely appreciated over the following three centuries, that the new 'modern' science had enormous advantages over the old, but that something was none the less lost in the replacement of the one by the other. As John Donne had previously and percipiently noted, 'if new things be found out, as many, and as good, that were known before, are forgotten and lost'.[45]

That same point is confirmed some two centuries later by the American essayist Ralph Waldo Emerson, who concluded that 'Society never advances. It recedes as fast on one side as it gains on the other . . . For everything that is given, something is taken.'[46] Recognition of that fundamental point lay at the root of some negative reactions to modernism, just as it no doubt accounts for some manifestations of pomophobia. It makes clear by implication that modernism is an intellectual fashion that will have its day but then in turn be superseded; the focus will change again, to take account of what's inevitably left out. 'New Systems of Nature', as Swift wrote, but as Montaigne had long since realised, were 'but new Fashions, which would vary in every Age'; each has a short time in which it flourishes, and then it's replaced. And historical sense encourages the insight that if Ptolemy's long-lasting cosmological system is finally displaced by that of Copernicus, then, in the longer term, Copernicus too is unlikely to have had the last word.[47]

So it's often, as Richard Baxter noted in 1667, 'the younger sort of ingenious men' who follow the latest philosophical fashion, being liable to be attracted by the 'meer novelty of some of these new-started notions'; notions that, Baxter believed (in company again with many current pomophobes), 'ere long . . . will grow out of fashion'.[48] Despite our best attempts to eliminate them, or to rule them out of court in our newly defined 'reality', fairies and ghosts – irreducible as they are to 'Mathematical Demonstration' – are likely to come back to haunt us, with another wisdom of their own.

6 Conclusion

The so-called 'scientific revolution' of the seventeenth century was far more than just a revolution in science. It did far more than reverse the respective roles (or rolls) of sun and earth, far more than simply mechanise the previously animate. When Galileo confronted the traditionalist philosophers from Padua, he was advocating not just a 'new science', but (in Charles Taylor's words) 'a revolution in the basic categories in [terms of] which we understand self'.[49] Galileo himself points out the wider dimensions and implications of his proposals when (through his modernist spokesman Sagredo) he indicates their *emotional* effects. It is the comforting aspects of Aristotelianism after which people continue to hanker – such notions as, for instance, physical incorruptibility – for these seem to have implications for their own condition as human beings. That is, as he explains: 'Those who so greatly exalt incorruptibility, inalterability, etc. are reduced to talking this way, I believe, by their great desire to go on living, and by the terror they have of death.'[50] It's not so much external nature *per se* that they are concerned with, but the way that a revised conception of that nature will impact upon their own understanding of *themselves*. An organic, animate, 'redeeming' nature seems (even now, perhaps) to hold more allure than its mechanised, mathematised, depersonalised replacement.

The history of science, therefore, the history of our changing conceptions of nature, becomes a history of changing conceptions of our 'self'. What is it that we want to make of the world? We can view it, perceive it, interpret and explain it, in many different ways; and those ways depend on *us* – on what we are, which is to say, on what we choose for ourselves to *be*. Our choice of world, and knowledge of the world, depends upon our choice of self; and since that choice is a moral one, 'epistemology', as Stephen M. Straker concluded some years ago in a highly interesting and suggestive paper, 'becomes ethics'.[51] The revolutionary modernists in the seventeenth century were not only promulgating a new view of nature, but also implicitly advocating a new sort of person.

For Bacon, Boyle and Descartes, as we have seen, that person would avoid the self-deceptions that arise from unthinking acceptance of earlier authorities; and for Galileo, in the example above, that person would be 'tough-minded' in the sense of pragmatically accepting as human such characteristics as change and mortality. But also, for all incipient modernists, the new relationship of the self to nature implied (especially in the eyes of feminist historians, as we have already intimated in Chapter 2) the subordination of feminine to *masculine* characteristics (or at least to those characteristics as they have been traditionally understood). So the essential Cartesian ploy of removing the self from the object of study in order to gain knowledge – of deliberately *detaching* the self from any (potentially contaminating) *involvement* in what is to be understood purely in its own terms – this modernist stance, on which science of any kind (not least historical) is posited, has been seen as a denial of the more subjective and intuitive approaches attributed to the 'feminine'. And it is, of course, the latter's blending of knower and known, subject and object, that marks (as I have suggested in Chapter 3) the organic model of mediaeval and Oriental thought, and which has been revived historically in versions of Romanticism, and currently postmodernism.

Citing Carolyn Merchant's assertion of 'the *death* of nature' in the scientific revolution, then, Susan Bordo has described how the 'female world-soul died – or more precisely was *murdered* – by the [early-modern] mechanist re-visioning of nature'.[52] And the imagery of a preferred *masculinity* is indeed much used by early modern natural philosophers themselves. Francis Bacon, as the arch-propagandist for the new science, referred to nature as a 'common harlot' – a woman awaiting penetration and domination; and as official historian of (and apologist for) the Royal Society, Thomas Sprat described her as a 'Mistress, that soonest yields to the forward, and the Bold'.[53] Potentially chaotic (as evidenced in wars, plagues, famines and all manner of natural disasters), nature had to be subdued – tamed and ordered, her secrets extracted if necessary by torture, so as to be properly serviceable to man. And through such a representation of their new model, methods and aspirations, the new scientists defined not only their preferred scientific methodology and epistemology, but also their very *selves* – as well as ours who follow them.

A recognition that the early modern intellectual revolution was essentially concerned with a redefinition of *self*, and of what it meant to be human, makes the emotional reactions to the process of transition from mediaevalism to modernism far more understandable; and of course it's just that crucial issue that is raised again in the case of postmodernism. Far from being merely a matter of 'theory' that can be put on one side and soon forgotten as irrelevant, it relates in practice to our very notions of what we are, or of what we believe that we should be, and of what therefore we now believe that it means to be human.

The need to make such fundamental choices – or to live with the uncertainties that derive from a disinclination to make them – will never be easy, and recognition of the need is bound (as shown, again, by Erich Fromm) to lead to some anxiety and fear. But though the problem won't go away, some awareness of its perennial nature may offer consolation. By seeing that the problematic advent of postmodernism had some parallels in modernism's own replacement of earlier thought, we may perhaps put our own anxieties and fears into some sort of perspective, and reduce the force of present pomophobia.

Part 3

FREEDOM (THE FUTURE)

5

OVERCOMING THE CONSTRAINTS OF MODERNISM

1 Introduction

May God us keep
From single vision and Newton's sleep.
(William Blake)

There will (presumably) always be those who prefer 'single vision', and who prefer to enjoy a 'sleep', whether induced, as Blake implies, by Newtonian modernism, or by any other all-embracing schema. The imposition of constraints can be reassuring; so that, as we have seen in Chapter 4, there is a tendency when external pressures on us are removed, not so much to rejoice as to recoil in horror and in fear. Instead of embracing new-found freedom, we are likely to avoid it, by imposing our own internal constraints. That's the only way that life seems manageable, liveable.

So through the centuries, we've seen 'Utopias' (or ideally ordered states) advocated (or just described) in the form of closed societies – societies in which internal order can remain unthreatened by any external influence, or any alternative visions of what might be. Plato, for example, takes his cue from the famously well-ordered state of Sparta – a state in which foreigners were never welcome and in which citizens were spared exposure to the potentially disruptive contact with alternatives that travel tends to bring. The rigid hierarchic structure of Plato's ideal state was proposed as a deliberate antidote to the perceived anarchy of his own democratic Athens; and, as with the later Utopian (or dystopian) visions of Aldous Huxley and George Orwell, it was to be insulated from any outside influence. For Plato and his successors well knew that it was only by such insulation that any structure – whether political or personal – can remain safely static, with its prescribed order unquestioned.

On the more personal level, to which Blake was referring in the quotation above, individual minds can be no less confined and closed than the societies they together comprise; and such confinements and closures may often appear as only common sense and positively virtuous. After all, Hamlet was so aware of complexity and of potential alternatives that he was disabled from acting at all – like spoilt consumers confronted by too much choice in their supermarkets: better surely, like John Locke (another of Blake's bêtes noires), to narrow down our field of vision, and restrict ourselves pragmatically to what lies within our immediate and existing visual range. Our 'life-tasks', as Zygmunt Bauman has ironically observed, have to be cut down 'to the size of human self-sufficiency', if only in order that the limits of that self-sufficiency can be kept safely out of sight.[1]

Just as in the early modern period, then, so too now, there are those who continue to evince nostalgia for the closed universe of pre-modernity, in the limits of which 'single vision' seems justified, and we can sleep. But Blake did have a point, and there remains the possibility of other visions, if not rude awakenings. 'We can become what we will', as Pico della Mirandola proclaimed in the context of his own 'rebirth'; or, in the more ambiguous words of Hamlet's Ophelia, 'Lord! we know what we are, but know not what we may be.'[2]

Those words of Ophelia can be taken as at once a statement and critique of the modernist position: that is, an assertion that in modernist terms we do indeed know what we are, but have lost sight of what we might be, or of what we could become. For modernism inspires both optimism and gloom. On the positive side, it provides enormous and potentially liberating advantages, but more negatively it shackles with its inbuilt constraints.

Those constraints, admittedly, are at one level unavoidable, because (as we have seen explicitly recognised by John Donne and William Temple in Chapter 4) any structure of thought, in attempting to circumscribe the infinite, inevitably falls short in one respect or another. As Emerson confirms, it's obvious that 'history and the state of the world at any one time [must be] directly dependent on the intellectual classification then existing in the minds of men',[3] for we can't get out of our own skins, or out of the 'paradigm' we've accepted in order to make some sense of our lives. But we know that any such accommodation is only a provisional arrangement, something that suits us for the moment; and we remain aware that the limitations of any such particular arrangement may come to seem excessive, bought at too high a price, and no longer acceptable. So it's worthwhile periodically to reassess the constraints under which we live, and to consider whether we're any longer prepared to accept their bondage, or the 'single vision' that they represent. In the following four sections, therefore, I'll consider a few modernist constraints, which might at least be loosened, and from which we might even be freed, in postmodernity.

2 Categorisation

Words strain,
Crack and sometimes break, under the burden,
Under the tension, slip, slide, perish,
Decay with imprecision, will not stay in place,
Will not stay still.

(T. S. Eliot)[4]

Modernism insistently categorises, by which I mean that it constrains things tidily within pigeon-holes (or at least persistently attempts to). So it forces the world (and our experience of it) into the orderliness of logic and language; it identifies and defines, differentiates and distances, and thereby imposes boundaries as well as expectations. We can tame the world, again, and make it manageable, if we can assign a name, with an allotted position and role, to its constituents; we need never be taken (as the expression revealingly puts it) by surprise.

But modernism's categories, which appear so safe and stable, are like the words in which they are expressed – constantly under strain, as T. S. Eliot suggests in the quotation above, threatening to break under the tension, slipping, sliding, perishing, decaying with imprecision, refusing to stay in place or still. Nicholas Lash has written similarly and more recently of the 'recognition that all language breaks, and fails, and crumbles' in the face both of divine mystery and of human love;[5] and that vulnerability of modernist language and categorisation is highlighted more generally by postmodernism – not, though, as something to be feared, but as a positively liberating prospect in the erosion of 'single vision'.

We have to note first, though, that the inclination to categorise manifests itself, unsurprisingly, in all departments of life – or in all those departments where order remains a priority (which surely is most). Chemistry provides one paradigm, where every material element can be ranged in tabular form, so that nothing – no known material constituent of the universe – need remain without its rightful place, or out of it; and if a new element is ever found, it can of course be duly slotted in, filed safely away in terms of what we already know. No less can the world of living things be appropriately reduced to order; or so it was believed by nineteenth-century taxonomists, who ensured that nothing eluded their classification into genus or species or lacked its proper place in nature. And as living things themselves, human beings could hardly plead exemption from such systematisation: they too could be readily classified, by reference to such physiognomic characteristics as size and shape of heads or chins or noses.

Certain physical types, it was clear, carefully catalogued with exemplary photographs, had propensities for insanity or criminality – essential information for the construction of a well-ordered society. It was useful, too, as a cultural shorthand. A painter such as William Powell Frith could enliven his crowd scenes, at horse-races or the railway station, with a deliberately chosen variety of 'types': the gentleman in reduced circumstances, waiting to board his train, could be clearly identified and differentiated from the villainous army recruit on the same platform, or from the insolent lower-class cabby demanding more money from his fare. Just as the members of each social class could be readily identified by the clothes in which they were portrayed, so the members of each generic human 'type' could be easily recognised by their assigned physical characteristics.[6]

Art's relationship with categorisation, however, could (and can) sometimes prove more ambiguous than science's; and even in the nineteenth century some problems did arise. There was, for example, some dispute about how to classify Degas's statue of *The Little Dancer, Aged Fourteen*. When exhibited in 1881, the girl-statue's projecting jaw and receding forehead reminded critics of those 'primitive' types whose characteristics they had seen illustrated in rogues' galleries of classificatory portraits. So was the statue 'art' at all, they wondered, and was it right to exhibit it as such: wouldn't it be more properly displayed in a popular museum of anatomical and physiognomic models?[7]

If Degas's statue provided provocation in the context of existing categories, the fragility of supposedly clear-cut distinctions in the realm of art was soon to be further exposed. When Marcel Duchamp exhibited a urinal as a work of art (suggestively named *Fountain*) in 1917, he was deliberately challenging the artistic conventions of his time – and challenging in particular the conventional categorisation of what constituted 'art'. Duchamp determinedly flouted convention by putting everyday objects into an unprecedented, and therefore unexpected, context. His choice of such objects, he explained, 'was based on a reaction of *visual indifference*, with a total absence of good or bad taste . . . in fact a complete anaesthesia'.[8] He had anaesthetised himself, in other words, against the cultural (aesthetic and moral) categories of his time. He would have delighted Blake by his refusal to be bound by 'single vision', and he has been rightly identified by Fredric Jameson as another precursor of postmodernism, or one of those 'who may be considered outright postmodernists, avant la lettre'.[9]

What is interesting, further, in the context of pomophobia is that Duchamp duly provoked a massive scandal (as he had intended), since he had, again, had the effrontery to question the cultural categories of his time. And people continue to be perturbed by such questioning. Duchamp's urinal has had many imitators, and piles of bricks, or unmade beds, or pickled sheep, or what in other contexts might be construed as pornographic videos still, in the twenty-first century, provoke heated discussions: 'Is this really art?' we hear repeated for the umpteenth time. 'Should this really be exhibited here, in what is meant to be a gallery of *art*?' Or paralleled in the world of music, 'Is this really classical' or 'only pop' – as the Bond quartet (or 'all-girl band') is shifted from one set of charts to another, more appropriate for the 'raunchy'; and the music critic Norman Lebrecht describes 'a highbrow [radio] station slipping off its blue stockings and jumping into bed with a funky jazz fest'. 'It won't be long', warned one of Josef Skvorecky's characters, 'before they're blowing the clarinet in Carnegie Hall like drunken Negroes in Chicago and calling it serious music' – and that was in 1986.[10]

History itself, of course, has become deeply and publicly embroiled in such demarcation disputes on its own account, in relation particularly to those supposedly polar opposites 'fact' and 'fiction'. The deliberate blurring of distinctions between history and fiction is nothing new. The first-century BC Roman poet Virgil, in his capacity as propagandist for the new Augustan Principate (and later Empire), blended such mytho-logical and historical accounts of Rome's past as would serve to forge a coherent and progressive identity for a nation and its new ruler. Theologically derived myths about the city's foundation by Romulus and Remus conspired with the human record of heroic exploits by historical figures to present an inspiring narrative that served to confirm and justify Rome's imperial and civilising mission. And such was Virgil's success and subsequent reputation that he was himself chosen – historical figure that he was – as mythical guide through the Underworld for the great mediaeval Italian poet Dante. In his *Divine Comedy* Dante again blended history with fiction, setting 'real' historical figures in an imaginary world – and serving thereby as a link in a still continuing tradition.[11]

But it has long been a presupposition – an absolutely unquestioned bedrock – of modernist history that it is concerned with *factual* presentations of the past, and that these can be sharply distinguished from any *fictional* usurpers. That founding-father Leopold von Ranke wrote that, as a historian, he 'turned away completely from fiction and resolved to

... keep strictly to the facts';[12] and since Ranke's time professional historians have had rules and procedures that supposedly enable them to make that fundamental distinction between 'fiction' and 'facts', and quickly to pounce upon any attempt to blur it. So numerous films have been criticised for presenting ahistorical, or partly fictionalised accounts of the past, often for political or nationalistic motives, but sometimes just in the cause of entertainment. 'Docudramas', similarly, reveal by their very name a disinclination to take seriously the traditional distinction between 'factual' documentary and 'fictional' drama; and that blurring of boundary lines between the two, enabling a dramatic story to be told that is only more or less tenuously 'based on fact', has been condemned, again, as misleadingly and dangerously ahistorical – a betrayal of what 'real' history should be.

Perhaps most significant of all has been the emergence of a new genre of literature, characterised as 'historiographic metafiction'. As its name implies, this is deliberately and explicitly concerned with the erosion of categories, the blurring of boundaries between (factual) 'historiography' (or history writing) and a 'fiction' whose normal conventions are transcended. One example is E. L. Doctorow's *Ragtime*, in which fictional characters, located in the early twentieth century, are provocatively mixed with historical individuals of the time; and, for example, two founding-fathers of psychoanalytic theory, Sigmund Freud and Carl Jung, are depicted riding through the Coney Island Tunnel of Love together, in a way, as Linda Hutcheon describes, that 'they *historically* did not, but *symbolically* perhaps always had'. Such deliberate erosion of the traditional fact/fiction distinction is effected specifically (as claimed by Robert F. Berkhofer) 'in order to highlight both the fictionality of fact and the truthfulness of fictional representation'; while Doctorow himself has insisted that, for him, 'history is a kind of fiction in which we live and hope to survive, and fiction is a kind of speculative history'.[13]

The commonality of many problems associated with the writing of both 'history' and 'literature' is demonstrated by other techniques already utilised in historiographic metafiction and potentially available for history, too: a multiplicity of viewpoints and visions can be presented, in place of a unitary narrative structure; a deliberate lack of coherence can be shown, with a choice of alternative perspectives, endings and meanings; and the narrating voice can be revealed as ideologically committed and manipulative, rather than supposedly detached and objective. In such ways the writers of 'literature' can re-emphasise and make transparent the difficulties and decisions by which not only they but historians are confronted; and they can clarify, as Linda Hutcheon claims, that 'both history and fiction are discourses, human constructs, signifying systems', concerned with the imposition of *meaning*.[14]

Indeed, historians themselves have become increasingly aware of how problematic attempted sharp distinctions between such categories as 'fact' and 'fiction' are. Writing of history at the turn of the nineteenth century, Jane Austen has one of her characters exclaim that 'a great deal of it must be invention' (which makes its dullness seem all the stranger to her);[15] and from a theoretical perspective Hayden White, most notoriously, has denied any possibility of maintaining 'fact' and 'fiction' as mutually exclusive categories. He argues that, since the past has no intrinsic meaning, historians have a choice of how to 'emplot' its traces. They may, for example, propose a tragic, comic or ironic mode on their material, and their choice will depend on the sort of message they want to convey. But whatever their preference, the form – the story as shaped – is *imposed* by them, and must therefore constitute a composition that inevitably includes elements of their own 'subjective' selves. No less than novelists, historians are concerned to present a coherent and interesting and persuasive story – a story that's aesthetically pleasing, with a beginning, middle, and end; so, despite their often extravagant claims to the contrary, what they produce is nothing more authoritative than an arbitrarily imposed narrative – hardly less fictional than a novel.

In seeming sympathy with that diagnosis, Simon Schama has in practical terms readily conceded that his histories include imaginative input. In *Dead Certainties* (significantly subtitled 'Unwarranted Speculations'), for instance, he invents a diary, and attempts to enter 'into the inner consciousness of some of his characters *like a novelist*'. Schama himself describes the book as 'a work of the *imagination* that chronicles historical events' – a work that includes 'purely imagined *fiction*', where 'the certainties of events [are dissolved] into the multiple possibilities of alternative narrations'.[16] As he accepts, histories of that kind verge on becoming works previously identified as 'historical novels' – a genre not greatly respected by professional and proper historians, but one that has often been popular, and not infrequently claimed as providing profounder insights into the past than more conventional scholarly accounts. Walter Scott is perhaps the best-known example, praised by Thomas Carlyle and G. M. Trevelyan for having brought *human* aspects of the past to life more effectively than many historians; and the novelist Thomas Hardy, too – described by J. M. Barrie in 1889 as the 'Historian of Wessex' – has recently been identified as 'a font of cultural history'.[17]

What is most interesting is the heat that these issues still generate: modernist categorisation continues as a cultural bedrock, in which any perceived instability seems bound to be a cause of apprehension, if not actual fear. And in the case of fact and fiction, that is not surprising, since 'fact' bears an authority of enormous political and ideological importance. As Robert F. Berkhofer has noted, 'the greatest power grab of all in professional history is to draw the line between what is true and what is fiction';[18] for by claiming 'fact' or 'truth' for oneself and one's own descriptions and explanations, one is by implication denying the validity of others' – relegating their alternative realities (like Hobbes with his fairies) to the realm of fantasy and fiction, 'unreality'.

Categories, then, are there to be accepted or transcended, to be seen as not only constraining but contingent, and so to be set aside or superseded at will – our will. That recognition may be central to postmodernism's programme, but again it's nothing new. As early as the seventeenth century, John Locke questioned the fixity of conventionally accepted categories. Even scientific categories, he observed, are not in fact *discovered* as essences inherent in the world, but are *invented* – specifically designed by us for our own benefit. The boundaries of species, for instance, which might give the appearance of being *fixed in* nature, are actually *imposed on* nature. Far from being defined by reference to any 'real essence', 'it is men, who . . . range them into sorts'. It's men who have fitted the natural world into their own categories, and even in the case of human beings themselves it's only by virtue of arbitrary definition 'that we can say: This is a man'.[19]

Locke's point was confirmed by the eighteenth-century Genevan naturalist Charles Bonnet. Concerning nature, Bonnet concluded similarly that 'it is evident that our classifications are not hers. Those which we form are purely nominal, and we should regard them as means relative to our needs and to the limitations of our knowledge'.[20] Categories, in other words, are simply human constructions – made and applied in the interests of humans and in terms of their own existing knowledge. Even food, then, as Fichte later came to recognise, can be envisaged as a human construct, defined in terms of humans' hunger: 'I am not hungry because food is placed before me; it is food because I am hungry for it.'[21]

On a larger scale, even the universe itself – the universe that we experience – is no less invented and constructed by humans; and the implication is, of course, that it (no less than 'food') could therefore appear in quite other ways. It's really up to us, as the German Romantic poet Friedrich Schiller concluded, and as postmodernists would agree: 'We can alter *anything*, even, perhaps, the laws of logic, as our *imagination* chooses.' That claim no doubt sounds extreme – especially with its reference to logic, since of all things logic (as we've seen) has often been thought to mirror the very construction of the universe. But Schiller's assertion of such human freedom has been central to the romantic tradition that has fed into postmodernism. 'All other things *must*: man is the being that *wills*', he wrote; or in Kant's later formulation, a human is not a mere 'turnspit' at the mercy of causal forces (or logical categories), but is an autonomous being who enjoys free will.[22]

That freedom of will relates, not least for the postmodernist, to the construction of the self (and its differentiation from the external world) and the constructedness (and historicity, and thence contingency) of such apparent essences as male and female identities. We may – as is evidenced daily on our streets – choose to dye our hair and change ourselves from blonde to brunette or to purple: 'Forget the hair you have. Get the hair you want!' as I read in Oxford Street in August 2001. And we may even, at choice it seems, change our sexual roles from male to female or vice versa. That is to free ourselves from the externally (and sometimes internally) imposed constraints of categorisation; and, as we have seen in Chapter 3, Luce Irigaray has claimed that women in particular do evade those constraints, and refuse to be bound by the specificities still (despite T. S. Eliot) expected from our language. 'It is', she suggests, 'useless to trap women into giving an exact definition of what they mean' (or, presumably, of who they are). Rather, in conversing with a woman:

> One must listen to her differently in order to hear an *'other meaning' which is constantly in the process of weaving itself, at the same time ceaselessly embracing words and yet casting them off to avoid becoming fixed, immobilised.* For when 'she' says something, it is already no longer identical to what she means.[23]

To evade being trapped in specific categories and immobilised in the fixity of linguistic expression need not be the prerogative of women alone: to define women specifically in such terms, and by implication men in this respect as 'others', may itself represent submission to a modernist convention and constraint. Postmodernism, rather, can propose a more universal prospect of liberation from the categories imposed by other people's (and one's own) often linguistically derived expectations. 'We discover, once again', as Nicholas Lash puts it, 'that we must live and tell our stories in *unlabelled* places'.[24]

That has to do not least with our own rigid labelling and self-definitions, and the way we differentiate ourselves from the 'other' – whether that other is the natural world external to us, or simply other people. For, in their quest for supposedly 'objective' knowledge, Western modernists have insisted on the adoption of a detached standpoint that has effectively isolated individuals from their natural and human surroundings. (This is typified by Descartes' diagrammatic representation of perception as a strictly mechanical process, with straight lines drawn between sense-organs and their objects of perception.) It's small wonder that that deliberate withdrawal of the self, and its categorisation as something clearly distinct from whatever is supposedly 'external', has often been criticised from Romantic and Oriental perspectives. Writing of characters in the novels of Jane Austen and George Eliot, Elizabeth Deeds Ermarth has described how Anne in the former's *Persuasion* assumes the role of a narrator, who is always detached, and how, while showing great insight in that role, she is none the less 'burdened with a kind of "deadness"'. The strain of appearing as a detached 'nobody' can prove too great, as it did too for the scholarly Casaubon in Eliot's *Middlemarch*. Such characters, Ermarth explains, while trying to capitalise on their detachment, 'eventually *die*'.[25]

A similar critique was offered (in the 1960s) in the field of psycho-therapy by the 'existential' psychotherapist R. D. Laing. Having spent some time with Buddhist teachers, Laing developed an approach to his subject that rejected conventional Western 'scientific' procedures, including the cultivation of 'detachment'; for that, he came to realise, was all too likely to result in the counter-productive *depersonalisation* of the 'other' whom he was trying to help. Far from forcing others into one's own conceptual framework, and seeking to understand them in one's own terms, the psychotherapist has to relax boundaries and try to enter and understand their other world: 'one has to orientate oneself as a person in the other's scheme of things, rather than only to see the other as an object in one's own world' – an altogether more subjective, intuitive, or even mystical approach.[26]

In this context it's interesting to note that Laing himself drew atten-tion to the fear that can result from that breakdown of traditional psychological categories that he was advocating. By repudiating clear distinctions between ourselves and the outside world, and by assimilating ourselves to nature and to other people, we might, he realised, jeopardise our own hard-won separate identities and expose ourselves to the risk of 'ontological insecurity' – of no longer being confident, that is, about who we are.

The essence of such a risky condition on a national scale has recently been diagnosed by Richard Kearney. Writing presumably in the earlier part of 2001, and certainly before 11 September, he describes a 'mounting millennial hysteria' in the United States, characterised by a 'wave of identity-questions – who are we? What is our nation?'[27] Such identity-questions, as has long been recognised, can best (or most easily) be answered by reference to an external 'other', an alien threatening force;

and noting a huge and increasing interest in extraterrestrial 'aliens' (with numerous claimed sightings), Kearney cites the pop comic *Captain America*, with its (uncannily prescient, as it now appears) message. Captain America reports to the nation:

> We have been the victims of a MASSIVE ALIEN INVASION ... of HORRIFYING PROPORTIONS. Systematically America has been invaded by an alien race bent on earth's destruction. They have taken our PLACES ... DISGUISED themselves as OUR KIND ... and now they lie in HIDING, lie in WAIT ... Today, with the FULL TRUST of the AMERICAN PEOPLE BEHIND me ... I have come forward to EXPOSE them before it is TOO LATE![28]

'It's US or THEM', the message concludes, and that message has, in the historical event, been taken up with (literally) a vengeance after '9/11', since when the peoples of the world have been divided between two mutually opposing categories – them and us, the evil and the good, those against us and those with us.

That Manichaean dispensation, with its categorial clarity, may serve to confirm both personal and national identities; but its simplistic presuppositions may lead to a conflict that leaves neither of those categories intact. And it's possible too that ontological insecurity itself might be construed as positively beneficial – as implying the possibility of self-determination, of individually determining the self and the self's relationship with the external world. Which is to make a grand assertion of human freedom, albeit necessarily linked with a recognition of responsibility. For the implication is that our manner of perceiving and experiencing the world (and ourselves) depends on our own choice of the categories by which we try to understand it; and in that case knowledge itself becomes again (as we have already seen indicated in Chapter 4) a matter of morality.

That point was clearly articulated in the twentieth century by other thinkers associated with existentialism – another philosophical tributary that flows into postmodernism. So the hero of Sartre's novel *Nausea*, Antoine Roquentin, comes to realise his personal responsibility for the construction of a meaningful life – which necessitates the construction of a meaningful narrative in which he can appear and play his part. It's hard, he explains, to accept the course of our lives as simply 'an inconsequential buzzing', and to view our lives as just growing 'in a haphazard way and in all directions'. Rather, he clarifies, 'I wanted the moments of my life to follow one another in an *orderly* fashion like those of a life remembered'. He wanted, that is, a personal history that would confer some sense of a continuing (and relatively stable) identity.[29]

Roquentin's anxieties, though, concern not only his personal identity, but also the whole of the external world. It's not only his self that is in constant danger of dissolution, but nature itself: material objects and entities that look as if they are solid and fixed could, he comes to believe, suddenly change in their very essence, and the so-called laws of nature could be transgressed at any moment. We may be offered 'proof, a hundred times a day, that everything is done mechanically, that the world obeys fixed, unchangeable laws', but Roquentin comes to realise that nature 'has no laws . . . It has nothing but habits, and it may change those tomorrow'; so that it is, as he concludes, 'out of laziness, I suppose, that the world looks the same day after day'; the exciting but frightening reality is that '*anything can happen*'.[30]

It's the *fear*, again, rather than the excitement engendered by such a prospect that was revealed by mid-twentieth-century psychological experiments designed to test people's reactions to anomalies – or situations where the application of conventional categorisations is denied. Experimental subjects were presented with a series of playing cards that, after a brief exposure, they were required to identify. Most of the cards were 'normal' (in the sense of being what anyone would expect them to be), but some 'anomalous' ones were inserted, where, for example, hearts and diamonds (normally red) were shown as black, and (conventionally black) clubs and spades were coloured red. With only brief exposures, anomalous cards were quickly (mis-)identified, being slotted in to conventionally accepted categories – so that, for instance, an (aberrant) black four of hearts was classified (or seen) as an (acceptable) four of spades. The data, that is, was initially made to fit existing categories. But after increasingly long exposures, the anomalies intruded, or could no longer be ignored. At least, for most of the experimental subjects that was the case, although a few remained unable to see outside, or to adjust, their habitual categorisations; and these latter, as is recorded, 'often experienced personal distress':

> One of them exclaimed: 'I can't make the suit out, whatever it is. It didn't even look like a card that time. I don't know what colour it is now, or whether it's a spade or a heart. I'm not even sure what a spade looks like. My God!'[31]

With the prospect of such disorientation – resembling the symptoms resulting from 'cognitive dissonance' described by Barbara Herrnstein Smith in Chapter 1 – it's small wonder that resort is often had to

Roquentin's 'laziness' – the laziness (now challenged by postmodernism) that enables us to see the world in the same way day after day, without distress. The psychologist Carl Duncker provided further experimental confirmation of such laziness, or of our propensity to give unquestioning acceptance to conventional categories. Having assigned his subjects the task of making a pendulum, he presented them with a pendulum-weight with cord attached, together with a nail. All they lacked was a hammer with which to drive the nail into the wall; and only half his subjects saw that the solution was to use the pendulum-weight as that hammer. That is, 50 per cent of an intelligent group of students were unable to break out from conventional categorisations in order to identify a 'pendulum-weight' as a potential 'hammer' (even when they needed one).[32]

Historians have similarly, through laziness or fear, been hidebound by conventional categories; but history itself, according to the Czech philosopher Jan Patočka (whom I shall claim as another honorary postmodernist), is particularly well placed to shake us out of such conformist habits. Patočka recalls how Heidegger had written that 'History is not a drama that unfolds before our eyes', not just 'a perception' to be passively received, but rather 'a responsibility', something that we can actually affect. For no more than nature do historical data have any inherent meaning: things 'have no meaning for themselves', but have to be assigned meaning by us; 'their meaning requires that someone "have a sense" for them'; and that sense (and hence their meaning and use) can constantly shift (even from pendulum-weight to hammer). For things necessarily present themselves to us one-sidedly. From another perspective, another side would be presented; so that our experience at any one time is inevitably limited. Other times offer an infinity of alternative perspectives, and so alternative perceptions and the possibility of alternative categorisations. 'We experience the world . . . as what opens itself to us', so that we ourselves need to remain constantly open to receive it; and our freedom enables us to do just that. So truth is never attained or attainable once and for all: it remains as the object of a life-long enquiry – as with the sceptics, the object of an endless and ongoing quest.[33]

For the Romantic, though, and for Heidegger and for Patočka, an openness to the apprehension of that truth constitutes what is effectively a religious position, more akin perhaps to Eastern than to Western philosophy. For Heidegger, it is our proper concern with phenomena that enables us to bring them to light (that facilitates enlightenment); and Patočka writes (in Socratic mode) of our life-long quest for truth constituting our 'care for the soul'. Souls, then, do not find rest: their goal and destiny are not, as in the Christian tradition, the attainment of an 'unshakeable' faith. On the contrary, spiritual life is to be envisaged as 'fundamental upheaval', and a veritable 'shaking' of old meaning and old categories (categories that 'will not stay still'), to reveal potentialities for new.[34]

3 Consistency

> I hope in these days we have heard the last of conformity and consistency . . . A foolish consistency is the hobgoblin of little minds . . . With consistency a great soul has simply nothing to do.
>
> (Ralph Waldo Emerson)[35]

In his attack on consistency, Emerson challenges a foundation stone of modernism. The 'rationality' on which modernity is constructed precludes the possibility of accepting, at one and the same time two 'inconsistent' propositions. As Galileo insists: 'Obviously two truths cannot contradict one another'; or in Joseph Glanvill's words, 'God cannot be the Author of Contradictions'.[36] If one claim is true, then the other, if inconsistent with it, must be false – that's how rationality and logic (and God himself) work; and it's on that rule that the whole edifice of modernist science, and Western thought more generally, rests.

Yet there have, of course, always been alternative traditions – more particularly, as we have seen, of Eastern and Romantic thought – that reject the narrowness that seems to be implied by the insistence on consistency. For them, consistency becomes a constraint to be accepted, as Emerson says, only by those with 'little minds'; it's not something to be countenanced by those with any aspirations to greatness of soul. 'Contradiction', Pascal had earlier written, but against the intellectual current of his time, 'is not a sign of falsity, nor the want of contradiction a sign of truth'; and Blake typically went further to insist more positively that, far from retarding thought, inconsistency alone advanced it: 'Without Contraries is no progression.'[37]

It is on the alternative tradition that postmodernists are now putting more emphasis, questioning the value and validity of consistency in relation both to general claims to knowledge (including historical knowledge), and to the construction and perception of the self. The former is related to the challenges being currently presented to the concept of a unitary truth. Once that concept is abandoned – on the grounds that any truth is necessarily bound to be relative, acquiring its status as 'truth' only within a provisional and contingent structure that has, or might have, numberless equally valid competitors – consistency itself becomes

128

obsolescent. For consistency, again, makes sense only within a single conceptual schema: a plurality of schemata validates a plurality of consistencies; and there's no reason why those alternatives should be mutually consistent.

One example of competing frameworks can be taken from the early modern period, when the new science was challenging traditional Christian theology. Aristotelian natural philosophy and Christianity had long since been moulded into a consistent whole, the two parts woven so closely together that any proposed change in one necessarily constituted a threat to the other. Hence Francis Bacon's advocacy of a separation of the two – to enable a new philosophy to be developed without posing any threat to the existing philosophy's religious doppel-gänger. But a 'double truth' – one for science, another for religion – proved uncongenial to later modernist reformers. 'Truth and truth can never jarre', as one insisted; and another synthesis was finally achieved, wherein scientific and religious truth could once more be seen as mutually consistent.

With the transition to postmodernity, the complications are compounded: it's no longer just two intellectual strands that need to be interwoven, but a host of competitors, each claiming equal validity and equal 'truth'; and it would seem to be desirable now to accept and even welcome ('celebrate') diversity, without even attempting, Procrustes-like, to force all or any into a single bed of consistency. In historical study it has long been clear (at least to some) that different approaches to the past, resulting in very different assessments – or versions of the truth – may all, rather than acting as mutual erasers, contribute to a fuller picture. For as the social historian G. M. Trevelyan, with a generosity not always emulated by his successors, recognised as long ago as 1930, his own was not the one and only possible approach – and nor was anybody else's:

> There are so many different ways in which things happen, or can be truly described as happening. Gibbon's is one, Carlyle's another, Macaulay's a third. Each is true, yet taken by itself each is false, for no one of them is the whole truth.[38]

Similarly, it's clear that 'alternative' therapies from China bear little relation to Western medical science, and are sometimes inconsistent with it; but that does not imply that either one (the Western or Chinese approach) should be rejected as invalid. They both might have their (complementary) 'truths'.

Similarly again with regard to the self, postmodernists can happily renounce traditional modernist models of consistency and positively embrace a greater and more exciting diversity. Thus, to give one example, Elizabeth Deeds Ermarth discusses the novelists Samuel Richardson and Daniel Defoe, and the fact that the 'disjunctive time schemes' used in their works liberate them from the modernist requirement of presenting characters with a consistent 'self'.[39] Consistency of self, or of personal identity, is usually seen as a major advantage gained from the modernist consensus. That is, modernism assumes the desirability and the possibility of a stable identity that endures not only through space, but also through time. In our characters, whether represented in fiction or met in 'real' life, we expect consistency; and identity seems to be guaranteed by an ability to position the self in a flow of time. That flowing time consists both of a past that can be accessed through recollection and of a future towards which one can aspire. Without memory, and without aspirations, we may well flounder, but by self-consciously positioning the self on a continuous conveyor belt through time, we gain confidence in the possible existence of a persisting and stable identity – a consistent self.

But identity thus becomes reliant on an agreement concerning the consistency of our experience of time and place. One presupposition of modernity is that we can all ultimately agree about these fundamentals, and it's that agreement that enables us to assume that our perspectives, however various, will ultimately (or at least in principle) cohere into a unified description, or explanation, or object, or identity. Any disagreement or disjunction between our relative schemata of time and place may lead, as Ermarth describes, to a parallel 'disjunctiveness in personality'. And that prospect – of a variety of individual perspectives that can't be made to cohere into a unified collective description – induces anxiety within a modernist context; for it threatens the precarious stability, and even the objective existence, of the self-consistent individual.

So pressures are exerted – pressures (as in Fromm's diagnosis of early modern individuals) not only external, but internal, too; for it's not only other people who want to understand and make sense of us, but (just as urgently) it's ourselves. Thus, as T. S. Eliot observed: 'It is human, when we do not understand another human being, and cannot ignore him, to exert an unconscious pressure on that person to turn him into something that we *can* understand.'[40] And just as emphatically we exert pressure on ourselves – reducing ourselves to something comprehensible, to something that we too can understand.

Yet that reduction, that comprehensibility, is, again, bought only at a price; for it implies the denial of what doesn't fit – of what appears as inconsistent. So, as Eliot continues, the effect on the pressurised person (the person pressurised to become comprehensible) 'is liable to be the repression and distortion, rather than the improvement, of the personality'. And as a corollary, it's only when such pressure is released that the 'real' personality has a chance to emerge: it's only by deferring our quest for intelligibility and consistency that we become freed to be ourselves – or as for Miss La Trobe, to act like Cleopatra.

So the modernist conception of an enduring entity may seem too good to risk, but it does have its disadvantages and its own implied constraints – in this case the limiting of potential for change and growth. We ourselves like to think that we can periodically act 'out of character', in ways that might surprise other people (and even ourselves): it's only by defying the constraints of other people's expectations that we can assert our freedom. That appearance of unpredictability may cause annoyance and even anxiety for those who like to 'pin people down' – to confine them in the straitjacket of a stereotypical role, whether of parent, teacher, artist, colleague or whatever. But, as the American anthropologist Elsie Clews Parsons confided to her journal in 1913, 'It is such a confounded bore to have to act one part endlessly'. For, as she explains, 'This morning perhaps I may feel like a male; let me act like one. This afternoon I may feel like a female; let me act like one.' As one of Salman Rushdie's characters unapologetically proclaims, 'I myself manage to hold large numbers of irreconcilable views simultaneously, without the least difficulty' – a prospect of ontological inconsistency that was positively welcomed by the intellectual historian Arthur Lovejoy, whose own conclusion resonated with that of Emerson as quoted at the beginning of this section: 'it is only the narrowest or the dullest minds that are – if any are – completely in harmony with themselves'.[41] Far better, then, surely, to repudiate the narrow and the dull, and aspire to that creativity and greatness of soul that 'has simply nothing to do' with any 'foolish consistency'.

4 Coherence

The knowledge imposes a pattern, and falsifies,
For the pattern is new in every moment.
(T. S. Eliot)[42]

The great advantage of modernism is that it makes sense of the world, affirming (indeed, presupposing) the reality of an external and autonomously existing entity (nature/the past), to which we have direct access, and of which we can then have knowledge. We may not enjoy immediate and total understanding of that world, but such understanding is not in principle ruled out. For the gaining of knowledge and understanding is a communal and cumulative enterprise: each individual nugget is necessarily less than wholly adequate, being circumscribed by the limits of our own adopted standpoint – an individual standpoint that inevitably rules out the simultaneous possibility of having innumerable others, all of which are needed for the completion of our task. But when enough of such partial nuggets have been accumulated, the prospect of a cohering treasure-trove of knowledge does await us.

Meanwhile, the value of each contribution is never in doubt. So long as appropriate methods – methods on which we are all agreed – are duly followed, then every contributory brick can be utilised for the completion of the final edifice. All bricks – or accounts that we present – are complementary; all (as we have just seen in the section above) must be mutually consistent; and where anomalies seem to occur, we may rest assured that in the longer term they will be able to be accommodated within the total structure. Just as, in providential terms, even sickness can ultimately be shown to be a good thing and beneficial for us (by, for example, physically warning us of greater dangers or teaching us a moral lesson), so in modernist terms any apparently inconsistent item of knowledge can in the end be seen to have contributed to our ideally total and coherent picture.

That all-embracing, comprehensive and coherent system, then, within which everything becomes explicable and has its place, is the ultimate goal of modernism; and in modernist terms it is, in principle, ultimately realisable – optimism for reason giving reason for optimism. But in practice we can see that T. S. Eliot did have a point – that the imposition of a '*pattern*', a coherent structure, is at once a prerequisite for knowledge *and* what inevitably 'falsifies'. For nothing is static: all is in constant flux, so that the requisite pattern to make sense of it all is necessarily itself 'new in every moment'.

That perpetual renewal does not suit the modernist conception of a 'body of knowledge' that is established (in science or history) and endures. But it clarifies that coherent understanding (or any aspiration to universal explanation) can be achieved only by defining things in such a way as to make such explanation possible. In other words, the promised universal explicability can be attained only at the price of redefining terms in such a way as to make the promise self-fulfilling. In particular, both 'universal' and 'explicable' need redefinition in such a (circular) way that 'universal explicability' becomes attainable – by definition. Having decided, for example, that what is meant by 'explicable' is what can be accounted for in terms of mechanistic science, it remains only to exclude from 'universal' (or the universe) whatever might defy such explanation. The classic statement of that convenient approach was made by Hobbes in 1651:

The *Universe*, that is, the whole masse of all things that are is Corporeall, that is to say, Body; and hath the dimensions of Magnitude, namely Length, Bredth, and depth: also every part of Body, is likewise Body, and hath the like dimensions; and consequently every part of the Universe, is Body; and that which is not Body, is no part of the Universe: And because the Universe is All, that which is no part of it, is *Nothing*; and consequently *no where*.[43]

Hobbes goes on immediately to clarify that he is not meaning to exclude 'Spirits' from the universe; but for them to be acceptable entrants into it, they do of course have to conform to his criteria by being 'really *Bodies*' themselves. What has been banished is whatever fails to meet Hobbes's mechanistic criteria for what constitutes reality; so that any incorporeal entity (such as a 'spirit' was traditionally conceived) is simply defined out of existence; it can't be explained in mechanistic terms, so it can form no part of universality, or of reality.

That narrowing down of reality, and so of the proper objects of human study, proved a convenient ploy for early modern thinkers confronting the then mounting problem of newly revived sceptical philosophy. Attempting to come to terms with the impossibility of ever attaining absolute certainty (a goal to be reserved henceforth for God), philosophers resigned themselves to the again limited capacities that they could enjoy as human beings. There was no point, it seemed, in aspiring beyond what was humanly possible and practicable.

One recommendation to circumscribe ambition and accept the inevitability of human limitations was expressed, for instance, by Samuel Parker in 1666:

Wise men, that consider the Nature and Inconstancy of things, will not designe to themselves more raised degrees of Blessednesse, then the World can afford: but will be content to be as happy as their own Capacities, and the present Condition of things will permit.[44]

And John Locke went on, in the opening pages of his hugely influential *Essay concerning Human Understanding*, to make another classic statement of the modernist position. Confronting again the impossibility of knowing everything with certainty, he urged humans to concentrate on what lay within their range, and to stop troubling themselves and others with matters that lay beyond their powers of comprehension. They should, he said, in words that (if remembered) might have consoled generations of students in examination halls, 'sit down in a quiet ignorance of those things, which upon examination, are found to be beyond the reach of our capacities'; for we should 'learn to content ourselves with what is attainable by us in this state'. As Pope was later to express the same point in his own poetic 'Essay on Man':

> The bliss of Man (could Pride that blessing find)
> Is not to act or think beyond mankind; . . .
> Why has not Man a microscopic eye?
> For this plain reason, Man is not a Fly.[45]

In this way, human beings were encouraged to accept confinement within their own self-constructed caves; and while they may have viewed with (albeit envious) equanimity their deprivation of microscopic fly-sight, to be reduced, in Blake's terminology, to 'single vision' (if not sleep), was a high price to pay for the Newtonian legacy. Modern science gave Enlightenment (and subsequent) thinkers enormous cause for optimism, but *scientism* (the belief in that science's universal applicability) was to take its toll on the extent of human aspiration. Whatever didn't fit the scientific model, whatever couldn't be squashed within the parameters that mechanistic science defined, was nullified – either quite literally defined as nothing (non-existent), or made amenable by pragmatic redefinition, or proscribed as an illegitimate object of human concern. As Wittgenstein later confirmed, 'What we cannot speak about we must consign to silence.'[46] Any residual traces of what was previously thought might lie beyond our ability to encompass in language became liable to provoke anxieties, and were consigned to such lesser breeds as 'Romantics' and devotees of Eastern mysticism.

For incoherence – our inability to contain some phenomenon or experience within existing structures – does unsettle. Coherence implies the imposition of meaning (at least for us), and it's disconcerting to encounter something that lies outside that safety-net (outside Mo's grid) – something that appears quite *meaningless*. If we see an incoherent jumble of lines, we try to read into those lines some semblance of order – to read them, perhaps, as a representation, whether of the 'real' world, or of some dream-world or fantasy. As often as not, even abstract art sports titles – and we may be happier when it does. For then at least we can claim to be able, or unable, to grasp what the artist is about, what he or she is intending, or meaning to convey. Then at least we have some parameters within which to assess or judge. And similarly with sounds, to hear an *incoherent* jumble of sounds (words even) is disquieting. So we desperately seek for clues – to ascertain the language, or the possible intention of the speaker – to enable us to bring together those sounds into a coherent whole again, into something we can make sense of, and fit into our existing categories of understanding.

Just so, historians cast their net of understanding and coherence over the potential chaos and absurdity of historical data – taming them, and making them conform to earlier accounts or current expectations; or when it does not *conform*, making it at least internally *coherent*. A time-scale is imposed – a beginning, middle, end – together with geographical limits – north, south, east, and west – to act as a space–time frame for meaning, and to ensure that, within those given constraints, some meaning is indeed possible. Ihab Hassan has written of 'warring empires, catastrophes and famine, immense hopes, faraway names . . . all fall[ing] into place on numbered pages'.[47] For you mustn't have pieces left over when you've finished the jigsaw puzzle. If they don't fit the picture you've already completed, the inclination is to throw them away, or forget them. But that can't be legitimate, since it is, of course, only within the frame of your present picture that they refuse to fit; and the frame itself was only an arbitrary imposition on what could have been a much bigger picture, including more people in the foreground and a background extending to infinity. It's only to make the picture's subject-matter coherent – to enable and enforce coherence – that the frame was imposed in the first place. Shift that frame ever so slightly to the right or left, or up or down, and the whole balance of what is enclosed – the relationship of one part with another and with the whole – will be destroyed, and the coherence of the composition threatened.

Coherence thus has to be seen as a modernist virtue, exemplifying 'knowledge', as T. S. Eliot recognised, through the imposition of 'a pattern'. But it is also a modernist and negative constraint, in that any pattern 'falsifies' – and so denies knowledge – through its assumed fixity and denial of the need to be 'new in every moment'. Some tension between competing alternatives – each internally coherent but with the appearance of mutual inconsistency – may need to be maintained and even prove creative; for, as T. S. Kuhn put it decades ago, it may sometimes be necessary for creative thinkers in any field (and whom should that exclude?) to 'be able to live in a world out of joint'.[48] What characterises postmodernity is, *inter alia*, its acceptance (welcoming even) of being 'out of joint', and its refusal to be seduced by the appearance of coherence, and the 'single vision' that entails.

5 Chronology

Time and Space died yesterday.
(Filippo Tommaso Marinetti)[49]

The self-styled 'futurist' Filippo Tommaso Marinetti was already, in
1909, straining against the constraints of modernist conceptions of time
and space; and in this section I want to consider in particular how
modernism is constrained by its emphasis on linear time. For modernism
assumes a straightforward consistent trajectory from past to present
to future, as providing the ideal (if not the only) chronological framework for its intellectual constructions, whether those constructions
are scientific, historical or literary. In modernist terms, linear time has
indeed come to be thought of as simply 'natural' – as something that is
just *given* (by God or human reason) and is therefore unquestionable; and
it can be seen as having the virtue of being something positive, inasmuch
as it implies another imposition of *order* on what might otherwise prove
threateningly chaotic. It provides us with a relatively stable structure
within which to locate or position our scientific, historical and literary
narratives.

And of course ourselves. That is to say, as we have seen above, our
very identities seem to presuppose awareness of a chronological structure,
which enables us to see a past self that has evolved into our present and
can be projected into the future. As Hume long since saw, it's only our
memory of the past that enables us to claim any continuing identity in
the present; and those who lose their memories, or even just their sense
of passing time, can suffer serious psychological problems. One psychiatrist
reported her patient's anxiety when she became so absorbed in some
spectacle that she lost her sense of time, and so her sense of self: 'I forgot
what time it was', she explained, 'and who and where I was . . . [and so]
I was frightened to death'. She needed to 'watch the clock' in order to
keep a grasp of her own identity and know who she was.[50]

And similarly, even looking from the outside, we can find someone's
mental 'absence' or half-absence disconcerting. As brilliantly depicted
in the film *The Deerhunter*, the presence in a bar of a veteran from
Vietnam – a man who was partly there and partly far away, in his own
incommunicable past – casts a cloud over the otherwise jolly proceed-
ings. The ex-soldier, still more than half living in his own world and
time, is remote, an unsettling intruder and an anomaly in the otherwise
agreed and accepted chronology – spatially only feet away, but temporally
distanced. He constitutes a threatening presence, destabilising others'
present – and of course his own. And that that destabilisation is common
in such situations is further suggested by the central character in *All*

Quiet on the Western Front, a book about an earlier war. Paul goes home on leave from the front, but feels himself distanced from his family and surroundings and the home that he had known before he left: 'There is my mother, there is my sister, there my case of butterflies, and there the mahogany piano – but *I am not myself there*. There is a distance, a veil between us.'[51] In another, literary example, Virginia Woolf's character Mrs Swithin is quickly written off as 'batty' by her maid, Grace. For Mrs Swithin has become so immersed in her reading about prehistoric monsters, that her sense of chronology has become confused:

> It took her five seconds in actual time, in mind time ever so much longer, to separate Grace herself, with blue china on a tray, from the leather-covered grunting monster who was about, as the door opened, to demolish a whole tree in the green steaming undergrowth of the primeval forest.

Mrs Swithin, who 'was given to increasing the bounds of the moment by flights into past or future', thus leaves Grace feeling confused by 'the divided glance that was half meant for a beast in a swamp, half for a maid in a print frock and white apron'; so that she is best identified as mad, or (as the expression significantly is) 'not quite all there'.[52]

But while Grace's and our own conventional structure of clock-watched linear time may protect us from the potential chaos of a chronologically structureless universe and self, that protection does again inevitably come only at a price; and as far as historical study more specifically is concerned, it can be seen to operate as another constraint, from which postmodernism may positively liberate. 'Narrative' has been defined by the eminent twentieth-century historian Lawrence Stone as, *inter alia*, 'the organisation of material in a *chronologically sequential order*'. But as the more poetic novelist Flaubert had recognised, ideally 'every-thing should sound simultaneously'; or as the literary critic James Wood has more recently noted, 'Narrative sequence, at bottom, is nothing other than the materiality of words, which forces us to order phrases in sequence, rather than on top of each other'.[53] For, as Virginia Woolf recognised in the example above, chronological sequence often defies human experience. It runs counter to our own jumbling of past and present, when memories intrude and overlap, and throw into ambiguity even supposedly straightforward apprehensions. Even (or perhaps especially) in the case of causation, causes and effects that seemed to have a natural relationship, running from one to the other through time, are found disconcertingly to twist and turn and loop back on each other. The chronological priority of chicken and egg remains forever in dispute, and we are forced, like the veterans from the First World War and Vietnam, to live in worlds that are temporally chaotic, and where past, present and future are inextricably blended.

That chronological chaos may be best represented in the visual arts, which circumvent 'the materiality of words', and may leave the 'phrases' or constituents available for reference in any order and at any time. A 'narrative portrait' of about 1596 (now in the National Portrait Gallery, London) shows *The Life and Death of Henry Unton* (Figure 5). As well as a conventional portrayal of his subject, the painter has shown a series of significant scenes from Unton's life and death. Reading anticlockwise from the bottom right-hand corner, there are his birth, his studies in Oxford, his foreign travels as a soldier and diplomat, and his actual death, with his body then brought back across the Channel (in the black ship), and on by hearse to his home in Faringdon, near Oxford. Other scenes show his life at home – sitting in his study, conversing, making music, and presiding at a banquet; and finally his funeral, with his wife's kneeling figure by his effigy in the local church. These scenes lack any restraining chronological 'sequence': it is more as if – as in some modern films – they had been piled 'on top of each other', all remaining simultaneously there, for viewers to refer to as they feel inclined.

Some viewers may well feel inclined to ignore, or go beyond, conventionally structured chronology – referring, perhaps, to the manner of the subject's death, and only then seeking illumination for the finale in earlier lifetime events. And we learn from an Australian historian, Howard Pederson, who has researched the Bunaba people's resistance to white colonisation, that 'Aboriginal perceptions of the past and explanations about why certain events occurred *do not sit easily within western historical chronology*'. It seems that once the need for multiple viewpoints has been conceded, there follows as a corollary the need for 'a multiplicity of times and therefore of histories'.[54]

That need has been recognised by some Western historians themselves. Ferdinand Braudel, in particular, famously distinguished three chronologies, or concepts of time, each requiring, or corresponding with, its own kind of history. First, he identified a traditional 'history of events', which focuses on individuals and relates to 'the rhythm of their brief lives'. With such an attenuated time-frame, history is usually centred on politics; but a second type might concentrate more on economies, societies, states, and civilisations – being associated with a chronology of 'gentle rhythms, of groups and groupings', which receives its form from conjunctures of trends and social structures in collective institutions. A third chronological form, with its associated history, is that *'longue durée'* which encompasses 'a history that is almost

Figure 5 Overcoming chronological constraints: narrative portraiture. *The Life and Death of Henry Unton* (c. 1596)
Source: National Portrait Gallery, London

changeless, the history of man in relation to his surroundings' – with endlessly renewed cycles, and very long demographic and ecological trends.[55]

Such differing and complementary 'strata' of chronology as those identified by Braudel, and recognised by most of us to some extent, and in varying situations, suggest that the more simplistic linear approach, usually associated with modernism, may be a further constraint from which the history of human experience might profitably be freed.

For from a negative standpoint, linear time can be seen as somehow *taming* the past – making it manageable and acceptable by normalising and reducing it to something uniformly bland. Peaks and troughs of experience are levelled out, and forced to fit the homogenising mould. Obstructive anomalies can't be allowed for too long to interrupt the genial flow of time. So if a peak or trough does appear, in the form, let us say, of a great war or Holocaust, it may admittedly appear initially to stand out starkly from its background and its context as an aberration, as something anomalous that fails to fit into our consensual view of what human beings are and how they act; or in chronological terms, it may appear as a veritable punctuation point in time, at which we need to stop and linger. But the seemingly inevitable flow of time denies such self-indulgence, and we convince ourselves, as we say in more personal crises of this kind, that time will no doubt prove to be 'the great healer'; and given time, the grossest anomalies can be smoothed down and appear as nothing less than 'normal' in the longer perspective. The First World War may have seemed at the time to be 'the war to end all wars' (another end of history); but, given time, we can assess it as just another stepping-stone (however gruesome) on the way to many others. And even the Holocaust, after which, it has been said, there could be no more poetry, can have its impact flattened by contextualisation in the smoothly running flow of time, until it too can be reduced to the banality of a prosaic (unpoetic) theme park.

Just, then, as we distance ourselves from personal disasters, assuring ourselves that the pain will go, if only we can view what is temporary in the longer term (or as long as it takes to diminish it to bearable proportions), so appropriate 'contextualisation' in uniform linear time will enable us to 'understand' historical events (however horrific) as legitimate (if not inevitable) events in a temporal (and causally connected) sequence. Historians, on the whole, have refrained from emulating the novelist Samuel Richardson's approach in *Pamela*, where, as Elizabeth Deeds Ermarth points out, no 'overarching patterns' – of the kind made possible by linear time – are provided, and as a consequence of such temporal discontinuity, 'every moment is a potential cliffhanger', where the reader, lacking the security of a continuous narrative thread, is kept 'in a prolonged "state of doubt and uneasiness"', and where for Pamela herself 'every moment is The Moment'.[56]

Some Romantics (Hamann was one example) may object to the way that time becomes fragmented in that sort of way, and reduced to isolated 'instants' that require some unifying 'thread'; but by adopting such an approach and repudiating the conventions of modernist chronology, Richardson is enabled to portray Pamela as experiencing a heightened awareness of what Goethe referred to as the 'historic moment' – a recognition that each moment in her life is a point of free decision, a moment that arrives in the present as the culmination of what has so far happened in the past, and is full of potential as being the point from which the future will proceed. As Ermarth explains in relation to Richardson's heroine, 'Any moment can be a supreme moment; properly conceived, every moment *is* a liminal moment'; and 'the ability to recognise the occasional value of all moments . . . is one of Pamela's major feats'.[57]

Pamela, then, perhaps to her surprise, would have pleased the philosophers Arthur Schopenhauer and Sören Kierkegaard. For they too emphasise the importance of a 'momentary present' – a present that (as the former puts it) 'alone is the form of all life', or which indicates for Kierkegaard 'the occasion of existential decision and resolution'.[58] The ability to seize that present moment, with the freedom that implies, may, however, be acquired again only at a price; and in Pamela's case one price is the reader's own feeling of anxiety. For lacking the rhythm that carries heroine and reader through a narrative that has been structured in the progressive sweep from past to future, both are confronted rather with 'a series of events without the benefits of continuity'; and the result, as we have seen above, is a floundering in a prolonged 'state of doubt and uneasiness' – that perception of an 'inconsequential buzzing' which Sartre's Roquentin preferred not to hear.[59]

Doubt and uneasiness are what pomophobia is all about, but for the postmodernist these may well seem preferable to certainty and a stable sense of self-identity. The avoidance of anxiety is not necessarily the greatest good: it can even constitute failure for one who sees every 'historic' moment as a possibility for further change and self-realisation. So that a denial of the constraints of modernist chronology may constitute one further step in facilitating free choices for our future.

Was it, then, yesterday, as Marinetti claimed in 1909, that 'Time and Space died' – or will it be tomorrow?

6 Conclusion

We must *be* nothing, but desire to *become* everything.
(Goethe)[60]

Goethe's prescription is a hard one to swallow, for it implies an endless restlessness, in our 'desire to *become* everything', that would seem to deny the traditional goal of much Western philosophy – philosophies that aspire to an established and fully integrated identity, a satisfactory completion of a life-long work of construction, a final arrival at a terminus, at the end of a difficult but ultimately finite journey. And what I've characterised as the 'constraints' of modernism may seem to provide the very bases of our lives. Neither socially nor intellectually could we order our experiences without recourse to categorising, without a belief in the consistency of selves and in ultimate coherence, and without acceptance of the past, present, and future of linear time. Without these alleged constraints, we may think, we wouldn't even know who or what we *are*, and civilisation would indeed revert to chaos.

And that is what provokes pomophobia. For postmodernism does challenge those conventions – asks us to question them, to view them not as 'natural' but as self- or culturally imposed and as contingent; and it requires us to consider (with Goethe) what it is that, in the light of possible alternatives, we might wish to *become*. In other words, postmodernism implies that, however difficult it may be to envisage a world without such constraints, we don't have to accept them as they are. Admittedly, the prospect of their removal may initially induce anxiety, but when they are seen (with Blake's eyes) as imposing 'single vision', it becomes clear that their removal opens up new possibilities – new vistas, new visions and new freedom. And that may be what it means to be awoken from 'Newton's sleep'?

6

HISTORY IN POSTMODERNITY

From fear to freedom

1 Introduction

There is another world to discover – and more than one! . . .
Perhaps there has never yet been such an 'open sea'.
(Friedrich Nietzsche)[1]

It's the openness of postmodernity that causes fear; and in the century
that has passed since Nietzsche was writing, the 'open sea' has flooded
yet more of the land on which intellectual foundations can be built.
Unsurprisingly, as there has never been more sea, there has never been
more fear. Our age has recently been characterised by one intellectual
historian as one of 'pervasive cultural disquietude', beset as it is
'with problems of anxiety, alienation, and emptiness'; and a theologian
has described how 'we have, for all our ingenuity, become increasingly
confused', no longer knowing 'what to say or do or value, or how to
realise the goals we seek . . . like children in the forest, lost'.[2] Yet, as
Nietzsche declares, openness can be viewed more positively: liberated
from 'single vision', it's possible to see, not just one, but a variety of
alternative 'world[s] to discover'.

Postmodernism, then, can be seen as a positively liberating force, not
so much inducing fear as encouraging further exploration – and it's that
claim that I'll try to substantiate in this concluding chapter.

2 The centre cannot hold

Things fall apart. The centre cannot hold.
Mere anarchy is loosed upon the world.
(W. B. Yeats)[3]

St Augustine envisioned God as a circle whose centre is everywhere
and circumference nowhere; and many mere humans have envisioned
themselves in rather similar terms. That is, they have considered

themselves to be in a privileged position, which, whatever their physical location, somehow remained permanently central to whatever concerned them. It was the centrality of their position that exemplified and underpinned their authority: from that position they could see it (any object of their concern – whether physical, ethical or historical), assess it and tell it as it was, 'objectively'.

Hence the importance of what we have already seen to be a major implication of postmodernity – a radical *decentring*; which is a denial of the validity of those quasi-theological foundational centres (geographical, chronological, cultural and so on) that modernity long took for granted. Those centres did of course enable standpoints and viewpoints to be easily established, and they in turn facilitated (and legitimated) a clarity and certainty that can come only from a narrowed focus and singleness of vision. Once those centres are challenged, dissolution follows, as Yeats describes in the quotation above. Any sense of order is lost, so that things fall apart, and are reduced to 'mere anarchy'.

We saw in Chapter 4 how the Copernican cosmological decentring implied the dissolution of the coherent cosmos derived from antiquity; and the latter half of the twentieth century witnessed a parallel geographical upheaval, as Eurocentrism fell to postcolonial challenges. Hugely unsettling, these revolutions can now be seen as contributing towards the postmodern perception that *no* centre can hold indefinitely – that we are left in the position described by Emerson in one of his essays, where 'All that we reckoned settled shakes and rattles'. 'Everything *looks* permanent', as he further describes, but only 'until its secret is known'. Once the secret is revealed, we realise that what we have taken to be an 'ultimate fact' (or foundation) is not ultimate (or foundational) at all, but is 'only the first of a new series', opening the way to another never-ending quest. We find again, in short, that we are, like Nietzsche's post-Copernican man, 'slipping faster and faster away from the centre', and we come to realise that 'this surface on which we now stand is not fixed, but sliding'.[4]

The point is that no given centre can hold as a uniquely privileged vantage-place, once it has been challenged by another, or any number of other possibilities. Mediaeval Christians may have been convinced of their own centrality, placing Jerusalem symbolically at the centre of their world maps, and believing faithfully in the exclusivity of their 'one, holy, catholic and apostolic church', outside of which was 'neither salvation nor remission of sins';[5] but by the later twentieth century Christian theologians had come to recognise the need for their own Copernican-style revolution, involving repudiation of 'the dogma that Christianity is at the centre', and acceptance of 'St John's vision of the heavenly city

. . . [where] it is said that there is no temple – no Christian church or chapel, no Jewish synagogue, no Hindu or Buddhist temple, no Muslim mosque, no Sikh gurdwara'.[6]

Our geographical and theological centres are now widely recognised as relative, and our horizons grow in number as our viewing points proliferate. What we had taken as an absolute 'end' (or even 'truth') dissolves into but one possibility among many, and that implies in turn that we can never reach the end of our quest for understanding. There is no final point from which and at which we can say, 'That's it!' For we can always move on to another point, from which it won't be it at all. So what is needed instead is what Nietzsche calls a 'continuous chain of ever-new interpretations',[7] with (in the style now of Gadamer) a constant *interaction* between ourselves and what we see. It no longer seems appropriate (or even meaningful) to search for a truth out there, which might (even must) ultimately be revealed: what is envisaged, rather, is an ongoing and indeterminate relationship, with the prospect of an ever-developing 'fusion' of conceptual horizons – between our own, that is, and that of whatever 'other' we confront (or aspire to).

That way may admittedly lead to uncertainty, and especially perhaps in relation to our own identity. For indeed, there must always be some tension between our twin desires, to explore new places and to remain safely at home. As Elizabeth Deeds Ermarth writes: 'The centrifugal forces of multiplicity, variety, disparity, ambiguity always exist in tension with centripetal forces of the centering, rationalising, synchronising motive.'[8] But there are compensating advantages for our exposure to multiplicity, variety, disparity, and ambiguity – all the effects of decentring. For that exposure forces us, if not to modify our views, at least to revisit them before either reaffirming or repudiating our commitment to them. In essence we are denied access to that cosy old refuge of habit, and are forced to remain aware and so alive. And in this context it's worth remembering Paul Valéry's suggestive identification of *disorder* as 'the condition of the mind's fertility'.[9]

Indeed, any reversion to chaos, as Derrida has more recently noted, is something not to be feared (in the customary manner as discussed in Chapter 1) but positively welcomed. For a recognition that order is never natural (but only imposed and contingent) opens up the possibility of change: things could be ordered differently, and better. So even in terms of doing history, it may be better *not* to conform to existing orderly models, adding our piece to the jigsaw puzzle or brick to the building – fitting in and cohering with an existing structure, in order to be professionally acceptable: better with Nietzsche to fight *against* it and start afresh, however much we may feel exposed upon an 'open sea'.

And in life more generally, there are potentially altruistic moral implications that are well brought out by Nicholas Lash. Primarily concerned with theology, Lash's fertile conclusions are (I shall claim) much more widely (if not universally) applicable, and are worth quoting at length:

> Perhaps the deepest reason for surrendering the modern search for safe and solid starting-points is that none of us, in fact, ever begins at the beginning. Finding ourselves somewhere, we do our best to work out where we are and what to do about it, to make some sense of things, to find our way around. Instead of wasting time casting about in search of absolutes, of a kind of safety, a possessed security, of solid ground beneath our feet that simply is not offered to us – neither by science nor Scripture, not by popes or presidents, not by proofs or private revelations – we would do better to get on with the business of trying to help each other take our bearings on a dark and dangerous road.[10]

Whatever our provisionally chosen central point, that at least would make a start towards some preferable circumference – the quality of the journey enhanced, even if the destination proves elusive.

3 Postmodern perceptions and perspectives

Perspective determines that point [i.e. the 'exact point . . . from which to look'] in the art of painting. But who shall determine it in truth and morality?

(Blaise Pascal)[11]

Pascal's point about perspective in painting seems obvious enough: the rules of perspective, developed during the Italian Renaissance, enabled painters to represent objects (nature, buildings, people) in a way that appeared to the viewer to be 'natural' or 'lifelike' or 'real' – in a way that made some sense of the notion of a 'truthful representation'. That 'truthfulness' was mathematically grounded, scientifically established. But there was, of course, an underlying presupposition – that viewers would place themselves directly in front of the painting, in just the same way as the painter had positioned himself in relation to his subject. Some shared standpoint, in other words, was presupposed.

That presupposition was questioned, and implicitly challenged, by the sixteenth-century painter William Scrots (fl. 1537–53), who painted his portrait (or so-called 'anamorphosis') of King Edward VI (now in the

National Portrait Gallery, London) in such a way that the viewer can 'make sense' of it only by looking from an extreme angle. From directly in front, the normal or conventional viewing point, the portrait head is barely recognisable as even human (Figure 6a). The grossly distorted features might just remind one of an attempt at caricature that has some-how gone too far – the skull deformed, and nose excessively long; but it doesn't, as a visitor noted in 1584, 'seem to represent a human being' at all. Yet looked at from another standpoint – not in front, but at an angle from the side – the portrait appears as perfectly lifelike (Figure 6b); from that stipulated point, as the sixteenth-century viewer noted, 'you will find the ugly face changed into a well-formed one'.

Scrots' clever manipulation of perspectival techniques (or of us) serves as a reminder that, even in the case of painting, 'truth' presupposes a *shared* viewpoint. If we – the painter or the viewer – don't 'play the game' in accordance with conventionally accepted rules, the result is a breakdown, a reversion to meaninglessness, and an inability to communicate. But at least there remains some possibility of agreement about where to stand in order to retain or regain some meaning and communication: Scrots does provide a key by which the 'truth' of his portrait can still be unlocked. But, to return to Pascal, who will provide such a key, to unlock the correct perspectival viewpoint, in the case of 'truth [itself] and morality'?

That's the question still faced in the context of historical study, where the possibility of countless perspectives, all yielding a meaningful narrative, evidently denies the concept of any unitary 'truth'. 'There is a . . . multiplicity of different universes', as Leibniz realised, 'according to the different points of view of each monad [or individual entity]'.[12] And as historians themselves have long recognised, they may provide narratives and explanations of past events that have every appearance of being true: the construction of a coherent causal chain of events lends plausibility to claims to have described things as they 'actually were'. But there always remains the possibility that another perspective will reveal another universe, with another story altogether; and then who is to decide between alternatives?

The contingency of historical narratives, and their problematic relationship with truth and morality, is well illustrated in a disturbing short story by Jean-Paul Sartre.[13] This emphasises the part that chance can play in human affairs, and at the same time indicates how easy it is for historians to ascribe neat causal connections, that seek to and seem to defy chance, but that can be refuted from another perspective.

Sartre's central character, Pablo Ibbieta, has been held in a cold prison cell overnight, awaiting execution in the morning. He and his friends

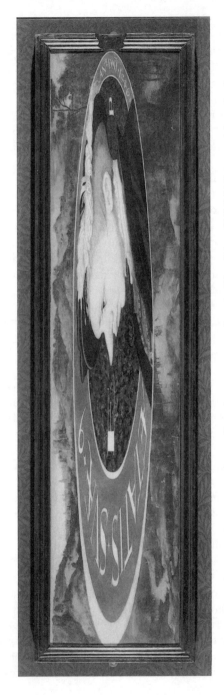

Figure 6a Perspective: choosing the viewpoint William Scrots, 'anamorphosis' of *King Edward VI* (1546), viewed from the front
Source: National Portrait Gallery, London

Figure 6b Scrots anamorphosis, viewed from the side

hear the regular shots of the firing-squad as they are taken from their cells
and led upstairs. Then, at the very last moment, Ibbieta alone is called
aside and taken to an office; and there he is offered his life, in exchange
for disclosing the whereabouts of his friend, Ramon Gris. 'It's his life
against yours', the interrogator explains; 'you can have yours if you tell
us where he is.' Our hero, of course, refuses to tell. He is well aware that
Gris was hiding with his cousins, some four kilometres from Madrid; but
he has no intention of betraying him. Then, given fifteen minutes more
to think about the interrogator's offer, he decides to play one last game
with his captors: 'He is hidden in the cemetery. In a vault or in the
gravediggers' shack.'

The soldiers go out to search accordingly, and when they return, Ibbieta expects to be shot. But instead he's taken to a courtyard, where he meets some other prisoners. One man, recently arrested, gives him the news: Gris has been captured. Apparently he had had an argument with his cousins; and not wanting to feel obligated to anyone else, he had declined offers from a number of other people who had been prepared to hide him. The one person he might have imposed upon had himself (as chance would have it) been captured; so he went to hide in the cemetery, and was found in the gravediggers' shack . . . On hearing the news, all that Ibbieta could do was laugh so hard that he cried.

But the story has a number of very serious points, of course: not least that chance plays a central part in our lives and deaths. However much in control we like to think we are, as we make our plans and go about our daily business, chance can get the better of us. And for the historian, that re-emphasises the difficulties of assigning causal explanations for events. For the casual observer (or historian), it would appear obvious that Ramon Gris had been betrayed by his friend: all the evidence seemed to point that way. Ibbieta had told the soldiers where to look, and they had found Gris there; and the self-interested motivation for the betrayal was absolutely clear. Yet in fact, of course, a far more complicated causal chain had operated, with some highly unlikely links; and it was one that would have been far more difficult for subsequent historians to trace. For them, the temptation would be to go for what was 'transparent', obvious, and understandable – and wrong.

History, in fact, no less than fiction, provides the comforting appearance of a certainty that we lack in real life – a forward thrust and sense of direction, an agreeable (whether tragic or comic) *plot*. And the loss of that plot may seem cause for lament, for it is, again, a loss of certainty that's implied, and a threat to our emotional security. Changing perceptions, therefore, may seem to be better avoided: they are what unsettle, and bring us back to the realisation of imminent chaos, where causal chains don't operate and chance determines life and death. We don't want Ramon Gris to be captured, any more than we want to see Edward VI as a distorted caricature rather than as 'in reality' he was.

But the unsettledness of perspectives in postmodernity can be seen as positively beneficial, in that it constantly challenges any comfortable status quo, and any tendency to ossify through the acceptance of claimed certainties. Earlier determinants of perspectival points, with their inbuilt canons, or accepted standards, had been imposed arbitrarily, whether for aesthetic or (not necessarily separable) ideological reasons; and by repudiating these, postmodernity opens up previously circumscribed perceptions and perspectives, liberating, in Zygmunt Bauman's words, 'the possibilities of life, which are infinite, from the tyranny of consensus'.[14] In that liberation the arts have often led the way as a subversive force against conformity, for they have questioned the very 'reality' that it was previously their function to represent. The ever-changing nature of what appears to us as the world's 'reality' was recognised, to give but one example, by the early twentieth-century painter Paul Klee: 'Standing on the earth', he wrote, 'he [the artist] says to himself: This world has looked different and in time to come it will look different again.'[15] What the artist attempts to do, therefore, is to look differently *now*, and so perceive and be enabled to represent an alternative aspect or *level* of 'reality'.

For some, that can be best achieved through abstract art, and Klee's contemporaries Kandinsky and Mondrian, for example, were inspired by their contacts with Eastern culture (with its alternative ways of looking) to penetrate beneath the mundane and material, and aspire to a more spiritual perception.[16] So rather than aspiring to ever-closer approximations to the outer appearance of the material world, or to representations that ever more closely resemble *physical* 'reality', late modern and postmodern art can be seen as a never-ending process of reinterpreting experience and phenomena, without being restricted to materiality at all. 'Reality' is not some objective entity, but rather, as Paul Feyerabend proposed in the context of science, 'We regard those things as real which play an important role in the kind of life we prefer.'[17]

That preferable life may turn out to be one in which 'reality' itself, then, is rethought. For postmodern perceptions imply the breakdown of those modernist categories and categorisations (discussed in Chapter 5) that have hitherto structured our experience of the world and of reality. In particular, such previously claimed polar opposites as good/bad, black/white, progress/regress, materiality/spirituality (and no doubt modernity/postmodernity) may need to be questioned, and 'reality' interpreted and experienced as something more akin to a continuum, potentially divisible in any number of equally valid configurations.

Thus, Minsoo Kang has recently written of how automata defy one of our most fundamental binary categorisations – that of life/death.[18] An automaton is a dead object that acts as if it is alive, or a quasi-living thing that is dead; it refuses to be neatly pigeon-holed as, in our habitual tidy-mindedness, we require. And so, by its ambivalence and ambiguity, it is liable to disturb us – a source of potential anxiety and fear that is frequently exploited by writers and film-makers of science fiction and horror stories.

Art's function then becomes endlessly to disturb in that way – to open up new visions (as Blake would have wished), and meanings and identities; or, in Bauman's words again, 'to stimulate the process of meaning-making and guard it against the danger of ever grinding to a halt'. This echoes T. S. Eliot, who writes of poetry that it 'may help to break up the conventional modes of perception and valuation which are perpetually forming, and make people see the world afresh, or some new part of it'. As Proust realised, 'The real voyage of discovery consists not in seeking new landscapes but in having new eyes.'[19]

Those new eyes, with their new perceptions from new perspectives, may seem to override and invalidate earlier interpretations, and render them fit to be discarded: in Emerson's words again, 'When we have new perception, we shall gladly disburden the memory of its hoarded treasures as old rubbish.'[20] But those hoarded treasures and old landscapes may still seem worth preserving: rather than rivals, they may be seen as alternatives – still with their own validity and still to be enjoyed. The analogy with history is obvious, and is made more or less explicit in an illustration proposed, in a theological context, by John Hick. He asks us to consider a piece of paper covered in writing. An illiterate savage, he suggests, might be able to discern that that object is something made by man. At the next level, a literate person, who does not know the particular language in which it is written, would interpret it as being some sort of document. But it would take someone who understands the language to find in it the expression of specific thoughts. Each observer would be seeking to answer the question 'What is it?', but each would be answering that question at different levels; and as the levels rose, each would presuppose, and so effectively incorporate, its less adequate predecessor.[21]

That sort of ascent, through progressive perspectives, or levels of understanding, can be seen too in the theories of other theologians who are no less concerned with history. Bernard Lonergan, for one, visualises humans as quasi-Faustian figures who have an innate aspiration towards complete understanding – a complete understanding that culminates (for him) in knowledge of a transcendent Being, or God. As constituting final and complete knowledge, the concept of God lies forever beyond reach. But it serves as a heuristic device – as a goal to which we may direct ourselves, and as a means of keeping us dissatisfied with the familiar world of phenomena and common sense, and dissatisfied with accounts of how things just *seem* to us. It impels us, Lonergan believes, through a sort of intellectual passion, or 'Eros of the mind', to continue striving towards knowledge of the world *as it is*.

Michel de Certeau similarly sees positive value in postulating a transcendent God, if only as a reminder of the limitations and inadequacies of our own human claims to knowledge. Once we define God in our own terms, within our own categories, we necessarily circumscribe and limit Him – fixing him in a way that enables us to apprehend and control Him. That, de Certeau claims, is tantamount to idolatry; and while that no doubt appeals in the context of our own quest for security, it limits our ability to respond to anything that might lie beyond, or outside the parameters of our existing structures of thought. What is needed, rather, are precisely challenges to those existing structures, facilitating new perspectives once more. So de Certeau refers to the necessity of *eruptions* that disturb us in our desire to settle down lazily into the conceptual frameworks that we're already in. For we need, he believes, to show continuing openness to alternatives; and an acceptance of transcendence – just as, for Karl Popper, an acceptance of 'objective truth' – will serve to keep us on our intellectual toes, indicating that something exists external to ourselves, and reminding us of our own limitations and contingency.

These theological approaches have clear relevance for historical study, where too, despite the absence of any tangible goal – or any goal that we can define in terms other than (indefinable) 'truth' – we may hope to ascend through different layers of intelligibility. That is, while remaining aware that any insights can only ever be partial, incomplete, inadequate, we may hope to find some ways of reducing chaos to intelligibility; and it is the very recognition of inadequacy (their falling short of 'truth'), that reinforces our ambition to know more. Only by having some conception of a transcendent 'other' – whether expressed as 'God', 'truth' or 'the sublime' – will we feel impelled onwards to further questioning.

No less than for Pyrrho and the sceptics, then, knowledge – and in this case historical knowledge – becomes for de Certeau not so much a goal of certainty as an ever-ongoing *process*. Historians remain forever on the unstable interface between past and present, negotiating some, admittedly temporary and contingent, vantage-point from which to make some sense of what they see. As they change their perspectives, so their perceptions will be modified – taking account of what has hitherto been concealed, overlooked or deliberately suppressed, and accepting as intrinsic to their world what has been previously relegated to the status of an extrinsic 'other'.

The prescription is, then, not for any assumed security of certitude, but for a never-ending inquiry – a quest for knowledge that has no destination, but constitutes a journey. '"This isn't it", "this isn't it"', as de Certeau writes, 'endlessly, till the end of one's strength.'[22] Whether in theology, or philosophy, or science, or history, or any other subject, the prospect is of an ongoing and dynamic *process*, without end. In postmodernity we are left with a positive acceptance of the continuing need for new perceptions from ever-new perspectives.

4 Imagining the unimaginable

Truly, we dwell happily in the Unimaginable.
(Ihab Hassan)[23]

Virginia Woolf describes in her novel *To the Lighthouse* how Mr Ramsay struggles desperately to transcend the limitations of his own thought processes.[24] Likening the mind to an alphabet, ranged with its twenty-six letters in order, he was well able to grasp them all – as far as the letter 'Q'. But there he stopped: despite his best efforts, the most heroic and determined efforts, he could never manage to penetrate beyond 'Q', to get as far as 'R'. Only very few people, he consoled himself, achieve as much as that; and only one person in a generation ever reaches 'Z'. But still Mr Ramsay felt frustrated at his inability to break through his own private conceptual barrier, and get beyond the extent of his everyday attainments – or, to return to our opening quotation, to dwell, however momentarily, in the unimaginable.

That has been the problem tackled by countless theologians in their quest for a similarly elusive 'God'. At least since early modern philosophy provided an intellectual model that seemed (as we have seen, by defining certain areas as out of bounds) to put knowledge in principle within our grasp, there has been a reluctance to admit the 'reality' of such things as defied comprehension through approved empirical procedures; and there has been scant attention paid to those aspects of experience that eluded a definitive 'fix'. Which leaves 'God' sick, if not, as Nietzsche realised, actually dead. I put the word 'God' there in quotes, to imply its variable definition as anything that serves as a transcendent and ineffable source of aspiration – such as Mr Ramsay's letter 'R', or 'truth' as used in science and history.

To reach our 'god', or get beyond 'Q', to imagine the unimaginable, or what lies just beyond our grasp – that is the problem. We are conscious, no less than Mr Ramsay, that it's there, that there's something we're striving to reach. But we can't quite get there. Like a word we can't remember, but that seems to hover 'on the tip of our tongue', it flits tantalisingly before us, but just eludes our grasp.

So how do we approach it? How do we bring the hitherto unimaginable within our present purview, in order to live there happily (or at least more happily than here)? The best answer on offer seems to be somehow to do the opposite of strive: better to relax or release those controls on our thought that bind us within modernist constraints – the constraints, again, of categorisation and consistency, and those structures of thought that, while enabling us conveniently to confine the complexity of experience, deprive us of access to that other world – those alternative realms of experience – which lie beyond, seemingly forever out of reach. Thus, for example, when confronted with the need to remember that elusive word, the more we grit our teeth and try to focus on it (or its absence) and apply our consciously controlling mind to its retrieval, the further from us it seems to recede; and we learn that the best technique is to leave the problem on one side, and think of something else. Then, if we're lucky, 'out of the blue', as we say, comes the solution – or in this case the word that we wanted. It was not for nothing that Archimedes found his solution to the problem, with which he'd long been wrestling, in the bath: it's by relaxing controls that we enable the normally excluded to enter and make its presence known.

Such laid-back invitation to imaginative input is unlikely to be gratefully accepted by modernist historians; for they, as we know, are concerned with how things were and not with how they might be. Speculations and imaginative flights are best left to poets and philosophers: history is a modernist-style science, the practitioners of which emulate the great Isaac Newton, who was once (and not unreasonably) described as 'the avowed Enemy to imaginary Systems'.[25] It is improper to speculate in subjects where the goal is an apprehension of something as solid as reality.

The functions of a philosophy that has declined to accept science as its model can then be defined in part by reference to what history is *not*; and vice versa. So Isaiah Berlin, for example, some fifty years ago, and in line with Aristotle's longstanding definitions, chose history as his benchmark of what philosophy is not. For philosophical questions, he asserted, can't be answered in the same manner as historical or scientific questions: they can't be answered, that is,

> by creating an army of experts, who, gifted with reasonable intelligence, assiduity, devotion, can set about performing the semi-mechanical work required, as routine scientists or *routine historians* can perform their work *without inspiration or genius or originality*.[26]

Berlin is here replicating also the Baconian image of the historian as plodding empiricist, detached observer, and patient collector of an interminable number of 'dry facts'. Such a person is happily able to make a positive contribution to historical knowledge, 'without inspiration, without the unpredictable leap of imaginative genius' that is, according to Berlin, required for the solution of philosophical problems. Like science, then, in this same Baconian tradition, history can be done 'as if by machinery'. It has no need of inspiration, genius or originality: in fact, those qualities should be positively discouraged, as being liable to seduce conscientious practitioners from their dispassionate pursuit of truth.

However seemingly contentious, that down-to-earth image of their subject has been perpetuated by historians themselves. Herbert Butterfield, for instance, typically insisted that

> the historian is essentially the observer . . . He deals with the tangible, the concrete, the particular . . . [So] it has generally happened that historians have reflected little upon the nature of things . . . They are not happy when they leave the concrete world and start reasoning in a general way.[27]

Butterfield's characterisation can then be usefully contrasted, as suggested by Berlin, with the philosopher Descartes, whose strength lay in his ability to shake himself free from the 'obsessive' intellectual framework in which he found himself, and to perform 'a great act of rebellion' against it. Like Mr Ramsay, Descartes battled hard against the strait-jacket of intellectual constraints; and unlike Mr Ramsay, he finally succeeded in freeing himself and getting past 'Q'. That is the essence of what it means to be a philosopher, who is, according to Berlin, intolerant of any status quo, and so liable 'to subvert, break through, destroy, liberate, let in air from outside'. 'Great philosophers', he concludes, 'always transform, upset and destroy.'[28]

Intellectual revolution of that kind is the last thing to be expected of Butterfield's historians, or of Geoffrey Elton's, who are described as having the virtues of 'a conservative temperament, [and being] willing to accept life on earth with all its imperfections'.[29] Such people prefer to remain unaware of Mr Ramsay's alphabet, or their own: neither disciplinary nor political boats are there to be rocked. In their determination to retrieve things as they were, they are prepared to go along unquestioningly with how things are. Elton was described by fellow-historian J. H. Plumb as being remarkable for 'implacability of vision and total rigidity';[30] and the desirability of such a psychological state was implicitly accepted by Elton himself, as he pondered the hazards of potentially transferable attitudes. For 'it is difficult', he realised, 'to promise that those who are revolutionary and irreverent in one sphere will remain docile and conformist in others'. Docility and conformity, it seems, have often been what is required of a historian, in spheres both academic and political (as well as personal).

That approach, typical as it has been of much modernist history, is now directly challenged in and by postmodernity. Such affected academic uninvolvement with the practicalities of everyday social and political life now seems an unlikely goal. Revolutionary irreverence replaces docile conformity as a virtue; intellectual presuppositions and habitual practices are there to be questioned. So, for example, Lyotard writes about the need to consider 'on what kinds of assumptions, what kinds of familiar, unchallenged, unconsidered modes of thought the practices that we accept rest'.[31] That implies a never-ending process of potential transformation – and constitutes an open invitation to go on trying at least to imagine (if not dwell in) the unimaginable.

5 Postmodernism: what future for the past?

Of our conceptions of the past, we make a future.
(Thomas Hobbes)[32]

History has been revealed as a modernist enterprise – indeed as a veritable core of modernism itself. With their scientistic aspirations, their objectification of the past and their repudiation of any moral or personal intrusions into their 'discipline', historians have constructed narratives that have served to confirm such underlying modernist conceptions as 'rationality' and 'progress'. But as an essentially modernist enterprise, history is now left stranded like some antediluvian beast on the beach of postmodernity, awaiting only nostalgic farewells and final submersion. Some postmodernists, as we have seen, have repudiated history altogether as an outdated and irrelevant activity. Resembling latter-day futurists, they effectively ask (rhetorically) with Filippo Tommaso Marinetti: 'Do you, then, wish to waste all your best powers in this eternal and futile worship of the past? . . . We want to free this land from its smelly gangrene of professors, archaeologists, ciceroni, and antiquarians.'[33] Others have more judiciously attempted to postpone the end by shifting the beast out of danger – even lopping off limbs if necessary and changing its essential character; and I shall join their number here, arguing that history, as a use of the past, can't simply be jettisoned as a modernist irrelevance. For it's from our conceptions of the past that we continue, as Hobbes claimed, to 'make a future'.

From whom, then, and from where and how do we derive our conceptions of the past? Our conceptions of the past, it must be noted, are not the same as the past itself (whatever that could mean): the past itself is gone, and forever eludes us, out of reach; we can never 'know' it. Yet we are, or can be, burdened by it – trapped in it, borne down by it.

'This', complains one of Virginia Woolf's characters, 'is the burden that the past laid on me . . .; what we must remember; what we would forget.'[34] For her there seemed no choice: memories intrude against her will. We may try to follow the advice of Elizabeth in Jane Austen's *Pride and Prejudice*, to 'Think only of the past as its remembrance gives you pleasure'. (For 'Why', as Emerson asked, 'drag about this corpse of your memory', if all it does is cause you pain?) But as Darcy explains to Elizabeth, 'painful recollections will intrude, which *cannot*, which *ought not* to be repelled'.[35]

To our *inability* to expel unpleasant memories, Darcy adds a *moral* dimension: some things, however unpleasant, we simply *should* remember. On a personal level, it could be claimed that we have a moral duty to remember actions that we should prefer to forget or should prefer had never happened; we owe it to our victims. And on a public level, we are constantly reminded of painful pasts – of wars and massacres and holocausts – by memorials and books and films, 'lest we forget'. As Nicholas Lash insists, 'all utopian fantasies, all simply sunlit futures forgetful of the past, are disallowed, subverted, by the silent witness of shed blood'.[36] We owe it, again, to those who died, sometimes on our behalf, to remember.

So from this mixed bag of the past, how are we to make a future? (For unless that future is to be literally deracinated, without roots, it's what we've got to make that future from.) Not, it is clear in postmodernity, by claiming to reach 'the truth' about it; not by objectifying it and endeavouring to remain remote and disinterested; not by excluding that part of us that seems to deny 'rationality'; not by trying to treat it as an entity in itself, 'for its own sake', denying any reference to ourselves. Instead, we need to take the future as our starting-point, and ask what it is that we're aiming at; for it's only by aiming at a future that we want to make, that we can form appropriate conceptions of the past. Once having determined the nature of that future, our histories can provide the paths we need to get there – those narrative trajectories that gain their authority, strength and nourishment through roots established deeply in the past, and thence lead forward to the future that we want.

That may well sound heretical – a reversion to the worst form of 'Whiggism', whereby historians have been accused of ahistorically moulding their material to show progression to an ideal present. And in a sense it is. Modernist historians have concentrated on modernist virtues, and seen a growth of rationality, or liberty, or capitalism, or socialism, or science, or technology, as the developments that have made some sense of what has happened in the past. If Rome is where we want to be, then all roads can be seen to lead there; and there has been widespread agreement (despite some obvious ideological divergencies) about the nature of the city to which we are travelling, as well as the (various) directions from which we approach it. However implicit, that is, and unstated (and denied), modernism itself has provided a model, a standard, a goal to which to aspire.

And it's that goal, and in particular its supposedly unitary nature, that has been (or is being) slowly but surely dismantled in postmodernity. The modernist virtues, so long taken for granted as indefinitely appropriate and universally applicable, have been exposed as relative and often a cover for less than virtuous ambitions. Heidegger long since insisted that 'thinking begins only when we have come to know that reason, glorified for centuries, is the most stiff-necked adversary of thought';[37] and conventionally defined 'rationality' is now widely recognised as excluding and inhibiting alternative approaches that (even in historical study) may claim their own validity. Technological progress, similarly, has been seen to have its downside, threatening, as it has come to do, environmental desolation; and the growth of capitalism has patently resulted, in both national and global contexts, in ever-increasing economic inequality. So with the demise of long-held modernist presuppositions, we are left with a proliferation of alternative goals and of potential futures; and it is the burden of postmodernity – or of historians in postmodernity – to choose between (or among) them, without necessarily rejecting all the rest.

That may, paradoxically, suggest a reversion to an earlier age – a pre-literate age even, when choices were legitimately left between different endings; when narratives were less directly linear as they zig-zagged through what was transiently important; and when meanings could be constantly redefined as individual viewpoints changed.[38] Such earlier oral history is interestingly linked by Robert Rosenstone with the possibilities of our contemporary representation of history on film. For freed from many of the constraints of other media, film has (as David Harvey has noted) 'of all the art forms, . . . perhaps the most robust capacity to handle intertwining themes of space and time [the themes of history surely] in instructive ways'. So it may be particularly well suited to show history in ways that postmodernist historians require – to show history as an open-ended process, as seen from a multiplicity of perspectives, and with the potentiality of a multiplicity of meanings (and so uses for the future). By the use of various cinematic techniques, including that most postmodern construction of 'collage', film can evade the constraints of literary representation that some postmodern historians have been striving to overcome – the constraints of linear chronology, for instance, and the structural expectations of a beginning, middle, and end (in that order). And better than any written text,

Rosenstone claims, film can convey 'the spirit of the past', 'the meaning rather than the literal reality of past events' – like the African 'griot', or traditional storyteller, who, as the guardian of tribal memory, conveys not so much chronological truths as moral truths.

Robert Rosenstone is not, of course, referring there to typical Hollywood products, with their commonsense notions of 'realism' and their 'satisfying sense of emotional closure', but rather to an avant-garde where history is portrayed as 'a series of disjunctive images and data, a kind of collage [again] or postmodern pastiche'. Significantly, too, for our theme of pomophobia, he notes how historians often 'dislike (or *fear*) ... the visual media'; for it's film, perhaps, that best shows the way forward for alternative modes of representation and future uses of the past. It's not writers but film-makers, as Rosenstone concludes, who 'have begun to create a kind of history that we can label truly postmodern'.[39]

At all events, as implied in the preceding section, the choice of our future (and so our use of the past) requires a faculty that has been long repressed as unworthy of historians: imagination. Imagination has traditionally been aligned rather with poets than prosaic historians. From the time of Greek antiquity, there is evidence for the supposedly prophetic powers of poets, linked with a sort of 'madness' that would debar them from any contact with the discipline of history. Plato, through his characterisation of Socrates, describes how the word for 'prophecy' (*mantike*) is really the same as that for 'madness' (*manike*), the insertion of the letter 't' in the former being, he explains, only a recent and tasteless addition. So the prophet needs to be in some sense mad, not rational; and because prophecy is obviously good, madness can be seen as superior to sanity; 'the sane man is nowhere at all when he enters into rivalry with the madman'.[40]

Any such preference for madness or the irrational would no doubt find short shrift with modernist historians. But there are increasing signs of a more sympathetic hearing from those who accept their own situation in postmodernity. We have seen how some historians explicitly recognise their own injections of imagination, and Minsoo Kang has gone so far as to claim illumination for his studies from a dream. In an interesting autobiographical fragment he describes how his perception of the relationship between funeral effigies and automata was inspired by a dream (which was in turn apparently provoked partly by his own recent experiences). For all its initial strangeness, the dream immediately provided a vital clue for his ongoing historical research. For the unconscious mind lacks such inhibiting restraints as binary categorisation, so is enabled to make those new connections and disjunctions between things that Francis Bacon had so disparagingly attributed to poetry.

Dreams, then, Kang suggests, might 'open up a whole new world of possibilities for thinking about the past'.[41]

The liberating function of dreams has, of course, been previously noted in other contexts, for it's in dreams (as well as baths) that access to the storehouse of the unconscious mind has been thought to be achieved. It was through a dream that the nineteenth-century German professor Kekulé claimed to have made his own important breakthrough in organic chemistry. He related how he had dozed off in front of the fire one afternoon, and dreamt of snake-like atoms, one of which suddenly seized hold of its own tail. That was the clue he needed, and 'as if by a flash of lightning I awoke'. His then revolutionary proposal was that 'the molecules of certain important organic compounds are not open structures but closed chains or "rings" – like the snake swallowing its tail'. Clearly, Kekulé, like Kang, had long been consciously pondering his problem, but he too attained his solution not by further conscious straining, but through the opposite – a relaxing of habitual controls and a consequent access to a more creative unconscious that lacked the restraints of scientific orthodoxy and convention. In similar mode to the historian, Kekulé concludes: 'Let us learn to dream'.[42]

Learning to dream, and so make contact with what lies normally beyond our reach, was a part of the Romantics' programme. Wordsworth, for example, writes of 'caverns in the mind which sun can never penetrate', and Goethe insists that 'Man cannot persist long in a conscious state; he must throw himself back into the Unconscious, for his roots live there'. And Coleridge provides the archetypal example of gaining access to those roots, when he claims that his poem 'Kubla Khan' was revealed to him after falling asleep in his Porlock farmhouse in 1797. He describes how he

> continued for about three hours in a profound sleep, at least of the external senses, during which time he has the most vivid confidence, that he could not have composed less than from two to three hundred lines; if that indeed can be called composition in which all the images rose up before him as *things* with a parallel production of the correspondent expressions, without any sensation or consciousness of effort.

On awaking, all he had to do was to write out what he distinctly recollected, and, as is well known, it was only unfortunate that he was interrupted before his transcription was complete.[43]

Science, poetry, and history, then, all have their examples of creative dreams, or of knowledge retrieved from the unconscious, when recreation becomes re-creation. One of the future functions of history more particularly, then, but (as we can see) in alignment with the other arts and sciences, becomes not least to facilitate such creative access, and so serve as a disrupting force against the orthodoxies that prevail in the modernist consciousness – the certitude and stagnancy of any status quo (both in personal and political terms) that has come to be perceived as nothing short of 'natural'. So as we have previously seen Jan Patočka insist: 'History is nothing other than the *shaken* certitude of pre-given meaning';[44] and, while he may not wish to be aligned with my blatant focus on the future, Stefan Collini too has insisted that one of the prime functions of the critical historian is to challenge historical orthodoxies as they relate to (and supposedly underpin) contemporary political positions. 'One of the services that the historian renders to society is to help prevent its members becoming the prisoners of any tendentious or partisan versions of "the national past".'[45] It is by shaking the certitude of what the past seems to imply (or what it has been interpreted as meaning) that historians are enabled, from that past, to construct their future.

For once the old modernist assumptions are challenged, a host of new possibilities is opened up and once released from some of their old disciplinary constraints, historians can unabashedly make some imaginative *use* of the past. It was some two hundred years ago that the Italian Romantic Ugo Foscolo pointed out that 'reality' (whether physical or historical) is not something out there awaiting our discovery but something rather that awaits our own imaginative construction: 'All that exists for men is but their own imagining . . . We fabricate reality after our own fashion.'[46] So historians are required to use their imaginations creatively to construct histories, as Thucydides long since advocated, with some positive purpose. Lyn Hunt has proposed that 'truth' is not to be seen as something 'objective', lying outside the historian's concerns and practices: it is something that must remain forever elusive, but that none the less (as some sort of ideal never-attainable goal, perhaps?) 'informs her work'; so that histories themselves become 'a field of moral and political struggle, in which we define ourselves in the present'.[47] For God may be dead, and angelic meta-narratives gone, too; but still some saving Ariadne with her thread – or even threads – is needed to guide us out of the fearful labyrinth to freedom. By openly helping to indicate directions, or 'fabricate reality' (or alternative realities), historians could show that their subject is still of practical relevance in relation to the future.

Nor is it only the function, but even the very form of histories that might change – or rather, is already changing. Historians have, for example, begun to imitate architects (so often invoked as the originators of postmodernism) in their playfulness – incorporating seemingly incompatible bits and pieces from the past, in order to present a novel form of whole in which the parts, by the very unexpectedness of their juxtapositions, provide mutual illumination. Robert F. Berkhofer, in his own exemplary work on historiography, has described how 'My text frequently resembles a *collage* . . ., because I build my arguments from the conceptual bricks most readily at hand, often extricating them from their customary intellectual context for my purpose'.[48] Modris Eksteins juxtaposes such seemingly diverse subjects as ballet, warfare, and solo transatlantic flights in his treatment of the Great War, *Rites of Spring*; and in his equally compelling story of the Baltic States in the twentieth century – a blend of autobiography, family history and an account of the fluctuating political and military fortunes of Eastern Europe – he describes his own 'pastiche of styles, an assemblage of fragments . . . a mélange of memory, reflection, and narrative'. He has, he explains, told a tale 'from the border, which is the new centre' – a tale that aspires to reveal 'the intimacy not of truth but of experience'.[49]

Others, too, have deliberately set out to challenge the old orthodoxies of modernist historical writing. Richard Price has described his experiments with the use of four different typefaces, with the aim of emphasising 'the inevitable perspectivality of my various historical sources'. Some of his work, he explains, is 'written in the form of a screenplay', some 'in the form of a diary set off against excerpts and fragments from other people's writings', and including pen-and-ink sketches, with 'the whole taking on the form of a collage or montage'. He has elsewhere confronted the challenge of modernist categorisations of time, using 'temporal shunts, flash-backs and cuts forward, [and] a wide range of photos that punctuate the text and accentuate rhythms'.[50] And in similarly experimental mode, Sven Lindqvist has recently written a history of bombing in the form of 399 short numbered passages. These passages are organised chronologically, but the reader is led through them not sequentially but via a number of alternative routes. 'This book is a labyrinth', the author explains – a labyrinth 'with twenty-two entrances and no exit'. Each entrance opens into a narrative or argument, through which one is directed by arrows; and the deliberate juxtapositioning of narratives is designed to facilitate their reciprocal illumination – with, for instance, bombers adjacent to their victims, and technology alongside evidence of its political and human dimensions:

> Wherever you are in the text, events and thoughts from that same period surround you, but they belong to narratives other than the one you happen to be following. That's the intention.

That way the text emerges as what it is – one of many possible
paths through the chaos of history.[51]

Such experimental multi-perspectival approaches enable historians,
at least to some extent, to show that the past is not something fixed,
finally caught and preserved and presented in some divine equivalent of
aspic. Historians make of the past what they will, or what they can; and
their function becomes to enable their readers to come away with a
realisation that 'history' is something much more than the representation of a single and coherent (however persuasive) narrative thread.

Indeed, it might be that narrative *disruptions* – breaks in narrative
and gaps in history – could represent what happened more convincingly
than that even flow that seems to take everything so comfortably and
comfortingly into its embrace. In the context of attempted representations of the Holocaust, for example, Richard Kearney has proposed
'a form of narrative which can entertain its own disruption as part of
its repertoire of possibilities'. It was, as he reminds us, their very
inarticulateness in the face of the inarticulable, their *silences* as they
strove to express in language the linguistically inexpressible, that
confirmed the credibility of the film-maker Claude Lanzmann's witnesses
in *Shoah*.[52]

The need for such silences returns us to the erosion of our fact/fiction
categories discussed in Chapter 5, since they might well, as Kearney
suggests, indicate a need for *fiction* – the admitted incorporation of
fiction, that is, into the historical record. For it's sometimes, as we've
seen, only (or best) through fiction that truth can be approached; it's
only through thinking in terms of imaginary fictions that we allow
ourselves to access those aspects of experience that we'd rather not have
had: fiction, in the words of one of Dermot Healy's narrators, 'becomes
the receptacle for those truths we would rather not allow into our tales
of the self'. And that psychological insight is one that historians may
need to take on board. For 'not every story has to involve processes of
integration, harmony and compensation': it may be that the very opposite
processes – involving narrative *dis*junction – are what, in Paul Ricoeur's
words, 'prevent . . . events from appearing as necessary', and so (as with
Derrida) offer (preferable) alternatives for the future.

The imaginative potential in narrative disruption or disjunction is
well shown in the work of the Canadian photographer and film-maker
Stan Douglas,[53] who deliberately demonstrates just how disconcerting
gaps in our narrative plots can be. One of his most striking photographs,
Michigan Theatre (Figure 7), shows the interior of a once-grand theatre
that has now been turned into an indoor car-park: against the backdrop

Figure 7 Narrative disruption: what intervened? Stan Douglas, *Michigan Theatre*
(1988)
Sources: Stan Douglas and David Zwirner Gallery, New York

of an elaborately decorated ceiling, cars are parked; but the viewer is left
with nothing to explain that incongruous juxtaposition – nothing to link
the building's splendid past with the banality of its present. We are left
to insert our own imaginative reconstruction of its intervening history –
to search for clues in such relevant archives as local newspapers, perhaps,
or the memories of those who live near by. Without such clues and
imaginative reconstructions – and this is the point, surely – we're left
uneasy, troubled in some way by the seeming inexplicability of the visual
anomalies; we can't understand what we're looking at – don't know quite
how to 'read' it.

Similarly with Stan Douglas's films, there are no conventional
beginnings or ends or intermediary narrative threads – no connections
or progressions or explanations, or references to any external 'reality' or
'truth'. Viewers, again, are required to react, each in their own way –
filling in gaps or silences, and providing their own story-line and meaning.

And that may suggest again that a function for history, a future for the
past, is (as Modris Eksteins puts it) to '*provoke, not dictate* meaning'. For

165

the task of imaginative reconstruction never ends. In his novel *Waterland* Graham Swift highlights the analogy between reclaiming land in the Fens and reclaiming the past in history. 'The Fens', it is explained, 'are still being reclaimed even to this day. Strictly speaking they are never reclaimed, only being reclaimed'. And so in postmodernity history is to be seen as a continuing *process* of reclamation – or (to revert to Eksteins) 'a vehicle rather than a terminus'.[54] That gives to the past a positive conception from which to make a future?

6 History and education in postmodernity

All history classes should ask, What is the point of history? Why history? Why the past?

(Graham Swift)[55]

To many modernist historians, the idea of *using* history, for anything other than a training of the mind (or of course for career progression) remains anathema; and advocacy of the study of the past 'for its own sake' is still pervasive. Such an unworldly stance can be assumed only by those who refuse (for their own political reasons) or are unable to see that the much-vaunted 'purity' of their subject is but a veil for their own ideological positioning: history has long been a 'discipline' that has served to confirm the 'reality' of a particular set of values in a particular world.[56] But the days of high-minded 'uselessness' in the humanities, and in historical studies more specifically, may anyway be numbered: as increasing numbers of prospective students default to subjects of perceived practical relevance and utility, it may be time openly to reconsider the questions posed by Graham Swift's ideal teacher (who lost his job), and even inject into history a modicum of practicality in the interests of political idealism. That might well resonate with members of younger generations, who could then see some *point* in their historical studies.

For encouragement to 'imagine the unimaginable' forms part of a *practical* rather than purely theoretical agenda: it constitutes an invitation to formulate some *vision* for the future; and in the attempted attainment of that vision, history might play an important, if not central, role. For it has to do, surely, with imagining the sort of society we would wish to encourage to develop, and the sort of individual of whom that society would be constituted. And to envision these, some historical perspective seems (to me) essential. For virtues can best (or even *only*) be assessed within a context. As Thucydides noted over two millennia ago, characteristics accounted virtues in peacetime, for instance, may come to seem positively vicious in times of war; and of course vice versa.

And it's not only the *language* – the linguistic descriptions we assign to those characteristics – but our very *perception* and *experience* of them that undergo modifications in the light of changing circumstances. Virtues, in short, are to be assessed, not in the abstract, but in concrete situations – which is to say, in their overall contexts. And contextualisation implies historicisation.

Thus, we might select such virtues as freedom, justice, toleration and equality; but fully to understand the force of those terms (and to promote them as desirable), we'd need to examine their application in specific contexts – to see how and when and where and why they'd been adopted or repudiated, enjoyed or denied, and what some effects had been. Students would need to locate themselves historically in relation to such virtues, in order to assess for themselves their desirability, the processes of their development, and the means to their attainment (and sometimes loss). In this way history would become highly politicised, helping to provide, as American educational theorist Henry A. Giroux has proposed, 'the opportunity to develop the critical capacity to challenge and transform existing social and political forms, rather than simply adapt to them'.[57]

Encouragement 'simply [to] adapt' has often been an unspoken goal of academic history. Why else do we hear calls for citizenship classes to include introductions to our historical heritage? The assumption is that a newly acquired ability to slot oneself into a prolonged historical narrative of nationhood will confer identity – a conforming identity that will facilitate the maintenance of a (supposedly) hitherto coherent society. The desirability of the maintenance of that society is presupposed: we are in some sense at the 'end' of history again – at the culmination of a historical progression, into which any sensible person would wish to be assimilated.

But then the choice of historical narrative becomes crucial. For it's possible to conceive of alternatives – an alternative, perhaps and for instance, that celebrates not so much homogeneity as diversity, and where it's accepted that 'identities and subjectivities are constructed in multiple and contradictory ways'. In relation to historical study that implies, in postmodern mode, the rejection of any single master narrative, and its replacement by a multiplicity of not competing but complementary narratives, conferring a diversity of not competing but complementary identities.

Those new historical narratives would then themselves enhance awareness of alternatives. Their contingency would indicate that things – people and their circumstances – *could be otherwise*; and a more open discussion of evolving goals and aspirations might then be encouraged,

with some prospect of their possible attainment. That sort of politici-
sation has been (and no doubt continues to be) anathema to modernist
historians, with their vested interest in the status quo, their own
conformist attitudes, and their disinclination to destabilise the vehicle
of their own advancement. But when more people in Britain vote
for some television pop-idol contest than for their parliamentary
representative, some rethinking seems in order.

'Human demoralisation and mass depoliticising' have been identified
as characteristics of totalitarianism,[58] and those characteristics are
more than ever evident in our own supposed democracies today. In
postmodernity, therefore, there is a vital educational role for historical
studies to play, in helping to counter that dangerous and depressing
situation. Echoes of William Blake can be found when Henry Giroux
writes of enabling students 'to read the world differently' and to 'summon
up the courage to imagine a different and more just world and to struggle
for it'. That could serve to answer the questions posed by Graham Swift's
history class, being at least one important part of what history is *for*?

7 Conclusion

People wish to be settled; only as far as they are unsettled is
there any hope for them.

(Ralph Waldo Emerson)[59]

Postmodernists have sometimes been accused of self-indulgence –
of indulging *themselves* at the expense of any external constraints, of
claiming for themselves the *pleasure* that freedom is supposed to bring.
Bryan D. Palmer, for example, has described their '*hedonistic* descent
into a plurality of discourses that decenter the world in a chaotic
denial of any acknowledgement of tangible structures of power and
comprehension of meaning'. And in relation more specifically to history,
Gertrude Himmelfarb has decried 'the *pleasure* principle' with which
postmodernists allegedly replace any more puritanically inspired 'reality
principle' – a pleasure principle that countenances 'history at the
pleasure of the historian'.[60] Yet everyone surely would agree with
Emerson's first claim, that 'people wish to be settled'. They take no
pleasure from being unsettled. For the most part, at least, we like stability
and certainty in our lives; and it's postmodernism's tendency to
challenge our (intellectual and emotional) stability and certainties – its
proneness to unsettle – that leads to the anxieties characterised by
pomophobia. Emerson's second point, relating *un*settledness with any
hope for the future, is more contentious; but it consists with a postmodern

perspective, in terms of which certainties are constantly challenged, and unsettledness becomes a positive virtue that gives cause for hope as enabling and facilitating greater freedom.

Jan Patočka, following Heidegger, has referred to the anxiety induced by confrontation with existential meaninglessness. When we realise that things have no inherent meaning – no meaning in and of themselves – we are left with the task of ascribing meaning to them, unable as we are simply to accept the prospect of their total lack of meaning. 'Where human life is confronted with absolute meaninglessness, it can only surrender and give itself up . . . life is only possible thanks to the perennial illusion of total meaning.'[61] Illusion it may be, but better to live by that than die; better, for practical purposes, to have a dogmatic faith in meaning than an equally dogmatic belief in nihilism.

The point is, then, that we have a choice: having confronted meaninglessness, we can either descend into the depths of 'dreadful immobility' or pick ourselves up and return to a world of meaning and significance. For Christians, that choice (if ever confronted) was unproblematic: any philosophical doubts could be stilled by faith in God, and meaning in both personal and public histories could be assured in the context of a narrative that led from creation to fall and ultimate salvation. And as Patočka describes:

> European humanity has become so accustomed to this Christian conception of the meaning of history and of the universe that it cannot let go of some of its substantive traits, even where fundamental Christian concepts such as God the creator, saviour, and judge have ceased to be significant for it, and that it continues to seek meaning in a secularised Christian concep-tion in which humans or humanity step into God's place.[62]

In what is by now a decisively post-Christian era, humans assume the role of God, and, however arrogantly, on their own responsibility make the choices that will enable them to transcend anxiety and fear by once more restoring some meaning to the world.

That may involve another seemingly paradoxical reversion to an earlier age, where 'faith' again becomes respectable, or intellectually acceptable. For the question of 'Truth' in history remains a major issue; and if the study of history is to continue in postmodernity – as it seems to me it must – then some sort of concept of historical 'truth' seems necessary, if not as an achievable goal, then at least as something to which aspirations may be directed. As Julian Barnes has written: 'We all know objective truth is not obtainable . . . But while we know this, we must still believe that objective truth is obtainable.'⁶³ The traditional modernist belief in the attainability (in principle) of an historical truth that somehow corresponds with the past 'as it was' is clearly no longer tenable, but that does not preclude the possibility of retaining some conception of a 'truth' that will provide some justification, motivation, and even possibly direction for historical study in the future.

In this context it may be helpful once more to relate historiography (or the philosophy of history) to religion (or theology). For theologians, the concept of a 'God' is not necessarily *fixed*, or stable, or conclusive, or even intelligible. As St Augustine explains, it is *in*comprehensibility that defines God's nature: 'Since it is God we are speaking of, you do not understand it. If you could understand it, it would not be God.'⁶⁴ It is for that very reason that *faith* in God is needful; and even so, for historians there may be some concept of a 'truth', similarly undefined and even fluid, in which some *faith* may be required. So even Derrida, often interpreted as having deconstructed truth beyond redemption or recall – as has been clarified in an interesting article by Hugh Rayment-Pickard⁶⁵ – continues to maintain the value of truth (and associated values), not least in the context of history. His apparent reduction of everything to 'textuality' does *not*, as Derrida himself explains, 'suspend reference – to history, of the world, of reality'. Far from any wholesale repudiation, 'we must maintain *faith* in historical and other truth'.

Now, with their 'urbane contempt for religion', as Hugh Rayment-Pickard puts it, postmodern academics might find 'faith' a difficult concept to handle; but for Derrida it is not something exclusively religious. For even in our everyday use of language, despite our awareness of the many theoretical pitfalls, we continue to have faith in our ability (at least to some extent) to communicate. There is, in Derrida's words, 'a link of trust which connects us with the other in general and with history'; and, as has long been recognised, 'good faith is the condition of testimony' (or of historical witnesses) – or at least the condition of our acceptance of it (and them).

For 'We cannot', as Mary Midgley has written, 'keep our minds open for ever'.⁶⁶ In order to go anywhere, we need some 'mental map' that will enable us to take our bearings and proceed in a direction that we want (a direction that answers our purpose). The potential chaos of experience has to be structured in *some* way – made some *sense* of – whether we're talking of individual experience, scientific data or historical evidence; and rather than going along with someone else's map (or vision, with its own implicit closures), or *blindly* (unthinkingly, through fear or habit) accepting the currently conventional, it's surely preferable to insist on *self*-determination – on choosing our own terminus (or at least direction). If our minds can't, finally, be kept forever open, we can at least ensure that they're not slammed shut in our own faces, and that we retain control of any handle on our own futures.

Like Derrida, Mary Midgley writes in the context of 'faith', which she defines as 'the acceptance of a map, a perspective, a set of standards and assumptions, an enclosing vision'. There is no necessary implication here of any finality, or of any claim to absolute foundations for that faith or for the meaning we've accepted: rather, it's something to be accepted on trust, as a way of enabling us to get around in the world, and go through it, again, without what she fittingly calls a 'fear of lostness', and in a direction that seems to us to be for the better. Among the host of competing (and sometimes apparently conflicting) alternatives, all we can do is act *as if* communication, or historical truth, were possible – just as Pyrrhonists, and sceptical theologians, continue to act *as if* the external world, or God, is real.

That does not, then, imply any 'closure' in respect to truth. Again, far from it: like love (and to revert to Derrida), truth is 'a many splendour'd thing', and not incidentally, as modernists have conventionally assumed, to be confined to what is purely rational. Indeed, as Hugh Rayment-Pickard explains, that would constitute a breach of faith; for 'to close down the idea of truth merely to what is rational – what Derrida calls "Logocentrism" – is an act of *in*fidelity to other possibilities of meaning'.

Those other possibilities remain alive – as can be seen even on a personal level, where ambiguities of self, and conflicting motivations, are simply parts of the human condition. In Rayment-Pickard's words, 'We can achieve a rational and integrated account of human intentions only by suppressing or eliminating alternative, non-rational, contradictory intentions.' As is the case more generally in the construction of historical narratives, we can give rational and coherent accounts of human intentions only by a gratuitous act of reduction, or exclusion again of that host of competing alternatives.

As evidence for the existence of such competing alternatives, Hugh Rayment-Pickard cites the historical example of Petrarch and his symbolic ascent of Mont Ventoux. While some historians (or philosophers of history) have claimed that it's possible to ascertain his motivation, Petrarch himself is better aware of his own psychological complexity. His is not a single, unambiguous self – any more than anybody else's is. 'A stubborn and still undecided battle has long been raging on the field of my thoughts for the supremacy of one of the two men within me.' Or as Derrida describes in an interesting parallel of self-analysis: 'I have remained the counter-example of myself . . . In the end the two

171

certainties do not exclude one another, for I am sure that they are as true as each other'.

Refusing closure of the self, then, can be paralleled by a refusal to impose closure on the past. But that doesn't imply that there isn't a self or past, or that there isn't a 'truth', or meaning (however multiple, self-contradictory, irrational, indefinable) that can be ascribed to both. Faith in such a truth or meaning need not (indeed, cannot) be blind, though, and will not, as Patočka saw, imply a return to where we were before. For:

> Passing through the experience of the loss of meaning means that the meaning to which we might perhaps return will no longer be for us simply a fact given directly in its integrity; rather, it will be a meaning we have thought through, seeking reasons and accepting responsibility for it.[67]

We'll be aware, that is, that meaning is not just there, ready to be taken: it's a relationship that we've adopted with the world; and like any other relationship, it has to be constantly worked at. We need constantly to shake ourselves out of the rut of habit, to engage in 'the shaking of all the naive "certainties" that would find a home among what-is'; and 'The constant shaking of the naive sense of meaningfulness is itself a new mode of meaning'.[68]

We thus discover a meaningfulness that is at once more free and more demanding. It's more *free*, because it's *not* just given, any more than any historical narrative is there as something given. Rather, it has to be looked for – and that's what makes it more *demanding*. For it can never be definitively grasped; the search is never concluded: salvation (or meaning) is to be found in the *seeking* itself. Thus, Patočka concludes:

> the shaking of naive meaning is the genesis of a perspective on an absolute meaning to which, however, humans are not marginal, on condition that humans are prepared to give up the hope of a directly given meaning and to accept meaning *as a way*.[69]

Emerson would surely have approved of that, and so too would the ancient sceptic Pyrrho. For the former, the ongoing search for meaning would have equated with 'unsettledness' – the sort of unsettledness that drives one ever on, and so gives cause for hope. For Pyrrho, too, it was the search that mattered: our inability ever to be certain of anything – our unsettledness, again – ensured that we would go on seeking, and it was in the seeking that we'd enjoy that 'ataraxia' or freedom from anxiety and fear that remains the goal of life in postmodernity.

In intellectual terms – or in terms of historical study more specifically – one can hardly do better than go back to that diffident, early modern sceptical chemist Robert Boyle, whose prescription for his own subject would do as well for any other. Looking at the great intellectual super-structures, built on supposedly secure foundations of absolute principles and axioms, he insisted rather on their relativity and contingency. They were, he suggested, as good as we can get for the moment, but our commitment to them should never be final; they should always be considered as open to future improvement:

> I would have such kind of superstructures look'd upon only as temporary ones, which though they may be preferr'd before any others, as being the least imperfect, or, if you please, the best in their kind that we yet have, yet they are not entirely to be acquiesced in, as absolutely perfect, or uncapable of improving Alterations.[70]

Scientific superstructures, then, resemble historical truths, or theo-logical notions of God. They are provisionally useful as being the best we have for the moment, but they are not to be relied upon for ever. Our acceptance of them remains tentative, our commitment something less than wholehearted, while we continue to search for something better to displace them. In whatever area of human aspiration, the ultimate goal – the 'truth' or 'god' or 'reality' – remains forever elusive, out of reach, beyond us; but our belief that it's there provides the necessary motivation for our continuing search. Our 'wish to be settled' acts as the mainspring for our actions and our lives. Without that wish we die. But settledness itself would also be a cause of death: only insofar as we are 'unsettled is there any hope', or life. That is the essential tension and paradox of postmodernity, occasioning not fear but freedom.

NOTES

1 POSTMODERNISM AND POMOPHOBIA

1 *Daily Telegraph*, 15 March 2000, p. 4.
2 G. R. Elton, *Return to Essentials*, Cambridge, Cambridge University Press, 1991, p. 41; Allan Bloom, *The Closing of the American Mind*, Harmondsworth, Penguin, 1988, p. 346; Felipe Fernández-Armesto, lecture at Institute of Historical Research, London, 15 November 2001 (my emphasis); *Truth: A History and a Guide for the Perplexed*, London, Bantam, 1997, pp. 7, 8, 162, 226; David Cannadine's review of Gertrude Himmelfarb's *The De-moralization of Society: From Victorian Virtues to Modern Values*, New York, 1995, is reprinted in David Cannadine, *History in Our Time*, London, Penguin, 2000, pp. 188–96 (my emphasis); John Clarke, *The Tao of the West*, London, Routledge, 2000, p. 193; Susan Pederson, lecture at Institute of Historical Research, London, 15 November 2001 (my emphasis).
3 Jean-François Lyotard, *The Postmodern Condition* (1984), quoted in Lawrence E. Cahoone (ed.), *From Modernism to Postmodernism: An Anthology*, Oxford, Blackwell, 1996, p. 482.
4 Keith Jenkins, 'On Disobedient Histories', draft article kindly shown to me before publication in *Rethinking History: The Journal of Theory and Practice*, forthcoming.
5 T. S. Eliot, 'The Hollow Men', in *Collected Poems 1909–1962*, London, Faber & Faber, 1963, pp. 91–2.
6 Zygmunt Bauman, *Postmodernity and its Discontents*, Cambridge, Polity, 1997, p. 3. Future quotations are from pp. 13, 26, 75, 89.
7 On personal autonomy and 'an ethic of authenticity', see Nikolas Rose, *Governing the Soul: The Shaping of the Private Self*, 2nd edn, London, Free Association Press, 1999 – a reference for which I thank Susannah Southgate.
8 Ihab Hassan, in Cahoone (ed.), *From Modernism*, p. 386 (my emphasis).
9 Bauman, *Postmodernity*, pp. 95, 89, 100 (my emphasis).
10 Norman Lebrecht in the *Daily Telegraph*, 31 October 2001.
11 Zachary Leader and Hal Foster in *London Review of Books*, 21 September 2000, pp. 13, 16–18 (respectively).
12 See Pausanias, the second-century travel-writer, in his *Guide to Greece*, transl. Peter Levi, 2 vols, Harmondsworth, Penguin, 1971, vol. 1, p. 446.

13 Lorraine Daston, *London Review of Books*, 1 November 2001, pp. 3, 6, to whom I am indebted for much of this paragraph.
14 Michael Keith and Steve Pile (eds), *Place and the Politics of Identity*, London, Routledge, 1993, p. 3.
15 T. S. Eliot, 'Four Quartets', in *Collected Poems*, p. 189.
16 John Forrester, *The Seductions of Psychoanalysis. Freud, Lacan and Derrida*, Cambridge, Cambridge University Press, 1990, p. 206.
17 T. S. Eliot, 'Four Quartets', in *Collected Poems*, p. 190; Rainer Maria Rilke, *Duino Elegies*, London, Hogarth, 1963, p. 25.
18 Joseph Conrad, *Heart of Darkness*, Ware, Wordsworth, 1999 (1902), p. 41.
19 Quoted by Simon Hornblower, 'Narratology and Narration Techniques in Thucydides', in Simon Hornblower (ed.), *Greek Historiography*, Oxford, Clarendon Press, 1996, p. 133, n. 5 (my emphases).
20 Richard Evans, *In Defence of History*, London, Granta, 1997; Elizabeth Fox-Genovese and Elisabeth Lasch-Quinn (eds), *Reconstructing History*, London, Routledge, 1999, p. xvi.
21 Elton, *Essentials*, p. 49; Keith Windschuttle, *The Killing of History: How Literary Critics and Social Theorists Are Murdering Our Past*, New York, Free Press, 1997, p. 231; C. Behan McCullagh, seminar at the Institute of Historical Research, London, 11 October 2001; Brenda Almond, 'Philosophy and the Cult of Irrationalism', in A. Phillips-Griffiths (ed.), *The Impulse to Philosophise*, Cambridge, Cambridge University Press, 1992, p. 215 – a reference for which I thank Martyn Keys; Bernard Williams, in *London Review of Books*, 18 April 1996, p. 17 (my emphasis).
22 Elton, *Essentials*, p. 24; Juliet Gardiner (ed.), *The History Debate*, London, Collins & Brown, 1990, p. 10.
23 Barbara Herrnstein Smith, *Belief and Resistance: Dynamics of Contemporary Intellectual Controversy*, London, Harvard University Press, 1997, pp. xiv, 148.
24 Thomas Browne, *The Garden of Cyrus* (1658), in *The Religio Medici and Other Writings*, London, J. M. Dent, 1906, p. 229; Hesiod, *Theogony* CXVI, quoted by G. S. Kirk and J. E. Raven, *The Presocratic Philosophers*, Cambridge, Cambridge University Press, 1971, p. 24; Plato, *Timaeus*, in B. Jowett (ed.), *The Dialogues of Plato*, 5 vols, Oxford, Clarendon Press, 1875, vol. 3, p. 614.
25 Plato, *Dialogues*, vol. 3, p. 653.
26 Max Weber (1949), quoted in Robert M. Burns and Hugh Rayment-Pickard (eds), *Philosophies of History: From Enlightenment to Postmodernity*, Oxford, Blackwell, 2000, p. 216.
27 Jenny Diski, *Rainforest*, Harmondsworth, Penguin, 1987. Quotations that follow come from pp. 137, 17, 169, 103, 129, 81–2.
28 See Galileo, *The Assayer* (1623), in Stillman Drake (ed.), *Discoveries and Opinions of Galileo*, New York, Doubleday, 1957, p. 238. But see also Goethe, who pointedly asks: 'What is there exact in mathematics except its own exactitude?' Quoted by Erich Heller, *The Disinherited Mind*, Harmondsworth, Penguin, 1961, p. 28.
29 Virginia Woolf, *Between the Acts*, London, Granada, 1978 (1941), p. 112.
30 Samuel Taylor Coleridge, 'Self Knowledge', in *The Poems of Samuel Taylor Coleridge*, London, Oxford University Press, 1907, p. 380.

NOTES

2 POSTMODERNISM AND HISTORY

1 Samuel Auguste Tissot, *De la Santé des gens de lettres* (1768), quoted by Carolyn Steedman, *Dust*, Manchester, Manchester University Press, 2001, p. 37, n. 44.
2 Norman Davies, *Europe: A History*, London, Pimlico, 1997, p. 6.
3 David Harvey, *The Condition of Postmodernity: An Enquiry into the Origins of Cultural Change*, Oxford, Blackwell, 1989, p. 98; Charles Jencks (ed.), *The Post-Modern Reader*, London, Academy, 1992; Lawrence E. Cahoone (ed.), *From Modernism to Postmodernism: An Anthology*, Oxford, Blackwell, 1996; Stuart Sim (ed.), *The Icon Dictionary of Postmodern Thought*, Cambridge, Icon, 1998; Zygmunt Bauman, *Postmodernity and its Discontents*, Cambridge, Polity, 1997. See too, for example, Barry Smart: 'Postmodernity is an issue in anthropology, sociology, philosophy, geography, theological studies, literary criticism and economics' – 'to mention only a few areas', he adds; but why not history? *Postmodernity*, London, Routledge, 1993, p. 11.
4 Geoffrey Elton, *Return to Essentials*, Cambridge, Cambridge University Press, 1991, p. 49; Gertrude Himmelfarb, in Elizabeth Fox-Genovese and Elisabeth Lasch-Quinn (eds), *Reconstructing History*, London, Routledge, 1999, pp. xvii, 75 (cf. pp. xvi, 50), and as quoted by Robert F. Berkhofer Jr, *Beyond the Great Story: History as Text and Discourse*, London, Harvard University Press, 1997, p. 18; Keith Windschuttle, *The Killing of History: How Literary Critics and Social Theorists Are Murdering Our Past*, New York, Free Press, 1997, pp. 2, 4, 36, 249; Arthur Marwick, *The New Nature of History: Knowledge, Evidence, Language*, Basingstoke, Palgrave, 2001, pp. xvi, 242, 253, 19.
5 Berkhofer, *Great Story*, p. 12 (my emphasis).
6 Modris Eksteins, *Walking since Daybreak: A Story of Eastern Europe, World War II, and the Heart of the Twentieth Century*, London, Macmillan, 2000, p. 15.
7 Thomas Carlyle, quoted by Eksteins, *Walking since Daybreak*, p. 15.
8 Jean-Yves Tadié, *Marcel Proust: A Biography*, transl. Euan Cameron, London, Viking, 2000, p. xvi.
9 John H. Arnold, *History: A Very Short Introduction*, Oxford, Oxford University Press, 2000, p. 54.
10 J. B. Bury, inaugural lecture as Regius Professor of Modern History at Cambridge, 1903, quoted by E. H. Carr, *What is History?*, Harmondsworth, Penguin, 1964, p. 57.
11 Thucydides, *The Peloponnesian War* I.3, 9–10; II.41; III.104; Lord Bolingbroke, *Letters on the Study and Use of History*, London, Alexander Murray, 1870 (1752), p. 130.
12 David Hume, quoted by Peter Gay, *The Enlightenment: An Interpretation*, 2 vols, London, Wildwood House, 1973, vol. 1, p. 74 (my emphasis).
13 Francis Bacon, *Novum Organum*, ed. F. H. Anderson, Indianapolis, Bobbs-Merrill, 1960 (1620), I.CIV.
14 Walter Charleton, *Two Discourses, the First, Concerning the Different Wits of Men*, 3rd edn, London, William Whitwood, 1692, p. 14.
15 Thomas Hobbes, *Leviathan*, London, J. M. Dent, 1914 (1651), Part 1, ch. 3, p. 10.
16 Condorcet, quoted by Robert Nisbet, *History of the Idea of Progress*, London, Heinemann, 1980, p. 209.

176

17 Albert Bushnell Hart (1910), quoted by Peter Novick, *That Noble Dream: The 'Objectivity Question' and the American Historical Profession*, Cambridge, Cambridge University Press, 1988, p. 38.

18 Novick, *Noble Dream*, p. 40; Fritz Stern (ed.), *The Varieties of History*, New York, Meridian, 1956, p. 215.

19 Peter Gay, *Style in History*, London, Jonathan Cape, 1975, p. 210.

20 Johann Eduard Erdmann, in *A History of Philosophy*, Preface to 2nd edn., English transl. W. S. Hough, 3 vols, London, Swan Sonnenschein, 1869, vol. 1, p. xiv.

21 T. S. Eliot, 'Ash Wednesday 1930', in *Collected Poems, 1909–1962*, London, Faber & Faber, 1963, p. 95.

22 Auguste Comte, quoted by Robert M. Burns and Hugh Rayment-Pickard (eds), *Philosophies of History: From Enlightenment to Postmodernity*, Oxford, Blackwell, 2000, pp. 115–16.

23 J. T. Merz, *A History of European Thought in the Nineteenth Century*, 4 vols, Edinburgh and London, William Blackwood & Sons, 1896–1914, vol. 1, pp. 3–4.

24 Terne L. Plunkett and R. B. Mowat, *A History of Europe* (1927), Preface, p. vii, quoted by Davies, *Europe*, p. 17; John Vincent, quoted by Richard Evans, *In Defence of History*, London, Granta, 1997, p. 178.

25 Herbert Butterfield, *The Whig Interpretation of History*, Harmondsworth, Penguin, 1973 (1931), p. 30.

26 John Hexter (1954) quoted by Novick, *Noble Dream*, p. 375.

27 Nennius, *Historia Brittonum*, ed. in the tenth century by Mark the Hermit, transl. Rev. W. Gunn, London, John & Arthur Arch, 1819, p. 1. The manuscript of this work had been recently (at the time of publication) discovered in the Vatican library, and was 'commonly attributed' to Nennius.

28 Nennius, *Historia*, p. 35.

29 Statement by Institut vuur Christelijke-nationale Onderwijs, 1948, quoted by Marc Ferro, *The Use and Abuse of History, or How the Past is Taught*, London, Routledge & Kegan Paul, 1984, p. 2; T. S. Eliot, 'The Rock', in *Collected Poems*, p. 177.

30 Joseph Conrad, *Heart of Darkness*, Ware, Wordsworth, 1999 (1902), p. 102.

31 William Shakespeare, *All's Well that Ends Well*, Act 1, scene 2, lines 19f. I am indebted for this example to James Wood's essay 'Rambling', in *London Review of Books*, 1 June 2000, pp. 36–7.

32 Alfred Tennyson, 'Ode to Memory', in *Poetical Works*, London, Oxford University Press, 1953, p. 11.

33 For more detailed accounts, see, for example, Keith Jenkins, *Rethinking History*, London, Routledge, 1991 and *Why History? Ethics and Postmodernity*, London, Routledge, 1999; Alun Munslow, *Deconstructing History*, London, Routledge, 1997.

34 Friedrich Nietzsche, *On the Genealogy of Morals*, transl. Walter Kaufmann and R. J. Hollingdale, New York, Vintage, 1969, p. 158.

35 Michel Foucault, in Cahoone (ed.), *From Modernism*, pp. 372–3.

36 See Bonnie G. Smith, *The Gender of History: Men, Women, and Historical Practice*, London, Harvard University Press, 1998, who concludes that we still 'inhabit a gendered profession' (p. 240).

37 Elton, *Essentials*, pp. 42–3, 55.

38 Marwick, *New Nature*, p. 6.

39 See Fox-Genovese and Lasch-Quinn (eds), *Reconstructing History*.
40 Evans, *Defence*, p. 9. For postmodernism's benefits, see esp. p. 248; following quotations (with my emphasis) are from pp. 64, 70, 90–1, 221, 223, 252.
41 For Simon Schama, see, for example, *Dead Certainties*, London, Granta, 1992 (where, however, he does emphasise that he doesn't scorn the fact/ fiction distinction, p. 322); and see also *Citizens: A Chronicle of the French Revolution*, London, Penguin, 1989, which he admits, 'Though in no sense fiction . . ., may well strike the reader as story rather than history (p. 6). Natalie Zemon Davis, *The Return of Martin Guerre*, Harmondsworth, Penguin, 1985, p. 5; Modris Eksteins, *Rites of Spring: The Great War and the Birth of the Modern Age*, London, Macmillan, 2000, pp. 3, xvi; Berkhofer, *Great Story*, p. 277, referring to Greg Dening, *Mr Bligh's Bad Language*, Cambridge, Cambridge University Press, 1992; Annabel Patterson, *Early Modern Liberalism*, Cambridge, Cambridge University Press, 1997; J. J. Clarke, The *Tao of the West*, London, Routledge, 2000, pp. 12, 13, and *The Oriental Enlightenment*, London, Routledge, 1997, p. 6.
42 See Homer, *Odyssey* IV.385f.; Virgil, *Georgics* IV.387f.
43 *Daily Telegraph*, 29 August 2000.
44 Himmelfarb quoted by Berkhofer, *Great Story*, p. 18. See also the comment by contemporary-art expert Andrew Renton on Kylie Minogue as a 'malleable [postmodern] icon': 'she can be anything you want her to be'. Significantly, she is reported to cry herself to sleep 'for not knowing who she is'. I am indebted for these cross-cultural references to Norman Lebrecht, *Daily Telegraph*, 31 October 2001.
45 Hans Kellner, '"Never Again" is Now', in Keith Jenkins (ed.), *The Postmodern History Reader*, London, Routledge, 1997, p. 406.
46 Michael Shermer and Alex Grobman, *Denying History*, London, University of California Press, 2000, p. 27; Saul Friedlander, *Probing the Limits of Representation*, London, Harvard University Press, 1992, p. 2 (cf. pp. 4–5). For another discussion, see Alex Callinicos, *Theories and Narratives: Reflections on the Philosophy of History*, Cambridge, Polity, 1995, pp. 65–75.
47 Jenkins, *Why History?*, p. 14.
48 Jenkins, *Why History?*, p. 17 (my emphases).
49 Arthur Danto, quoted by Hans Kellner, 'Triangular Anxieties: The Present State of European Intellectual History', in D. La Capra and S. L. Kaplan (eds), *Modern European Intellectual History: Reappraisals and New Perspectives*, London, Cornell University Press, 1982, p. 120.
50 Jacques Derrida, quoted by Jenkins, *Why History?*, p. 40.
51 Quotations from Jenkins, *Why History?*, pp. 59, 71, 103 (my emphases).
52 Quotations from Jenkins, *Why History?*, pp. 173, 166, 174, 154.
53 Jan Patočka, *Heretical Essays in the Philosophy of History*, ed. James Dodd, Peru, Illinois, Open Court, 1996, p. 118 (my emphasis); Windschuttle, *Killing*, p. 154. See also p. 3 on his belief that 'history can be studied in an objective way and that there are no philosophical obstacles to the pursuit of truth and knowledge about the human world'. Since drafting this, Patrick Joyce has written of postmodern history's potential to provide 'a constant invitation to intellectual and therefore political critique': *Times Literary Supplement*, 26 October 2001.

3 POSTMODERN PERSPECTIVES: SOME ANTECEDENTS

1 Umberto Eco, quoted by Linda Hutcheon, A Poetics of Postmodernism: History, Theory, Fiction, London, Routledge, 1988, p. 42.
2 Stuart Sim, 'Postmodernism and Philosophy', in Stuart Sim (ed.), The Icon Critical Dictionary of Postmodern Thought, Cambridge, Icon, 1998, p. 13.
3 Sextus Empiricus, Against the Professors, transl. R. G. Bury, London, Heinemann, 1949, I.268.
4 Cicero used Carneades' arguments in his Republic III.
5 Dio Chrysostom, Discourses, transl. J. W. Cohoon, 5 vols, London, G. P. Putnam, 1932, vol. 1, pp. 517, 541, 561.
6 François La Mothe Le Vayer, Du peu de certitude qu'il y a dans l'Histoire, in Deux Discours, Paris, L. Billaine, 1668, p. 77.
7 Pierre Le Moyne, Of the Art Both of Writing and Judging of History, London, R. Sare & J. Hindmarsh, 1695, p. 76.
8 Thomas Hobbes, Human Nature (1640), in Richard S. Peters (ed.), Body, Man, and Citizen, London, Collier-Macmillan, 1962, p. 243.
9 John Sergeant, The Method to Science, London, W. Redmayne, 1696, pp. 108–12.
10 John Tillotson, The Rule of Faith . . ., London, S. Gellibrand, 1666, p. 138.
11 On Perizonius and historical pyrrhonism, see Paul Hazard, The European Mind, 1680–1715, transl. J. Lewis May, Harmondsworth, Penguin, 1973, pp. 52–4; Pierre Bayle, Historical and Critical Dictionary, ed. R. H. Popkin, New York, Bobbs-Merrill, 1965, pp. 194–5 (my emphasis), and his Dictionary, English transl., 4 vols, London, C. Harper, 1710– , vol. 2, p. 543.
12 John Leland, Reflections on the Late Lord Bolingbroke's Letters on the Study and Use of History, London, B. Dod, 1753, p. 155. G. M. Trevelyan's edition of the letters (which omits the first five) is significantly entitled Bolingbroke's Defence of the Treaty of Utrecht, Cambridge, Cambridge University Press, 1932.
13 Henry St John, Lord Bolingbroke, Letters on the Study and Use of History, London, A. Millar, 1752, pp. 98–9, 109–10 and The Substance of Some Letters . . . to M. de Pouilly (c. 1720), in The Works, 4 vols, Edinburgh, Carey & Hart, 1841, vol. 2, p. 469.
14 Joseph Glanvill, 'Of Scepticism and Certainty', in Essays on Several Important Subjects in Philosophy and Religion, London, 1676, p. 47; Bolingbroke, Letters, pp. 108, 136, and Works, vol. 2, p. 467.
15 Bolingbroke, Letters, p. 135.
16 Bolingbroke, Letters, pp. 71, 79.
17 Anon, Some Remarks on the Letters of the Late Lord Bolingbroke, London, 1752, pp. 14, 30–1.
18 Robert Clayton, A Vindication of the Histories of the Old and New Testament, London, W. Bowyer, 1752, pp. 28, 66f.
19 Leland, Reflections, pp. iv, vii, 21.
20 Leslie Stephen, History of English Thought in the Eighteenth Century, 2 vols, London, Smith, Elder & Co., 1876, vol. 1, p. 58; J. A. Froude, Short Studies on Great Subjects, 5 vols, London, Longmans Green, 1907, vol. 1, p. 1.
21 Aristotle, Metaphysics 1062.b.13 (my emphasis).
22 Herodotus, The History III.38.

23 Sextus Empiricus, *Outlines of Pyrrhonism*, transl. R. G. Bury, London, Heinemann, 1968, I.148.

24 Diodorus Siculus, quoted by D. R. Kelley, 'Historia Integra', *Journal of the History of Ideas* 25, 1964, p. 53 (my emphases).

25 Juan Luis Vives (1531), quoted by J. H. Franklin, *Jean Bodin and the Sixteenth-Century Revolution in the Methodology of Law and History*, New York, Columbia University Press, 1963, p. 94, n. 13.

26 Thomas Baker, *Reflections upon Learning*, London, A. Bosvile, 1699, p. 141.

27 Joseph Glanvill, *The Vanity of Dogmatizing*, London, Henry Eversden, 1661, p. 195 (emphasis in original); Bernard de Fontenelle, *A Week's Conversation on the Plurality of Worlds*, London, A. Bettesworth, 1737, pp. 180–1.

28 Herder, quoted in Robert M. Burns and Hugh Rayment-Pickard (eds), *Philosophies of History: From Enlightenment to Postmodernity*, Oxford, Blackwell, 2000, p. 60 (Herder's emphasis); see also p. 77, where Herder ironically exclaims how 'Soon there will be European colonies everywhere! [and] Savages all over the world will become ripe for conversion . . . and become, so help me God, good, strong and happy men, just like us!' See also Leslie Stephen who, as an intellectual historian in the following century, noted how, after the geographical discoveries of the early modern period, it had become quite clear that 'Christendom was but a fragment of the world' (*History*, vol. 1, p. 81).

29 Jonathan Richardson, *Richardsoniana: or, Occasional Reflections on the Moral Nature of Man*, London, J. Dodsley, 1776, p. 3.

30 Richardson, *Richardsoniana*, pp. 10–11.

31 Richardson, *Richardsoniana*, p. 32.

32 *The Prison House of Language* was the title of a book by Fredric Jameson, published in 1972. John Keane has more recently written of authors being 'prisoners of the discourse within whose boundaries they take pen in hand' ('More Theses on the Philosophy of History', in James Tully (ed.), *Meaning and Context: Quentin Skinner and his Critics*, Cambridge, Polity, 1988, p. 205).

33 See R. W. Southern, who describes how, in the Middle Ages in particular, 'logic was an instrument of order in a chaotic world' (*The Making of the Middle Ages*, London, Grey Arrow, 1959, p. 187).

34 Galileo, *The Assayer* (1623), in Stillman Drake (ed.), *Discoveries and Opinions of Galileo*, New York, Doubleday, 1957, pp. 237–8.

35 Ralph Cudworth, 'A Sermon preached before the House of Commons, 31 March 1647', in C. A. Patrides (ed.), *The Cambridge Platonists*, London, Edward Arnold, 1969, p. 92.

36 Luce Irigaray, quoted in Lawrence Cahoone (ed.), *From Modernism to Postmodernism: An Anthology*, Oxford, Blackwell, 1996, p. 465.

37 Genesis 11.4–9.

38 Quoted by Elizabeth Deeds Ermarth, *Realism and Consensus in the English Novel*, Edinburgh, Edinburgh University Press, 1998, p. 223.

39 Thucydides, *History of the Peloponnesian War* III.82.

40 Stephen, *History*, p. 5; Richard Rorty, *Contingency, Irony, and Solidarity*, Cambridge, Cambridge University Press, 1989, p. 21.

41 Isaiah Berlin, *The Magus of the North*, ed. Henry Hardy, London, John Murray, 1993, pp. 87, 88.

42 John Locke, *An Essay concerning Humane Understanding*, London, Thomas Basset, 1690, III.2, 5.

43 Rorty, *Contingency*, p. 9.
44 Berlin, *Magus*, pp. 40, 42; William Blake, quoted in Alfred Kazin (ed.), *The Portable Blake*, New York, Viking, 1946, p. 30.
45 G. Chatterton-Hill (1942), quoted by Arthur O. Lovejoy, *Essays in the Historiography of Ideas*, Baltimore, Johns Hopkins, 1948, pp. 230–1.
46 Carlyle, quoted in J. R. Hale (ed.), *The Evolution of British Historiography*, London, Macmillan, 1967, p. 36.
47 Carlyle, quoted in Hale, *Evolution*, p. 42.
48 Macaulay, review of 1828, in *Miscellaneous Writings*, ed. T. F. Ellis, 2 vols, London, Longman & Co., 1860, vol. 1, p. 275.
49 For this assessment of Chamberlain, see Modris Eksteins, *Rites of Spring: The Great War and the Birth of the Modern Age*, London, Macmillan, 2000, pp. 78–9. Chamberlain's *The Foundations of the Nineteenth Century* (1899) was translated into English by John Lees, 2 vols, London, John Lane, 1911.
50 G. M. Trevelyan, quoted by R. C. Richardson, *The Debate on the English Revolution*, London, Methuen, 1977, p. 81 (my emphasis).
51 J. J. Clarke, *The Oriental Enlightenment: The Encounter between Asian and Western Thought*, London, Routledge, 1997, p. 211.
52 David Hall, 'Modern China and the Postmodern West', in Cahoone (ed.), *From Modernism*, p. 701 (emphasis in original).
53 Tao Te Ching, quoted by David Hall, in Cahoone (ed.), *From Modernism*, p. 701; Laozi, quoted by J. J. Clarke, *The Tao of the West: Western Transformations of Taoist Thought*, London, Routledge, 2000, p. 18.
54 Clarke, *Oriental Enlightenment*, p. 60.
55 Clarke, *Oriental Enlightenment*, pp. 118, 107–8, 115.

4 POSTMODERN PARALLELS: THE TRANSITION TO MODERNITY

1 Simplicio, in Galileo, *Dialogue concerning the Two Chief World Systems*, transl. Stillman Drake, Berkeley and Los Angeles, University of California Press, 1970 (1967), p. 112.
2 François Lyotard, quoted by Robert F. Berkhofer, Jr, *Beyond the Great Story: History as Text and Discourse*, London, Harvard University Press, 1997, p. 220.
3 Berkhofer, *Great Story*, p. 224.
4 Pico della Mirandola, *Oration on the Dignity of Man* (c. 1486), in Ernst Cassirer, Paul Oskar Kristeller, John Herman Randall Jr. (eds), *The Renaissance Philosophy of Man*, London, University of Chicago Press, 1948, pp. 224–5 (my emphases).
5 Justus Jonus, quoted by James Wood, *The Broken Estate: Essays on Literature and Belief*, London, Jonathan Cape, 1999, pp. 10–11 (my emphasis).
6 René Descartes, *Principles of Philosophy* (1644), in *The Philosophical Writings of Descartes*, transl. John Cottingham *et al.* 2 vols, Cambridge, Cambridge University Press, 1985, vol. 1, pp. 205–6 (my emphasis); Kant and Sartre, quoted by Nicholas Lash, *The Beginning and the End of 'Religion'*, Cambridge, Cambridge University Press, 1996, pp. 83, 239.

7 J. Huizinga, *The Waning of the Middle Ages*, Harmondsworth, Penguin, 1965, p. 207; Keith Wrightson, *English Society 1580–1680*, London, Hutchinson, 1982, p. 17.

8 See Elizabeth Deeds Ermarth, *Realism and Consensus in the English Novel*, Edinburgh, Edinburgh University Press, 1998, pp. 12–13.

9 Saint Anselm, quoted by R. W. Southern, *The Making of the Middle Ages*, London, Grey Arrow, 1959, p. 109.

10 William Shakespeare, *Troilus and Cressida*, Act 1, scene 3, lines 109–10.

11 Erich Fromm, *The Fear of Freedom*, London, Routledge, 1960, p. 143.

12 Thomas Edwards, *Gangraena: or a Catalogue and Discovery of many of the Errors, Heresies, Blasphemies, and Pernicious Practices of the Sectaries of this Time*, London, 1646.

13 Blaise Pascal, *Pensées*, transl. W. F. Trotter, London, J. M. Dent & Sons, 1931 (1670), no. 205.

14 Pascal, *Pensées*, no. 427.

15 Pascal, *Pensées*, no. 72.

16 John Donne, *Ignatius His Conclave*, facsimile reprint, Norwood, NJ, Walter J. Johnson, 1977 (1611), p. 14; 'An Anatomie of the World: The First Anniversary', line 213, in H. J. C. Grierson (ed.), *The Poems of John Donne*, London, Oxford University Press, 1929, p. 214; Nietzsche, *On the Genealogy of Morals*, transl. Walter Kaufmann and R. J. Hollingdale, New York, Vintage, 1969, p. 155.

17 Sir John Fortescue, quoted by E. M. W. Tillyard, *The Elizabethan World Picture*, London, Chatto & Windus, 1945, p. 24.

18 *De Stella Nova* (where Kepler was referring to Bruno's speculations about infinity), quoted by Paolo Rossi in A. G. Debus (ed.), *Science, Medicine and Society in the Renaissance*, 2 vols, New York, Science History Publications, 1972, vol. 2, p. 144.

19 John Milton, 'Paradise Lost' (1669), Book II, lines 891–4.

20 Bernard de Fontenelle, *A Week's Conversation on the Plurality of Worlds*, London, A. Bettesworth, 1737, pp. 127, 129.

21 Jacques Monod, *Chance and Necessity*, Glasgow, William Collins & Sons, 1972, pp. 161, 160, 167.

22 Stephen Jay Gould, *Wonderful Life*, London, Hutchinson, 1990, p. 323.

23 John Dryden, *Of Dramatick Poesie*, ed. James T. Boulton, London, Oxford University Press, 1964 (1668), p. 44.

24 Leonardo and Kepler are helpfully juxtaposed by John Hedley Brooke, *Science and Religion: Some Historical Perspectives*, Cambridge, Cambridge University Press, 1991, p. 120; Friedrich Hoffmann, *Fundamenta Medicinae*, transl. Lester S. King, London, Macdonald, 1971 (1695), p. 5 (my emphasis); Fontenelle, *Plurality of Worlds*, p. 10; E. J. Dijksterhuis, *The Mechanization of the World Picture*, Oxford, Oxford University Press, 1961.

25 Robert Boyle, *The Christian Virtuoso* (published 1690, but written years earlier), in *The Works*, ed. T. Birch, 6 vols, London, J. and F. Rivington, 1772, vol. 5, p. 41; see also vol. 4, pp. 76f., where Boyle claims *inter alia* that 'Mathematical and mechanical principles are the alphabet in which God wrote the world'.

26 Boyle, *The Excellency and Grounds of the Corpuscular or Mechanical Philosophy* (1674), in *The Works*, vol. 4, pp. 68–70.

27 Descartes, *Principia* (1644), quoted by Ron Millen, 'The Manifestation of Occult Qualities in the Scientific Revolution', in Margaret J. Osler and

Paul Lawrence Farber (eds), *Religion, Science, and Worldview*, Cambridge, Cambridge University Press, 1985, p. 198.

28 Fontenelle, *Plurality*, p. 10.

29 Descartes, *L'homme* (1662), quoted by A. C. Crombie, *Augustine to Galileo*, 2 vols, London, Heinemann, 1959, vol. 2, p. 246.

30 Henry Power, *Experimental Philosophy*, London, Johnson Reprint Corporation, 1966 (1664), pp. 192–3.

31 Herder, quoted in Robert M. Burns and Hugh Rayment-Pickard (eds), *Philosophies of History: From Enlightenment to Postmodernity*, Oxford, Blackwell, 2000, p. 76; David Hume, *Dialogues concerning Natural Religion*, ed. Norman Kemp Smith, Oxford, Clarendon Press, 1935, p. 176.

32 Max Weber, quoted in Lawrence E. Cahoone (ed.), *From Modernism to Postmodernism: An Anthology*, Oxford, Blackwell, 1996, p. 175; Keats, 'Lamia', Part II, line 233.

33 William Blake, 'Marginalia 1', in Alfred Kazin (ed.), *The Portable Blake*, New York, Viking, 1946, p. 583.

34 Méric Casaubon, *Of Credulity and Incredulity* (1668), pp. 25–6, quoted by Michael R. G. Spiller (ed.), *'Concerning Natural Experimental Philosophie': Méric Casaubon and the Royal Society*, The Hague, Martinus Nijhoff, 1980, p. 129.

35 Casaubon, *On Learning* (1667), and *A Letter to Peter du Moulin Concerning Natural Experimental Philosophie* (1669), in Spiller, *Casaubon*, pp. 212, 175, 174, 205.

36 Francis Bacon, *Novum Organum*, ed. F. H. Anderson, Indianapolis, Bobbs-Merrill, 1960 (1620), Epistle Dedicatory, Proem, pp. 5, 4; Descartes, *Principles of Philosophy*, Preface to the French edition, Cottingham *et al.* (eds), *Philosophical Writings*, vol. 1, p. 183; Galileo, *Dialogue*, 'To the Discerning Reader', p. 7.

37 Robert Boyle, *Certain Physiological Essays*, London, Henry Herringman, 1661, 'A Proemial Essay', p. 35.

38 Quoted by Douglas Grant, *Margaret the First: A Biography of Margaret Cavendish, Duchess of Newcastle, 1623–1673*, London, Rupert Hart-Davis, 1957, p. 143.

39 John Sergeant, *Solid Philosophy*, London, Roger Clavil, 1697, Epistle Dedicatory; Thomas Sprat, *History of the Royal Society*, London, J. Martyn, 1667, p. 340; John Sheffield, *An Essay on Poetry* (1682), as quoted by John Rogers in G. A. J. Rogers and Alan Ryan (eds), *Perspectives on Thomas Hobbes*, Oxford, Clarendon Press, 1988, p. 5.

40 Leibniz, quoted by Hugh Kearney, *Science and Change, 1500–1700*, London, Weidenfeld & Nicolson, 1971, p. 195.

41 Thomas Manningham, *Two Discourses*, London, 1681, pp. 95–6.

42 Galileo, *Dialogue*, p. 56; see also p. 112.

43 Alexander Ross, *Arcana Microcosmi*, 1652, Epistle Dedicatory, quoted by R. F. Jones, *Ancients and Moderns*, Berkeley and Los Angeles, University of California Press, 1965, p. 122.

44 Sir William Temple, 'An Essay upon the Ancient and Modern Learning', *The Battle of the Books*, ed. A. Guthkelch, London, Chatto & Windus, 1908, p. 67.

45 John Donne, 'Sermon for Whitsunday', 1628.

46 Ralph Waldo Emerson, 'Self-Reliance', in *The Works of Ralph Waldo Emerson*, 2 vols, London, G. Bell & Sons, 1913, vol. 1, p. 45.

47 Jonathan Swift, *Gulliver's Travels*, London, J. M. Dent & Sons, 1940 (1726), p. 211; see also Montaigne, 'Apology for Raimond Sebond', in D. M. Frame (ed.), *The Complete Works of Montaigne*, London, Stanford University Press, 1958, p. 429.

48 Richard Baxter, *The Reasons of the Christian Religion*, London, R. White, 1667, p. 498.

49 Charles Taylor, quoted by Stephen M. Straker, 'What is the History of Theories of Perception the History of?', in Osler and Farber (eds), *Religion*, p. 257.

50 Galileo, *Dialogue*, p. 59.

51 Straker, in Osler and Farber (eds), *Religion*, p. 259.

52 Susan Bordo, 'The Cartesian Masculinization of Thought', in Cahoone (ed.), *From Modernism*, p. 643 (emphases: first quote mine; second quote Bordo's).

53 Sprat, *History*, p. 124. See also Brian Easlea, *Witch-hunting, Magic and the New Philosophy*, Brighton, Harvester, 1980, esp. pp. 246f.; Mary Midgley, *Science as Salvation: A Modern Myth and its Meaning*, London, Routledge, 1992, chs 7 and 8.

5 OVERCOMING THE CONSTRAINTS OF MODERNISM

1 Zygmunt Bauman, *Postmodernity and its Discontents*, Cambridge, Polity, 1997, p. 168.

2 William Shakespeare, *Hamlet*, Act 4, scene 5, lines 43–4. See Pico's 'Oration on the Dignity of Man', in Ernst Cassirer, Paul Oskar Kristeller and John Herman Randall Jr (eds), *The Renaissance Philosophy of Man*, London, University of Chicago Press, 1948, p. 225.

3 Ralph Waldo Emerson, 'Circles', in *The Works of Ralph Waldo Emerson*, London, G. Bell & Sons, 1913, p. 166.

4 T. S. Eliot, 'Four Quartets', in *Collected Poems, 1909–1962*, London, Faber & Faber, 1963, p. 194.

5 Nicholas Lash, *The Begining and the End of 'Religion'*, Cambridge, Cambridge University Press, 1996, p. 170.

6 See, for example, Frith's painting, *The Railway Station*, 1862.

7 The Musée Depuytre already existed for this purpose (Hayward Gallery, London, exhibition notes, October 2000).

8 Marcel Duchamp, quoted by Edward Lucie-Smith, in C. B. Cox and A. E. Dyson (eds), *The Twentieth Century Mind*, 3 vols, Oxford, Oxford University Press, 1972, vol. 2, p. 481 (emphasis in original).

9 Fredric Jameson, quoted in Lawrence E. Cahoone (ed.), *From Modernism to Postmodernism: An Anthology*, Oxford, Blackwell, 1996, p. 559.

10 News reports, October 2000. See also questions raised concerning the London Jazz Festival, November 2000: 'Should pop stars sing jazz?', Norman Lebrecht in the *Daily Telegraph*, 31 October 2001. Josef Skvorecky is quoted by Linda Hutcheon, *A Poetics of Postmodernism: History, Theory, Fiction*, London, Routledge, 1988, p. 132.

11 See Richard Kearney, *On Stories*, London, Routledge, 2002, pp. 9, 84–5.

12 Leopold von Ranke (1885), quoted by John H. Arnold, *History: A Very Short Introduction*, Oxford, Oxford University Press, 2000, p. 34.

13 Hutcheon, *Poetics*, pp. 225 (my emphases), 112; Robert F. Berkhofer Jr, *Beyond the Great Story: History as Text and Discourse*, London, Harvard University Press, 1997, p. 67.

14 Hutcheon, *Poetics*, p. 93 (emphasis in original). See also Richard Kearney, who suggests that if mythic narrative 'mutated over time into two main branches: *historical* and *fictional*', then historiographic metafiction may represent their cyclical mutation back to their original unitary (mythic) origins (*On Stories*, p. 9).

15 Catherine Morland in *Northanger Abbey* (c. 1803), ch. 14 – a quotation used by E. H. Carr at the head of his *What is History?*, Harmondsworth, Penguin, 1964.

16 Berkhofer, *Great Story*, p. 280 (my emphasis); Simon Schama, *Dead Certainties (Unwarranted Speculations)*, London, Granta, 1991, pp. 327, 320 (my emphases).

17 See Shannon L. Rogers, 'The Historian of Wessex', *Rethinking History: The Journal of Theory and Practice* 5, 2001, pp. 217–32.

18 Berkhofer, *Great Story*, p. 197.

19 John Locke, *An Essay concerning Human Understanding*, London, Thomas Basset, 1690, Book 3, ch. 6, para. 36.

20 Charles Bonnet, *Contemplation de la Nature* (2nd edn, 1769), I, 28, quoted by Arthur O. Lovejoy, *The Great Chain of Being*, New York, Harper & Row, 1960, p. 231.

21 Johann Gottlieb Fichte, quoted by Isaiah Berlin, *The Sense of Reality: Studies in Ideas and their History*, ed. Henry Hardy, London, Chatto & Windus, 1996, p. 243.

22 Friedrich Schiller, quoted by Berlin, *Sense of Reality*, pp. 184, 238 (my emphases).

23 Luce Irigaray, quoted in Cahoone (ed.), *From Modernism*, pp. 465–6 (emphasis in original).

24 Lash, *Beginning and End*, p. 112 (my emphasis).

25 Elizabeth Deeds Ermarth, *Realism and Consensus in the English Novel*, Edinburgh, Edinburgh University Press, 1998, pp. 165–6, 56.

26 R. D. Laing, *The Divided Self*, Harmondsworth, Penguin, 1990 (1960), p. 26. A similar point has been made in relation to anthropology, where too it is necessary to abandon the position of 'transcendental observer'. So R. S. Khare: 'It is as if the anthropologist's self requires the Other to sacrifice itself, to let the anthropologist become a distinct "text-maker"' (quoted by Berkhofer, *Great Story*, p. 196).

27 Kearney, *On Stories*, p. 102.

28 Captain America, quoted by Kearney, *On Stories*, p. 114.

29 Jean-Paul Sartre, *Nausea*, transl. Robert Baldick, Harmondsworth, Penguin, 1965, pp. 124, 63.

30 Sartre, *Nausea*, pp. 113–15, 225 (my emphasis).

31 The experimental results of J. S. Bruner and Leo Postman (1949) are recorded by T. S. Kuhn, *The Structure of Scientific Revolutions*, London, University of Chicago Press, 1964, pp. 63–4.

32 Cited by Arthur Koestler, *The Act of Creation*, London, Hutchinson, 1964, p. 189.

33 Jan Patočka, *Heretical Essays*, ed. James Dodd, Peru, Illinois, Open Court, 1996, pp. 49, 56–7, 99. I am grateful to Aviezer Tucker for drawing my attention to Patočka's work.

34 Patočka, *Heretical Essays*, pp. 46, 82, 141, 143; cf. also pp. 103, 134.

35 Emerson, 'Self-Reliance', in *Works*, pp. 31–2, 30.

36 Galileo, *Dialogue concerning the Two Chief World Systems*, transl. Stillman Drake, Berkeley and Los Angeles, University of California Press, 1970 (1967), p. 55; Joseph Glanvill, 'The Agreement of Reason and Religion', in *Essays on Several Important Subjects in Philosophy and Religion*, London, 1676, p. 22.

37 Blaise Pascal, *Pensées*, transl. W. F. Trotter, London J. M. Dent & Sons, 1931 (1670), no. 384; William Blake, 'The Marriage of Heaven and Hell', in Alfred Kazin (ed.), *The Portable Blake*, New York, Viking, 1946, p. 250.

38 G. M. Trevelyan, quoted by Stefan Collini, 'Writing "the National History": Trevelyan and after', in *English Pasts: Essays in History and Culture*, Oxford, Oxford University Press, 1999, p. 37.

39 See Ermarth, *Realism and Consensus*, pp. 128f.

40 T. S. Eliot, quoted by Adam Phillips, 'The Soul of Man under Psychoanalysis', *London Review of Books*, 29 November 2001, p. 20.

41 Elsie Clews Parsons, quoted by Barbara Taylor, *London Review of Books*, 3 January 2002, p. 3; Salman Rushdie, quoted by Hutcheon, Poetics, p. 227; Arthur O. Lovejoy, *Essays in the Historiography of Ideas*, Baltimore, Johns Hopkins, 1948, p. xvi.

42 Eliot, *Collected Poems*, p. 199.

43 Thomas Hobbes, *Leviathan*, London, J. M. Dent, 1914 (1651), Part 4, ch. 46, pp. 367–8 (emphasis in original)

44 Samuel Parker, *A Free and Impartial Censure of the Platonick Philosophie*, Oxford, 1666, p. 11.

45 Locke, *Essay*, Book 1, ch. 1, paras 4 and 5; Alexander Pope, 'Essay on Man', Epistle 1, lines 189–90, 193–4, in *The Poetical Works*, ed. Adolphus W. Ward, London, Macmillan, 1908, p. 197.

46 Ludwig Wittgenstein, *Tractatus Logico-Philosphicus*, London, Routledge, 1961 (1921), p. 151.

47 Ihab Hassan, quoted in Cahoone (ed.), *From Modernism*, p. 383.

48 Kuhn, *Structure*, p. 79.

49 Filippo Tommaso Marinetti, 'Manifesto of Futurism' (1909), quoted in Cahoone (ed.), *From Modernism*, p. 187.

50 L. Dooley's report, quoted by Laing, *Divided Self*, p. 109.

51 Erich Maria Remarque, *All Quiet on the Western Front* (1929), transl. A. W. Wheen, London, Putnam, 1954, p. 139 (my emphasis).

52 Virginia Woolf, *Between the Acts*, London, Granada, 1978 (1941), p. 11.

53 Lawrence Stone (1987), quoted by Anna Green and Kathleen Troup (eds), *The Houses of History*, Manchester, Manchester University Press, 1999, p. 204 (my emphasis); Flaubert, quoted by David Harvey, *The Condition of Postmodernity: An Enquiry into the Origins of Cultural Change*, Oxford, Blackwell, 1989, p. 263; James Wood, *The Broken Estate: Essays on Literature and Belief*, London, Jonathan Cape, 1999, p. 100.

54 Howard Pederson, quoted in Green and Troup, *Houses of History*, p. 285 (my emphasis); and on the need for a multiplicity of times, see Berkhofer, *Great Story*, p. 271.

55 Braudel's chronologies, as formulated in the Preface to his *The Mediter-ranean and the Mediterranean World in the Age of Philip II*, are discussed by Berkhofer, *Great Story*, pp. 271–2.
56 Ermarth, *Realism and Consensus*, pp. 101–3.
57 Ermarth, *Realism and Consensus*, pp. 143, 112.
58 See Burns and Rayment-Pickard (eds), *Philosophies of History*, pp. 131–2.
59 Ermarth, *Realism and Consensus*, p. 125.
60 Goethe, quoted by Idris Parry, *Animals of Silence*, London, Oxford University Press, 1972, p. 68 (emphasis in original).

6 HISTORY IN POSTMODERNITY: FROM FEAR TO FREEDOM

1 Friedrich Nietzsche, *The Gay Science* (1882), quoted by J. J. Clarke, *The Tao of the West: Western Transformations of Taoist Thought*, London, Routledge, 2000, p. ix.
2 J. J. Clarke, *Tao*, p. 28, and *The Oriental Enlightenment: The Encounter between Asian and Western Thought*, London, Routledge, 1997, p. 160; Nicholas Lash, *The Beginning and the End of 'Religion'*, Cambridge, Cambridge University Press, 1996, p. 181.
3 W. B. Yeats, 'The Second Coming', in *The Collected Poems*, London, Macmillan, 1950, p. 211.
4 Ralph Waldo Emerson, 'Circles', in *The Works of Ralph Waldo Emerson*, London, G. Bell & Sons, 1913, vol. 1, pp. 167, 162, 168 (my emphasis); Friedrich Nietzsche, *On the Genealogy of Morals*, transl. Walter Kaufmann and R. J. Hollingdale, New York, Vintage, 1969, p. 155; see also Chapter 4 above.
5 Boniface VIII in 1302, quoted by John Hick, *God and the Universe of Faiths: Essays in the Philosophy of Religion*, London, Macmillan, 1973, p. 120 – a reference for which I am indebted to John Ibbett.
6 Hick, *God and Universe*, pp. 131, 141.
7 Nietzsche, quoted by Clarke, *Tao*, p. 10.
8 Elizabeth Deeds Ermarth, *Realism and Consensus in the English Novel*, Edinburgh, Edinburgh University Press, 1998, p. 47.
9 Paul Valéry, 'The Course in Poetics: First Lesson, transl. Jackson Matthews (1940), in Brewster Ghiselin (ed.), *The Creative Process: A Symposium*, Berkeley and Los Angeles, University of California Press, 1952, p. 105.
10 Nicholas Lash, *Beginning and End*, p. 162.
11 Blaise Pascal, *Pensées*, transl. W. F. Trotter, London, J. M. Dent & Sons, 1931 (1670), no. 381.
12 Gottfried Wilhelm Leibniz, quoted by Arthur O. Lovejoy, *The Great Chain of Being*, New York, Harper & Row, 1960, p. 294.
13 Jean-Paul Sartre, *The Wall* (1939), in Walter Kaufmann (ed.), *Existentialism from Dostoevsky to Sartre*, New York, Meridian, 1956, pp. 223–40.
14 Zygmunt Bauman, *Postmodernity and its Discontents*, Cambridge, Polity, 1997, p. 111.
15 Paul Klee (1879–1940), exhibition at the Hayward Gallery, London, January 2002.

16 See Clarke, *Oriental Enlightenment*, p. 103.

17 Paul Feyerabend, quoted by Ian Hacking, *London Review of Books*, 22 June 2000, p. 29.

18 Minsoo Kang, 'The Use of Dreaming for the Study of History', *Rethinking History: The Journal of Theory and Practice* 5, 2001, 275–83.

19 Bauman, *Postmodernity*, p. 107; T. S. Eliot, *The Use of Poetry and the Use of Criticism*, London, Faber & Faber, 1933, p. 155; Marcel Proust, quoted in Natural History Museum publicity, March 2000.

20 Emerson, 'Self-Reliance', in *Works*, p 36.

21 John Hick, *Faith and Knowledge*, 2nd edn, London, Macmillan, 1967, p. 103. I am grateful to John Ibbett for letting me read and make use of his unpublished M.Phil. thesis, 'The Concept of Faith in Relation to Epistemology', University of Leeds, 1980. I am particularly indebted to him for the following paragraphs referring to the works of John Hick, Bernard Lonergan and Michel de Certeau.

22 Michel de Certeau, *Mystic Fable*, p. 289, quoted by Lash, *Beginning and End*, pp. 180–1.

23 Ihab Hassan, quoted in Lawrence E. Cahoone (ed.), *From Modernism to Postmodernism: An Anthology*, Oxford, Blackwell, 1996, p. 395.

24 Virginia Woolf, *To the Lighthouse*, London, J. M. Dent, 1938 (1927), pp. 38f.

25 Francesco Algarotti, *Sir Isaac Newton's Philosophy Explained for the Use of the Ladies*, transl. Elizabeth Carter, London, E. Cave, 1739, vol. 1, p. 231.

26 Isaiah Berlin, *The Sense of Reality: Studies in Ideas and Their History*, ed. Henry Hardy, London, Chatto & Windus, 1996, p. 59 (my emphases).

27 Herbert Butterfield, *The Whig Interpretation of History*, Harmondsworth, Penguin, 1973 (1931), pp. 52–3.

28 Berlin, *Sense of Reality*, pp. 60, 67, 70.

29 G. R. Elton, *Return to Essentials*, Cambridge, Cambridge University Press, 1991, p. 24.

30 J. H. Plumb, quoted in Elton's obituary, *Daily Telegraph*, 23 October 2001.

31 Jean-François Lyotard, quoted by Bauman, *Postmodernity*, p. 168.

32 Thomas Hobbes, *Human Nature* (1650), in Richard S. Peters (ed.), *Body, Man, and Citizen*, London, Collier-Macmillan, 1962, p. 194.

33 Filippo Tommaso Marinetti, 'The Founding and Manifesto of Futurism', quoted in Cahoone (ed.), *From Modernism*, p. 188.

34 Virginia Woolf, *Between the Acts*, London, Granada, 1978 (1941), p. 114.

35 Jane Austen, quoted by Anna Green and Kathleen Troup (eds), *The Houses of History*, Manchester, Manchester University Press, 1999, p. 236 (my emphases); Emerson, 'Self-Reliance', in *Works*, p. 30.

36 Lash, *Beginning and End*, p. 207.

37 Martin Heidegger, quoted by J. Appleby, L. Hunt and M. Jacob, *Telling the Truth about History*, New York, W. W. Norton, 1994, pp. 210–11.

38 See Walter J. Ong, *Orality and Literacy*, London, Routledge, 1982.

39 David Harvey, *The Condition of Postmodernity: An Enquiry into the Origins of Cultural Change*, Oxford, Blackwell, 1989, p. 308; Robert A. Rosenstone, *Visions of the Past: The Challenge of Film to Our Idea of History*, London, Harvard University Press, 1995, pp. 187, 133, 39, 63, 47 (my emphasis), 199.

40 Plato, *Phaedrus* 244–5, in B. Jowett (ed.), *The Dialogues of Plato*, 5 vols, Oxford, Clarendon Press, 1875, vol. 2, pp. 121–2.

41 Minsoo Kang, 'Use of Dreaming', p. 281.
42 Friedrich August von Kekulé, quoted by Koestler, *Act of Creation*, p. 118.
43 See Koestler, *Act of Creation*, pp. 166–7.
44 Jan Patočka, *Heretical Essays in the Philosophy of History*, ed. James Dodd, Peru, Illinois, Open Court, 1996, p. 118 (my emphasis); see Chapter 2 above.
45 Stefan Collini, 'Writing "the National History": Trevelyan and after', in *English Pasts: Essays in History and Culture*, Oxford, Oxford University Press, 1999, p. 18.
46 Ugo Foscolo (1802), quoted in A. K. Thorlby, *The Romantic Movement*, London, Longmans Green, 1966, p. 151.
47 Lyn Hunt, quoted by Robert F. Berkhofer Jr, *Beyond the Great Story: History as Text and Discourse*, London, Harvard University Press, 1997, pp. 74–5.
48 Berkhofer, *Great Story*, p. x (my emphasis).
49 Modris Eksteins, *Walking since Daybreak: A Story of Eastern Europe, World War II, and the Heart of the Twentieth Century*, London, Macmillan, 2000, p. xxi.
50 Richard Price, 'Practices of Historical Narrative', *Rethinking History: The Journal of Theory and Practice* 5, 2001, pp. 359, 361.
51 Sven Lindqvist, *A History of Bombing*, transl. Linda Haverty Rugg, London, Granta, 2001, 'How to read this book' (unpaginated).
52 I am obviously indebted, in this and the following paragraph, to Richard Kearney's fascinating study, *On Stories*, London, Routledge, 2002; quotations are taken from pp. 65, 25, 169, 172.
53 An exhibition of Stan Douglas's work was held at the Serpentine Gallery, London, in March 2002. For an insightful review, see Richard Dorment, *Daily Telegraph*, 6 March 2002.
54 Eksteins, *Walking since Daybreak*, p. 16 (my emphasis); Graham Swift, *Waterland*, London, Picador, 1992, p. 10 – a reference for which I thank John Ibbett, from whose paper 'The Significance of the Past' it is taken.
55 Swift, *Waterland*, p. 106.
56 See further Patrick Joyce, 'The Return of History: Postmodernism and the Politics of Academic History in Britain', *Past and Present* 158, 1998, 207–35.
57 Henry A. Giroux, 'Modernism, Postmodernism, and Feminism: Rethinking the Boundaries of Educational Discourse', in Henry A. Giroux (ed.), *Postmodernism, Feminism, and Cultural Politics: Redrawing Educational Boundaries*, Albany, State University of New York Press, 1991, p. 47. Further quotations from pp. 48, 49, 52.
58 By A. Michnik, quoted by Giroux, 'Modernism', p. 45.
59 Emerson, 'Circles', in *Works*, p. 172.
60 Bryan D. Palmer and Gertrude Himmelfarb, quoted by Berkhofer, *Great Story*, pp. 15 and 67 respectively (my emphases).
61 Patočka, *Heretical Essays*, pp. 58–9.
62 Patočka, *Heretical Essays*, p. 69.
63 Julian Barnes, *A History of the World in 10½ Chapters*, Basingstoke, Picador, 1990, p. 245.
64 St Augustine, sermon quoted by Adam Phillips, 'The Soul of Man under Psychoanalysis', *London Review of Books*, 29 November 2001, p. 22.
65 Hugh Rayment-Pickard, 'Derrida and Fidelity to History'. This paper, given at a conference in June 2001, is forthcoming in *The Journal for the History of*

European Ideas. I am grateful to the author for giving me a typescript before publication, and am obviously indebted to him for the following paragraphs.

66 Mary Midgley, *Science as Salvation*, London, Routledge, 1992, p. 50. Further quotations from pp. 57 and 65.
67 Patočka, *Heretical Essays*, p. 60.
68 Patočka, *Heretical Essays*, pp. 49, 61.
69 Patočka, *Heretical Essays*, p. 77 (my emphasis).
70 Robert Boyle, 'A Proemial Essay', in *Certain Physiological Essays*, London, Henry Herringman, 1661, p. 9.

FURTHER READING

This highly selective list is designed to be not too dauntingly off-putting but to include books (and a few articles) that can be recommended as readable and/or intellectually stimulating on the main issues treated in this book – a book that derives from my own earlier thinking on the nature(s) and purpose(s) of history, on which see *History: What & Why?: Ancient, Modern, and Postmodern Perspectives*, 2nd edn, London, Routledge, 2001 (1996), and *Why Bother with History?: Ancient, Modern, and Postmodern Motivations*, Harlow, Longman, 2000.

On postmodernism itself, there is of course by now a vast library. Barry Smart, *Postmodernity*, London, Routledge, 1993, provides one short entrée; but the best overall introduction that I've found is David Harvey, *The Condition of Postmodernity*, Oxford, Blackwell, 1989 – a readable historical/cultural contextualisation, with wide-ranging interdisciplinary references. As evidenced in this book, a wonderful quarry of source-material can be mined from Lawrence E. Cahoone (ed.), *From Modernism to Postmodernism: An Anthology*, Oxford, Blackwell, 1996; and other helpful collections are provided in Thomas Docherty (ed.), *Postmodernism: A Reader*, Hemel Hempstead, Harvester Wheatsheaf, 1993 – including what are claimed as 'the most influential and the most substantial essays which have shaped the postmodern question'; Charles Jencks (ed.), *The Post-Modern Reader*, London, Academy, 1992; Stuart Sim (ed.), *The Icon Critical Dictionary of Postmodern Thought*, Cambridge, Icon, 1998; and Joyce Appleby *et al.* (eds), *Knowledge and Postmodernism in Historical Perspective*, London, Routledge, 1996 – including texts from the seventeenth century to the present. Particularly recommendable from the standpoint of social/cultural theory are the works of Zygmunt Bauman: see, for example, *Postmodernity and its Discontents*, Cambridge, Polity, 1997; also interesting is Anthony Giddens, *Modernity and Self-Identity: Self and Society in the Late Modern Age*, Cambridge, Polity, 1991;

and Nikolas Rose, *Governing the Soul: The Shaping of the Private Self*, 2nd edn, London, Free Association Books, 1999. On pomophobia specifically, I know of no book that addresses the matter directly, but there is some extremely interesting material that bears on this issue in Barbara Herrnstein Smith, *Belief and Resistance: Dynamics of Contemporary Intellectual Controversy*, London, Harvard University Press, 1997; and so far as history is concerned manifestations can be found in such works as Keith Windschuttle, *The Killing of History: How Literary Critics and Social Theorists are Murdering Our Past*, New York, Free Press, 1997 – an impassioned and readable plea to save history and Western culture more generally; Elizabeth Fox-Genovese and Elisabeth Lasch-Quinn (eds), *Reconstructing History*, London, Routledge, 1999 – a collection of essays by historians bonded by their common concern to transcend postmodernity; and Arthur Marwick, *The New Nature of History: Knowledge, Evidence, Language*, Basingstoke, Palgrave, 2001 – a case-study for those interested in assessing responses to 'theory' by the older generation of empirical historians.

On postmodernism and history, the classic introduction remains Keith Jenkins, *Rethinking History*, London, Routledge, 1991; and see also the development of Jenkins' provocative thought in *On 'What is History?'*, London, Routledge, 1995; *Why History? Ethics and Postmodernity*, London, Routledge, 1999 – which includes helpful introductions to such central thinkers as Derrida, Baudrillard, Lyotard and Hayden White; and *Refiguring History*, London, Routledge, 2002. Other possibilities include Alun Munslow, *Deconstructing History*, London, Routledge, 1997 – a clear introduction to current debates; Lutz Niethammer, *Posthistoire: Has History Come to an End?*, transl. Patrick Camiller, London, Verso, 1992; and for an interesting assessment of postmodernism's relationship with history, together with its wider implications in and for the academy, Patrick Joyce, 'The Return of History: Postmodernism and the Politics of Academic History in Britain', *Past and Present* 158, 1998, 207–35. The works of Hayden White are central to any consideration of history's relationship with postmodernism: see especially *Metahistory*, Baltimore, Johns Hopkins, 1973; *Tropics of Discourse: Essays in Cultural Criticism*, London, Johns Hopkins, 1978; *The Content of the Form* Baltimore, Johns Hopkins, 1987; *Figural Realism: Studies in the Mimesis Effect*, Baltimore, Johns Hopkins, 1999. On the development of American historiography up to postmodernity, see the detailed and readable account (focused as the subtitle implies) in Peter Novick, *That Noble Dream: The 'Objectivity Question' and the American Historical Profession*, Cambridge, Cambridge University Press, 1988; and another excellent historiographical overview is provided by Robert F. Berkhofer Jr, *Beyond the Great Story: History as Text and Discourse*, London, Harvard University Press, 1997. On Foucault more specifically, see Alec McHoul and Wendy Grace, *A Foucault Primer: Discourse, Power and the Subject*, London, UCL Press, 1995; and for Foucault in relation specifically to history, the useful and diverse collection of essays in Jan Goldstein (ed.), *Foucault and the Writing of History*, Oxford, Blackwell, 1994. An invaluable collection of texts representing the main positions in contemporary debates is provided by Keith Jenkins (ed.), *The Postmodern History Reader*, London, Routledge, 1997; Ewa Domanska, *Encounters: Philosophy of History after Postmodernism* Charlottesville, University Press of Virginia, 1998, presents a collection of interviews with eminent practitioners, reasonably claimed as 'the best meditation that you are likely to find on the state of historiography at the end of the twentieth century'; and for a philosophical heavyweight to carry you into the twenty-first, try Frank Ankersmit, *Historical Representation*, Stanford, Stanford University Press, 2001 – which includes discussion of such vital historiographical topics as language, narrative, memory and (centrally) representation.

For feminist and postcolonial undermining of history's centrism, useful introductions can be found in Anna Green and Kathleen Troup (eds), *The Houses of History: A Critical Reader in Twentieth-Century History and Theory*, Manchester, Manchester University Press, 1999. On feminism, a particularly lucid entrée is provided by Chris Weedon, *Feminist Practice and Poststructuralist Theory*, Oxford, Blackwell, 1987; while the more adventurous could progress to Judith Butler, *Gender Trouble: Feminism and the Subversion of Identity*, London, Routledge, 1990; Joan Kelly, *Women, History and Theory: The Essays of Joan Kelly*, Chicago, University of Chicago, 1984; Diane Elam and Robyn Wiegman (eds), *Feminism Beside Itself*, London, Routledge, 1995 (including essays on the identity and history of feminism); Joan Wallach Scott (ed.), *Feminism and History*, Oxford, Oxford University Press, 1996; and (particularly interesting in relation to the history of historiography – and accessible, too) Bonnie G. Smith, *The Gender of History: Men, Women, and Historical Practice*, London, Harvard University Press, 1998. (We await Keith Jenkins and Sue Morgan (eds), *The Feminist History Reader*, London, Routledge, forthcoming.) For postcolonialism, Patrich Williams and Laura Chrisman (eds), *Colonial Discourse and Post-colonial Theory: A Reader*, Hemel Hempstead, Harvester Wheatsheaf, 1993, provides a useful collection of texts, with introductions that commendably aim at overall accessibility; Edward Said, *Orientalism*, London, Routledge, 1978, marks a turning- or starting-point for postcolonial studies; and see also his

Culture and Imperialism, London, Chatto & Windus, 1993. More difficult, but potentially rewarding, are Homi K. Bhabha, *The Location of Culture*, London, Routledge, 1994; and Robert Young, *White Mythologies: Writing History and the West*, London, Routledge, 1990.

Some of the antecedents claimed for postmodernism in Chapter 3 (together with other wider implications) can be studied further in Stuart Sim (ed.), *Postmodern Thought*, Cambridge, Icon, 1998; works by Richard Rorty are important – as, for example, *Contingency, Irony, and Solidarity*, Cambridge, Cambridge University Press, 1989, and essays collected in *Philosophy and Social Hope*, Harmondsworth, Penguin, 1999; and a selective use can be made of the intellectual quarry presented by Robert M. Burns and Hugh Rayment-Pickard (eds), *Philosophies of History: From Enlightenment to Postmodernity*, Oxford, Blackwell, 2000. For the development of scepticism more specifically, the classic is Richard H. Popkin, *The History of Scepticism from Erasmus to Spinoza*, Berkeley and Los Angeles, University of California Press, 1979; and see also Barbara Shapiro, *Probability and Certainty in Seventeenth-Century England*, Princeton, Princeton University Press, 1983. Those interested in getting to the sources should try Sextus Empiricus, *Outlines of Pyrrhonism*, transl. R. G. Bury, London, Heinemann, 1967; for the early modern period, Montaigne's essay 'Apology for Raymond Sebond', in Donald M. Frame (ed.), *The Complete Works of Montaigne*, London, Stanford University Press, 1958, pp. 318–457. For incipient historical pyrrhonism, particularly interesting are Henry St John, Lord Bolingbroke, *Letters on the Study and Use of History*, London, A. Millar, 1752 (reprinted Alexander Murray, 1870); and Friedrich Nietzsche, 'On the Uses and Disadvantages of History for Life', in Daniel Breazeale (ed.), *Untimely Meditations*, Cambridge, Cambridge University Press, 1997. On language, a treatment that is both readable and relevant to historians is provided by Walter J. Ong, *Orality and Literacy: The Technologizing of the Word*, London, Routledge, 1982; while the braver might try D. Attridge, 'Language as History/History as Language', in D. Attridge, G. Bennington and R. Young (eds), *Post-structuralism and the Question of History*, Cambridge, Cambridge University Press, 1987. For Romanticism, H. G. Schenk, *The Mind of the European Romantics: An Essay in Cultural History*, Oxford, Oxford University Press, 1979, is culturally wide-ranging and considers some central themes of Romanticism as a European movement; while a more nation-orientated approach is adopted by Maurice Cranston, *The Romantic Movement*, Oxford, Blackwell, 1994, who has chapters on German, English, French, Italian, and Spanish varieties, and by Roy Porter and Mikuláš Teich (eds), *Romanticism in National Context*,

Cambridge, Cambridge University Press, 1988, where the picture is extended to include Wales, Ireland, Greece, Switzerland, Scandinavia, the Netherlands, Hungary, Russia and Poland. On Oriental thought, see (for its early recognition of the East's importance) Fritz Capra, *The Tao of Physics: An Exploration of the Parallels between Modern Physics and Eastern Mysticism*, Oxford, Fontana, 1976; and the lucid, suggestive expositions by J. J. Clarke: *Oriental Enlightenment: The Encounter between Asian and Western Thought*, London, Routledge, 1997; and *The Tao of the West: Western Transformations of Taoist Thought*, London, Routledge, 2000.

On the claimed parallel early modern intellectual revolution, T. S. Kuhn, *The Copernican Revolution*, Cambridge, Massachusetts, Harvard University Press, 1966, remains a useful guide to astronomy and cosmology; and for early feminist approaches to the scientific revolution more generally, Carolyn Merchant, *The Death of Nature: Women, Ecology, and the Scientific Revolution*, San Francisco, HarperCollins, 1980; and Brian Easlea, *Magic, Witch-hunting and the New Philosophy*, Brighton, Harvester, 1980. On Renaissance individualism, Ernst Cassirer, Paul Oskar Kristeller, and John Herman Randall (eds), *The Renaissance Philosophy of Man*, London, University of Chicago, 1948, contains some central texts; and the classic on the angst-ridden response to modern individualism remains Erich Fromm, *The Fear of Freedom*, London, Routledge, 1960.

Some constraints of modernism are disposed of by Elizabeth Deeds Ermarth, *Sequel to History: Postmodernism and the Crisis of Representational Time*, Princeton, Princeton University Press, 1992, which presents some intellectually exciting ideas on time in postmodernity; and on possible futures (or not) for history in postmodernity, see Frank Ankersmit and Hans Kellner (eds), *A New Philosophy of History*, London, Reaktion Books, 1995; Alex Callinicos, *Theories and Narratives: Reflections on the Philosophy of History*, Cambridge, Polity, 1995; Brian Fay, Philip Pomper and Richard T. Vann (eds), *History and Theory: Contemporary Readings*, Oxford, Blackwell, 1998; Frank Füredi, *Mythical Past, Elusive Future*, London, Pluto, 1992; and Jan Patočka, *Heretical Essays in the Philosophy of History*, ed. James Dodd, Peru, Illinois, Open Court, 1996.

For inter-disciplinary perspectives on fictionality and narrative, Richard Kearney, *On Stories*, London, Routledge, 2002, is particularly good; and (though perhaps less immediately accessible in parts) Linda Hutcheon, *A Poetics of Postmodernism: History, Theory, Fiction*, London, Routledge,

1988. Further stimulating thoughts on possible future directions for historical study in relation to film can be seen in a collection of essays by Robert A. Rosenstone, *Visions of the Past: The Challenge of Film to Our Idea of History*, London, Harvard University Press, 1995; and for postmodern experimentation with narrative, a good example is Sven Lindqvist, *A History of Bombing*, transl. Linda Haverty Rugg, London, Granta, 2001. Those interested in theological parallels and models should try Nicholas Lash, *The Beginning and the End of 'Religion'*, Cambridge, Cambridge University Press, 1996, which is more readable and thought-provoking than its title might suggest. Finally, for up-to-the-minute theory and some examples of practice, see *Rethinking History: The Journal of Theory and Practice*, ed. Alun Munslow (UK) and Robert A. Rosenstone (USA); and we await Keith Jenkins and Alun Munslow (eds) *The Nature of History Reader*, London, Routledge, forthcoming.

Most of the above contain their own bibliographies and/or suggestions for further reading; so that should suffice for one lifetime . . .

BIBLIOGRAPHY

Algarotti, Francesco, *Sir Isaac Newton's Philosophy Explained for the Use of the Ladies*, transl. Elizabeth Carter, London, E. Cave, 1739.

Anon, *Some Remarks on the Letters of the Late Lord Bolingbroke*, London, 1752.

Appleby, J., Hunt, L. and Jacob, M., *Telling the Truth about History*, New York, W. W. Norton, 1994.

Aristotle, *Metaphysics*, transl. H. Tredennick, London, Harvard University Press, 1933.

Arnold, John H., *History: A Very Short Introduction*, Oxford, Oxford University Press, 2000.

Bacon, Francis, *Novum Organum*, ed. F. H. Anderson, Indianapolis, Bobbs-Merrill, 1960 (1620).

Baker, Thomas, *Reflections upon Learning*, London, A. Bosvile, 1699.

Barnes, Julian, *A History of the World in 10½ Chapters*, Basingstoke, Picador, 1990.

Bauman, Zygmunt, *Postmodernity and its Discontents*, Cambridge, Polity, 1997.

Baxter, Richard, *The Reasons of the Christian Religion*, London, R. White, 1667.

Bayle, Pierre, *Dictionary*, English transl., 4 vols, London, C. Harper, 1710– .

Bayle, Pierre, *Historical and Critical Dictionary*, ed. R. H. Popkin, New York, Bobbs-Merrill, 1965.

Berkhofer, Robert F. Jr, *Beyond the Great Story: History as Text and Discourse*, London, Harvard University Press, 1997.

Berlin, Isaiah, *The Magus of the North*, ed. Henry Hardy, London, John Murray, 1993.

Berlin, Isaiah, *The Sense of Reality: Studies in Ideas and Their History*, ed. Henry Hardy, London, Chatto & Windus, 1996.

Bloom, Allan, *The Closing of the American Mind*, Harmondsworth, Penguin, 1988.

Bolingbroke, Lord Henry St John, *The Works*, 4 vols, Edinburgh, Carey & Hart, 1841.

Bolingbroke, Lord Henry St John, *Letters on the Study and Use of History*, London, A. Millar, 1752.

Boyle, Robert, *Certain Physiological Essays*, London, Henry Herringman, 1661.

Boyle, Robert, *The Works*, ed. T. Birch, 6 vols, London, J. & F. Rivington, 1772.

Brooke, John Hedley, *Science and Religion: Some Historical Perspectives*, Cambridge, Cambridge University Press, 1991.

Browne, Thomas, *The Religio Medici and Other Writings*, London, J. M. Dent, 1906.

Burns, Robert M. and Rayment-Pickard, Hugh (eds), *Philosophies of History: From Enlightenment to Postmodernity*, Oxford, Blackwell, 2000.

Butterfield, Herbert, *The Whig Interpretation of History*, Harmondsworth, Penguin, 1973 (1931).

Cahoone, Lawrence E., (ed.), *From Modernism to Postmodernism: An Anthology*, Oxford, Blackwell, 1996.

Callinicos, Alex, *Theories and Narratives: Reflections on the Philosophy of History*, Cambridge, Polity, 1995.

Cannadine, David, *History in Our Time*, London, Penguin, 2000.

Carr, E. H., *What is History?*, Harmondsworth, Penguin, 1964.

Cassirer, Ernst, Kristeller, Paul Oskar and Randall, John Herman Jr (eds), *The Renaissance Philosophy of Man*, London, University of Chicago Press, 1948.

Chamberlain, Houston Stewart, *The Foundations of the Nineteenth Century*, transl. John Lees, 2 vols, London, John Lane, 1911 (1899).

Charleton, Walter, *Two Discourses, the First, Concerning the Different Wits of Men*, 3rd edn, London, William Whitwood, 1692.

Clarke, J. J., *The Oriental Enlightenment: The Encounter between Asian and Western Thought*, London, Routledge, 1997.

Clarke, J. J., *The Tao of the West: Western Transformations of Taoist Thought*, London, Routledge, 2000.

Clayton, Robert, *A Vindication of the Histories of the Old and New Testament*, London, W. Bowyer, 1752.

Coleridge, Samuel Taylor, *The Poems of Samuel Taylor Coleridge*, London, Oxford University Press, 1907.

Collini, Stefan, *English Pasts: Essays in History and Culture*, Oxford, Oxford University Press, 1999.

Conrad, Joseph, *Heart of Darkness*, Ware, Wordsworth, 1999 (1902).

Cox, C. B. and Dyson, A. E. (eds), *The Twentieth Century Mind*, 3 vols, Oxford, Oxford University Press, 1972.

Crombie, A. C., *Augustine to Galileo*, 2 vols, London, Heinemann, 1959.

Davies, Norman, *Europe: A History*, London, Pimlico, 1997.

Davis, Natalie Zemon, *The Return of Martin Guerre*, Harmondsworth, Penguin, 1985.

Debus, A. G. (ed.), *Science, Medicine and Society in the Renaissance: Essays to Honor Walter Pagel*, 2 vols, New York, Science History Publications, 1972.

Dening, Greg, *Mr Bligh's Bad Language: Passion, Power and Theatre on the Bounty*, Cambridge, Cambridge University Press, 1992.

Descartes, René, *The Philosophical Writings*, transl. John Cottingham, Robert Stoothoff and Dugald Murdoch, 2 vols, Cambridge, Cambridge University Press, 1985.

Dijksterhuis, E. H., *The Mechanization of the World Picture*, Oxford, Oxford University Press, 1961.

Dio Chrysostom, *Discourses*, transl. J. W. Cohoon, 5 vols, London, G. P. Putnam, 1932.

Diski, Jenny, *Rainforest*, Harmondsworth, Penguin, 1987.

Donne, John, *Ignatius His Conclave*, facsimile reprint, Norwood, NJ, Walter J. Johnson, 1977 (1611).

Drake, Stillman (ed.), *Discoveries and Opinions of Galileo*, New York, Doubleday, 1957.

Easlea, Brian, *Witch-hunting, Magic and the New Philosophy*, Brighton, Harvester, 1980.

Edwards, Thomas, *Gangraena: or a Catalogue and Discovery of many of the Errors, Heresies, Blasphemies, and Pernicious Practices of the Sectaries of this Time*, London, 1646.

Eksteins, Modris, *Rites of Spring: The Great War and the Birth of the Modern Age*, London, Macmillan, 2000.

Eksteins, Modris, *Walking since Daybreak: A Story of Eastern Europe, World War II, and the Heart of the Twentieth Century*, London, Macmillan, 2000.

Eliot, T. S., *The Use of Poetry and the Use of Criticism*, London, Faber & Faber, 1933.

Eliot, T. S., *Collected Poems 1909–1962*, London, Faber & Faber, 1963.

Elton, G. R., *Return to Essentials*, Cambridge, Cambridge University Press, 1991.

Emerson, Ralph Waldo, *The Works of Ralph Waldo Emerson*, London, G. Bell & Sons, 1913.

Erdmann, Johann Eduard, *A History of Philosophy*, English transl. W. S. Hough, 3 vols, London, Swan Sonnenschein, 1869.

Ermarth, Elizabeth Deeds, *Realism and Consensus in the English Novel*, Edinburgh, Edinburgh University Press, 1998.

Evans, Richard, *In Defence of History*, London, Granta, 1997.

Fernández-Armesto, Felipe, *Truth: A History and a Guide for the Perplexed*, London, Bantam, 1997.

Ferro, Marc, *The Use and Abuse of History, or How the Past is Taught*, London, Routledge & Kegan Paul, 1984.

Fontenelle, Bernard de, *A Week's Conversation on the Plurality of Worlds*, London, A. Bettesworth, 1737.

Forrester, John, *The Seductions of Psychoanalysis. Freud, Lacan and Derrida*, Cambridge, Cambridge University Press, 1990.

Fox-Genovese, Elizabeth and Lasch-Quinn, Elisabeth (eds), *Reconstructing History*, London, Routledge, 1999.

Frame, D. M. (ed.), *The Complete Works of Montaigne*, London, Stanford University Press, 1958.

Franklin, J. H., *Jean Bodin and the Sixteenth-Century Revolution in the Methodology of Law and History*, New York, Columbia University Press, 1963.

Friedlander, Saul, *Probing the Limits of Representation*, London, Harvard University Press, 1992.

Fromm, Erich, *The Fear of Freedom*, London, Routledge, 1960.

Froude, J. A., *Short Studies on Great Subjects*, 5 vols, London, Longmans Green, 1907.

Galileo, *Dialogue concerning the Two Chief World Systems*, transl. Stillman Drake, Berkeley and Los Angeles, University of California Press, 1970 (1967).

Gardiner, Juliet (ed.), *The History Debate*, London, Collins & Brown, 1990.

Gay, Peter, *The Enlightenment: An Interpretation*, 2 vols, London, Wildwood House, 1973.

Gay, Peter, *Style in History*, London, Jonathan Cape, 1975.

Ghiselin, Brewster (ed.), *The Creative Process: A Symposium*, Berkeley and Los Angeles, University of California Press, 1952.

Giroux, Henry A. (ed.), *Postmodernism, Feminism, and Cultural Politics: Redrawing Educational Boundaries*, Albany, State University of New York Press, 1991.

Glanvill, Joseph, *The Vanity of Dogmatizing*, London, Henry Eversden, 1661.

Glanvill, Joseph, *Essays on Several Important Subjects in Philosophy and Religion*, London, 1676.

Gould, Stephen Jay, *Wonderful Life*, London, Hutchinson, 1990.

Grant, Douglas, *Margaret the First: A Biography of Margaret Cavendish, Duchess of Newcastle, 1623–1673*, London, Rupert Hart-Davis, 1957.

Green, Anna and Troup, Kathleen (eds), *The Houses of History: A Critical Reader in Twentieth-Century History and Theory*, Manchester, Manchester University Press, 1999.

Grierson, H. J. C. (ed.), *The Poems of John Donne*, London, Oxford University Press, 1929.

Hale, J. R. (ed.), *The Evolution of British Historiography*, London, Macmillan, 1967.

Harvey, David, *The Condition of Postmodernity: An Enquiry into the Origins of Cultural Change*, Oxford, Blackwell, 1989.

Hazard, Paul, *The European Mind, 1680–1715*, transl. J. Lewis May, Harmondsworth, Penguin, 1973.

Heller, Erich, *The Disinherited Mind*, Harmondsworth, Penguin, 1961.

Herodotus, *The History*, transl. G. Rawlinson, 2 vols, London, J. M. Dent & Sons, 1910.

Herrnstein Smith, Barbara, *Belief and Resistance: Dynamics of Contemporary Intellectual Controversy*, London, Harvard University Press, 1997.

Hick, John, *Faith and Knowledge*, 2nd edn, London, Macmillan, 1967.

Hick, John, *God and the Universe of Faiths: Essays in the Philosophy of Religion*, London, Macmillan, 1973.

Hobbes, Thomas, *Leviathan*, London, J. M. Dent, 1914 (1651).

Hoffmann, Friedrich, *Fundamenta Medicinae*, transl. Lester S. King, London, Macdonald, 1971 (1695).

Hornblower, Simon (ed.), *Greek Historiography*, Oxford, Clarendon Press, 1996.

Huizinga, J., *The Waning of the Middle Ages*, Harmondsworth, Penguin, 1965.

Hume, David, *Dialogues concerning Natural Religion*, ed. Norman Kemp Smith, Oxford, Clarendon Press, 1935.

Hutcheon, Linda, *A Poetics of Postmodernism: History, Theory, Fiction*, London, Routledge, 1988.

Ibbett, John, 'The Concept of Faith in Relation to Epistemology', unpublished MPhil thesis, University of Leeds, 1980.

Jameson, Fredric, *The Prison House of Language*, Princeton, Princeton University Press, 1972.

Jencks, Charles (ed.), *The Post-Modern Reader*, London, Academy, 1992.

Jenkins, Keith, *Rethinking History*, London, Routledge, 1991.

Jenkins, Keith, *Why History? Ethics and Postmodernity*, London, Routledge, 1999.

Jenkins, Keith, 'On Disobedient Histories', *Rethinking History: The Journal of Theory and Practice*, forthcoming, 2003.

Jenkins, Keith (ed.), *The Postmodern History Reader*, London, Routledge, 1997.

Jones, R. F., *Ancients and Moderns*, Berkeley and Los Angeles, University of California Press, 1965.

Jowett, B. (ed.), *The Dialogues of Plato*, 5 vols, Oxford, Clarendon Press, 1875.

Joyce, Patrick, 'The Return of History: Postmodernism and the Politics of Academic History in Britain', *Past and Present* 158, 1998, 207–35.

Kang, Minsoo, 'The Use of Dreaming for the Study of History', *Rethinking History: The Journal of Theory and Practice* 5, 2001, 275–83.

Kaufmann, Walter (ed.), *Existentialism from Dostoevsky to Sartre*, New York, Meridian, 1956.

Kazin, Alfred (ed.), *The Portable Blake*, New York, Viking, 1946.

Kearney, Hugh, *Science and Change, 1500–1700*, London, Weidenfeld & Nicolson, 1971.

Kearney, Richard, *On Stories*, London, Routledge, 2002.

Keith, Michael and Pile, Steve (eds), *Place and the Politics of Identity*, London, Routledge, 1993.

Kelley, D. R., 'Historia Integra: François Baudouin and his Conception of History', *Journal of the History of Ideas* 25, 1964, 35–57.

Kirk, G. S. and Raven, J. E., *The Presocratic Philosophers*, Cambridge, Cambridge University Press, 1971.

Koestler, Arthur, *The Act of Creation*, London, Hutchinson, 1964.

Kuhn, T. S., *The Structure of Scientific Revolutions*, London, University of Chicago Press, 1964.

La Capra, D. and Kaplan, S. L. (eds), *Modern European Intellectual History: Reappraisals and New Perspectives*, London, Cornell University Press, 1982.

Laing, R. D., *The Divided Self*, Harmondsworth, Penguin, 1990 (1960).

La Mothe Le Vayer, François, *Du peu de certitude qu'il y a dans l'Histoire*, in *Deux Discours*, Paris, L. Billaine, 1668.

Lash, Nicholas, *The Beginning and the End of 'Religion'*, Cambridge, Cambridge University Press, 1996.

Leland, John, *Reflections on the Late Lord Bolingbroke's Letters on the Study and Use of History*, London, B. Dod, 1753.

Le Moyne, Pierre, *Of the Art Both of Writing and Judging of History*, London, R. Sare & J. Hindmarsh, 1695.

Lindqvist, Sven, *A History of Bombing*, transl. Linda Haverty Rugg, London, Granta, 2001.

Locke, John, *An Essay concerning Humane Understanding*, London, Thomas Basset, 1690.

Lovejoy, Arthur O., *Essays in the Historiography of Ideas*, Baltimore, Johns Hopkins, 1948.

Lovejoy, Arthur O., *The Great Chain of Being*, New York, Harper & Row, 1960.

Macaulay, Thomas Babington, *Miscellaneous Writings*, ed. T. F. Ellis, 2 vols, London, Longman & Co., 1860.

Manningham, Thomas, *Two Discourses*, London, 1681.

Marwick, Arthur, *The New Nature of History: Knowledge, Evidence, Language*, Basingstoke, Palgrave, 2001.

Merz, J. T., *A History of European Thought in the Nineteenth Century*, 4 vols, Edinburgh and London, William Blackwood & Sons, 1896–1914.

Midgley, Mary, *Science as Salvation: A Modern Myth and its Meaning*, London, Routledge, 1992.

Monod, Jacques, *Chance and Necessity*, Glasgow, William Collins & Sons, 1972.

Munslow, Alun, *Deconstructing History*, London, Routledge, 1997.

Nennius, *Historia Brittonum*, transl. Rev. W. Gunn, London, John & Arthur Arch, 1819.

Nietzsche, Friedrich, *On the Genealogy of Morals*, transl. Walter Kaufmann and R. J. Hollingdale, New York, Vintage, 1969.

Nisbet, Robert, *History of the Idea of Progress*, London, Heinemann, 1980.

Novick, Peter, *That Noble Dream: The 'Objectivity Question' and the American Historical Profession*, Cambridge, Cambridge University Press, 1988.

Ong, Walter J., *Orality and Literacy: The Technologizing of the World*, London, Routledge, 1982.

Osler, Margaret J. and Farber, Paul Lawrence (eds), *Religion, Science, and Worldview*, Cambridge, Cambridge University Press, 1985.

Parker, Samuel, *A Free and Impartial Censure of the Platonick Philosophie*, Oxford, 1666.

Parry, Idris, *Animals of Silence*, London, Oxford University Press, 1972.

Pascal, Blaise, *Pensées*, transl. W. F. Trotter, London, J. M. Dent & Sons, 1931 (1670).

Patočka, Jan, *Heretical Essays in the Philosophy of History*, ed. James Dodd, Peru, Illinois, Open Court, 1996.

Patrides, C. A. (ed.), *The Cambridge Platonists*, London, Edward Arnold, 1969.

Patterson, Annabel, *Early Modern Liberalism*, Cambridge, Cambridge University Press, 1997.

Pausanias, *Guide to Greece*, transl. Peter Levi, 2 vols, Harmondsworth, Penguin, 1971.

Peters, Richard S. (ed.), *Body, Man, and Citizen*, London, Collier-Macmillan, 1962.

Pope, Alexander, *The Poetical Works*, ed. Adolphus W. Ward, London, Macmillan, 1908.

Power, Henry, *Experimental Philosophy*, London, Johnson Reprint Corporation, 1966 (1664).

Price, Richard, 'Practices of Historical Narrative', *Rethinking History: The Journal of Theory and Practice* 5, 2001, 357–65.

Rayment-Pickard, Hugh, 'Derrida and Fidelity to History', *Journal for the History of European Ideas*, 28, 2002, 13–20.

Remarque, Erich Maria, *All Quiet on the Western Front*, transl. A. W. Wheen, London, Putnam, 1954 (1929).

Richardson, Jonathan, *Richardsoniana: or, Occasional Reflections on the Moral Nature of Man*, London, J. Dodsley, 1776.

Richardson, R. C., *The Debate on the English Revolution*, London, Methuen, 1977.

Rilke, Rainer Maria, *Duino Elegies*, London, Hogarth, 1963.

Rogers, G. A. J. and Ryan, Alan (eds), *Perspectives on Thomas Hobbes*, Oxford, Clarendon Press, 1988.

Rogers, Shannon L., 'The Historian of Wessex', *Rethinking History: The Journal of Theory and Practice* 5, 2001, 217–32.

Rorty, Richard, *Contingency, Irony, and Solidarity*, Cambridge, Cambridge University Press, 1989.

Rose, Nikolas, *Governing the Soul: The Shaping of the Private Self*, 2nd edn, London, Free Association Press, 1999.

Rosenstone, Robert A., *Visions of the Past: The Challenge of Film to Our Idea of History*, London, Harvard University Press, 1995.

Sartre, Jean-Paul, *Nausea*, transl. Robert Baldick, Harmondsworth, Penguin, 1965.

Schama, Simon, *Dead Certainties (Unwarranted Speculations)*, London, Granta, 1991.

Schama, Simon, *Citizens. A Chronicle of the French Revolution*, London, Penguin, 1989.

Sergeant, John, *The Method to Science*, London, W. Redmayne, 1696.

Sergeant, John, *Solid Philosophy*, London, Roger Clavil, 1697.

Sextus Empiricus, *Against the Professors*, transl. R. G. Bury, London, Heinemann, 1949.

Sextus Empiricus, *Outlines of Pyrrhonism*, transl. R. G. Bury, London, Heinemann, 1968.

Shermer, Michael and Grobman, Alex, *Denying History*, London, University of California Press, 2000.

Sim, Stuart (ed.), *The Icon Critical Dictionary of Postmodern Thought*, Cambridge, Icon, 1998.

Smart, Barry, *Postmodernity*, London, Routledge, 1993.

Smith, Bonnie G., *The Gender of History: Men, Women, and Historical Practice*, London, Harvard University Press, 1998.

Southern, R. W., *The Making of the Middle Ages*, London, Grey Arrow, 1959.

Spiller, Michael R. G. (ed.), *'Concerning Natural Experimental Philosophie'*: *Méric Casaubon and the Royal Society*, The Hague, Martinus Nijhoff, 1980.

Sprat, Thomas, *History of the Royal Society*, London, J. Martyn, 1667.

Steedman, Carolyn, *Dust*, Manchester, Manchester University Press, 2001.

Stephen, Leslie, *History of English Thought in the Eighteenth Century*, 2 vols, London, Smith, Elder & Co., 1876.

Stern, Fritz (ed.), *The Varieties of History*, New York, Meridian, 1956.

Swift, Graham, *Waterland*, London, Picador, 1992.

Swift, Jonathan, *Gulliver's Travels*, London, J. M. Dent & Sons, 1940 (1726).

Tadié, Jean-Yves, *Marcel Proust: A Biography*, transl. Euan Cameron, London, Viking, 2000.

Temple, William, *The Battle of the Books*, ed. A. Guthkelch, London, Chatto & Windus, 1908.

Tennyson, Alfred, *Poetical Works*, London, Oxford University Press, 1953.

Thorlby, A. K., *The Romantic Movement*, London, Longmans Green, 1966.

Thucydides, *The Peloponnesian War*, transl. R. Crawley, London, J. M. Dent & Sons, 1910.

Tillotson, John, *The Rule of Faith* . . ., London, S. Gellibrand, 1666.

Tillyard, E. M. W., *The Elizabethan World Picture*, London, Chatto & Windus, 1945.

Tully, James (ed.), *Meaning and Context: Quentin Skinner and his Critics*, Cambridge, Polity, 1988.

Windschuttle, Keith, *The Killing of History: How Literary Critics and Social Theorists Are Murdering Our Past*, New York, Free Press, 1997.

Wittgenstein, Ludwig, *Tractatus Logico-Philosophicus*, London, Routledge, 1961 (1921).

Wood, James, *The Broken Estate: Essays on Literature and Belief*, London, Jonathan Cape, 1999.

Woolf, Virginia, *To the Lighthouse*, London, J. M. Dent, 1938 (1927).

Woolf, Virginia, *Between the Acts*, London, Granada, 1978 (1941).

Wrightson, Keith, *English Society 1580–1680*, London, Hutchinson, 1982.

Yeats, W. B., *The Collected Poems*, London, Macmillan, 1950.

INDEX

Aborigines, Australian 15
Abraham 40
Acton, Lord 35
Adam 40
Africa 38, 160
Alexander the Great 72
Almond, Brenda 18
Alsop, Will 43
Amazons 72, 77
American Historical Association
    35
Anaximander 62
Ancients and Moderns 90
Ankersmit, Frank 58
anomalies 126, 132, 136, 140, 165
Anselm, Saint 93
anthropology 28, 185 n. 26
aporia 5–6
Archimedes 11, 155
architecture 27, 42–3, 162
Ariadne 162
Aristotle 39, 71, 88, 105, 155;
    Aristotelianism 73, 89–90, 100,
    102, 104, 107, 109, 129;
    Aristotelians 99
Arnold, John H. 31
Arnold, Matthew 10
Arthur, King 40
Asia 38
Athene, Greek goddess 61
Athens 115; Athenians 19, 64
atomism 101–2, 107, 161
Augustine, Saint 143, 170
Austen, Jane 121, 124, 158
authenticity, personal 8

Babel, Tower of 76
Bacon, Francis 33, 78, 104–5,
    109–10, 129, 160; Baconianism
    35, 155–6
Baker, Thomas 72–3
balance ix, 6, 35, 50; emotional 4, 18
Barrie, J. M. 121
Barnes, Julian 169
Barton, Glenys 22–3
Baudrillard, Jean 57
Bauman, Zygmunt 7–9, 28, 116, 150,
    152
Baxter, Richard 108
Bayle, Pierre 67
Berkhofer, Robert F., Jr. 29, 89, 120,
    122, 163
Berlin, Isaiah 78, 155–6
biography 22, 30
Blair, Tony, British Prime Minister 3,
    6, 16–17, 80, 85
Blake, William 79, 84, 104, 115–16,
    128, 134, 142, 151, 168
Bloom, Allan 4
Bolingbroke, Lord Henry St John
    67–70
Bonnet, Charles 122
Bordo, Susan 110
Boyle, Robert 102, 104–6, 109, 173,
    182 n. 25
Braudel, Ferdinand 138, 140
Britain 3, 40, 53, 89, 168
Browne, Thomas 20
Buddhism 85–6, 124, 145
Bury, J. B. 31, 35, 44
Butterfield, Herbert 39, 156

post-colonialism 13, 18, 38, 45–8, 72, 86, 144; proto-postcolonialism 73, 180 n. 28
power 16, 45, 48, 63, 77; of history 29
Power, Henry 103
Price, Richard 163
probability, degrees of 68–9
Procrustes 129
progress 5, 29–30, 36, 42, 46, 48, 107, 157, 159; progression 7, 9, 30, 36, 42, 46, 75, 97, 128, 158, 165, 167; progressive trajectory 30, 36, 56, 84, 90–1, 141
Protagoras 71
Proteus 41, 53
Proust, Marcel 30, 152
Providence 40, 77, 89, 132; providential plan 97
psychology 33–4, 49, 95, 164
Ptolemy 108
Pyrrho of Elis 63, 67, 72–3, 153, 172
Pyrrhonism 65, 68, 171; historical 65, 67–8, 70

Ranke, Leopold von 31, 119
Rayment-Pickard, Hugh 170–1
reason 30, 50, 62–3, 74, 76, 81, 107, 132, 136, 159; rationalism 79; rationality ix, 48, 74, 128, 157–60, 171
Reformation 92
relativism 9, 11, 56–7, 71–5, 77, 86, 128, 173; relativisation 19, 159
Remarque, Erich Maria 137
Renaissance 11, 46, 85, 91–2, 101, 146
representations 5–6, 11–13, 31, 49, 53
revolution 16; intellectual 99, 110, 156; scientific 46–7, 76, 85, 95, 98, 109–10; technological 7
rhetoric 6, 64, 68, 77; history as 17
Richardson, Jonathan 73–4
Richardson, Samuel 130, 140–1
Ricoeur, Paul 164
Rilke, Rainer Maria 16, 21
Romans 47, 64, 74
Romanticism 79–82, 85–6, 96, 110, 124, 127–8, 134, 141, 161–2

Rome 74, 119, 158; Roman history 65
Rorty, Richard 56, 78
Rosenstone, Robert A. 159–60
Ross, Alexander 107
Royal Society 104, 106, 110
Rushdie, Salman 131

Said, Edward 82
Sartre, Jean-Paul 92–3, 125–6, 141, 147, 149–50
scepticism 4, 22, 55, 62–70, 75, 86, 127, 133, 153; see also Pyrrhonism
Schama, Simon 51, 81, 121, 178 n. 41
Schiller, Friedrich 122
Schopenhauer 85, 141
science 18, 22, 30, 33–6, 67, 71, 73, 75–6, 96, 98, 104, 106, 109–10, 118, 132, 134, 146, 151, 153–6, 158, 161–2; historicity of 44; history as 31, 57, 65, 82; as model 31–3, 44, 81; new 90, 102, 105, 108, 129; popularisation of 98
scientism 31–6, 44–5, 79, 86, 134, 157
Scott, Sir Walter 80, 121
Scrots, William 146–9
Seabrook, John 10
Second World War see World War II
secularisation 5, 169; secularism 48
self 8–9, 14, 39, 54, 84, 92, 110, 124, 126, 128–30, 136–7, 142, 164, 172; ambiguities of 171; -analysis 171; -centredness 37; -creation 84–5, 92, 123; -definition 14, 93, 123, 162; -denial 44; -determination 91–2, 125, 170; -effacement 44–5, 55; -expression 3; -hood 24, 141; -indulgence 44, 140, 168; -knowledge 87; -realisation 141; reflexivity 67; -sufficiency 116
Sergeant, John 66–7
Sextus Empiricus 63, 65
Shakespeare, William 41, 94
Sheffield, John 106
Shelley, Percy Bysshe 85
Shermer Michael 56
Sim, Stuart 62